TAKING UP A FRANCHISE

TAKING UP A FRANCHISE
The Daily Telegraph Guide
Fourth Edition

Colin Barrow and Godfrey Golzen

KOGAN
PAGE

The authors

Colin Barrow is a senior lecturer at Cranfield School of Management and is the author of **Financial Management for the Small Business**, also published by Kogan Page, and of other books on business and management.

Godfrey Golzen is a specialist writer on business and employment. He is the author of several highly successful Kogan Page/*Daily Telegraph* guides and writes regularly for the *Daily Telegraph* and the *Sunday Times*.

Advertisement sales by Manor House Press, 01-609 9373

First and second editions © Godfrey Golzen, Colin Barrow and
    Jackie Severn 1983, 1984
Third and fourth editions © Godfrey Golzen and Colin Barrow
    1986, 1987

First edition 1983
Second edition 1984
Third edition 1986
Fourth edition 1987
Published by
Kogan Page Limited
120 Pentonville Road
London N1 9JN

British Library Cataloguing in Publication Data

Barrow, Colin
    Taking up a franchise: the Daily Telegraph guide. – 4th edn.
    1. Franchises (Retail trade) – Great Britain
    I. Title   II. Golzen, Godfrey
    658.8'708'0941   HF5429.235.G7
    ISBN 1-85091-435-4
    ISBN 1-85091-342-0

Printed and bound in Great Britain by
Biddles Ltd, Guildford and King's Lynn

Contents

9

Introduction

Arriving at the airport, having spent the previous night at a *Holiday Inn,* Mr Smith goes to the *Budget Rent A Car* office to pick up a car since his was out of action the day he left home. On the way into town he stops at a *Wimpy* bar for some breakfast. He goes straight to his office, where his secretary has typed up the copy for some promotional leaflets. A hundred of these are to go out to his Midlands sales office and he takes them round to *Prontaprint* to be printed up. There is no time to send them through the post, so he takes them round to *TNT,* who operate a fast delivery service.

On the way back to his office, he stops at an *Olivers Hot Bread Shop* to buy a couple of cakes by way of thanking his secretary for the work she stayed late to finish. He then phones home, where his wife tells him that she has been discussing redecorating the sitting room with *Colour Counsellors* and also the previous afternoon she had arranged for someone from *Home Tune* to check the family car. In exchange for this service she asks him to bring home some soft drinks from *Sperrings* convenience store for a children's party the next day; and while he's at it, could he buy her a certain health food which she needs for the diet she's starting? The place to get it is *Holland & Barrett,* a health food store. This will not take him out of his way because it is just a couple of doors down from *Fotofast*, the film processing service in the High Street, where he might as well see if the snaps from their summer holiday are ready. Mr Smith has a lot of paperwork to catch up with before he sets off for home, though. Rather than go out for lunch, he asks an office junior to pop round to *Perfect Pizza* and bring him a pizza. It will come in a box so he can eat it at his desk without causing too much mess for the cleaners from *Global* to deal with when they come round in the evening. His wife has also started a new cleaner from an agency called *Poppies*.

Each service or outlet Mr Smith has used or referred to in his morning's activities is a business format franchise and he could probably fill a large part of his week using one or other of the 400 or so types of business format franchise now in operation in the UK.

H·Plan
Fitted Bedrooms

Contact: Paul Whicher,
H·Plan Fitted Bedroom Furniture Ltd,
Dallow Road, Luton LU1 1SP.
☎ 0582-424222
Fax: 0582 452423

Some of them are new. Others are so well established that they have become part of the High Street landscape to the extent that one is apt to forget that what is probably the best known name in British franchising, Wimpy, is scarcely 25 years old and that the whole concept spread only slowly in the decade after Wimpy got going.

Since then, however, development has been very rapid; more rapid, perhaps, than most people realise because, until you look at the names and details of franchises given on pages 150-293 you may not have been aware that some of these firms are franchises at all. It is a fair bet that if you look at your local High Street or shopping centre with that list in your hand, you will find several business format franchises in operation. Probably you will also see a site where a new one is being started up because the growth in UK franchising is now very rapid indeed. According to a survey commissioned by the British Franchise Association in 1986, since 1978 the number of franchise outlets has grown from under 2000 to around 20,000. Annual sales have grown at a similar rate to something in excess of £2000 million. In the same survey, it is forecast that retail sales through franchised outlets in the UK will top £5000 million by 1990.

This is a bold forecast but it can be supported by trends in the USA. Europe tends to follow America in commercial practices and there franchising has established for itself a position of dominance in the retail trade. Sales from franchising now account for 32 per cent of all US retail sales. There are thought to be some 350,000 business format franchise outlets in operation in the USA at present.

The cult of owning your own business is perhaps more strongly established in the USA than in some other countries, but as far as Britain is concerned there are very good reasons why franchising can be expected to grow in popularity. Some of these have to do with the fact that setting up one's own business may be the only alternative to unemployment, though curiously enough, a survey by the British Franchise Association shows that only 8 per cent of franchisees* are drawn from the ranks of the redundant. However, it is clearly the insecurity of the job market and the difficulty of even getting a foothold in it that attracts many into franchising.

What many of them find particularly helpful is that it is ideal for those with little experience of running their own business. It operates in a way that takes some of the sting and isolation out of going it absolutely alone. We will deal with this aspect in more detail in Chapter 4. The most compelling reason of all, however, for the growth both of franchising and interest in it as a way of going into business is its success. It is reckoned that as many as 90 per cent of all

---

*A *franchisee* is the person who operates the franchise. A *franchisor* is the party who owns the rights to the franchise which he assigns to the franchisee under a franchise contract.

new businesses fail, whereas 90 per cent of new franchises succeed. That they sometimes succeed because it is in the interests of the franchisor to pull out all the stops to prevent them from failing – so it is said – is an argument in their favour rather than against. It helps to be able to turn to someone who will not only be there to advise you, but in whose interests it is to do so, because clearly, the difficulties of an outlet have to be resolved by the franchisor. Otherwise it reflects on his whole operation. No wonder then, that when regular employment is diminishing, taking up a franchise looks like an attractive alternative for someone who has money to invest in running his* own business.

However, while franchising eliminates some of the more costly and at times disastrous bumps in the learning curve of working for yourself, it is not an easy way to riches either. Furthermore, there are stresses and dangers as well as advantages in some of the compromises it offers between self-employment and working for someone else. Some of these could be exploited by unscrupulous operators who tend to emerge whenever there are inexperienced people around with money to invest in business ventures. Though some of the less savoury versions, or rather perversions, of franchising are now subject to legislation – pyramid selling for instance – it is quite possible for an unscrupulous franchisor to stay within the law and give the franchisee very little in return for his fee. This book has been written, not only to tell intending franchisees what exactly franchising is, how it operates and who the main franchisors are, but also to alert them to the pitfalls. They can be avoided if you ask the right questions. Once you have signed on the dotted line and parted with your fee, though, it is too late to turn back and the person who is wise before the event rather than after it is in an infinitely better position. To impart some of the necessary wisdom is the object of *Taking Up A Franchise.*

---

*'He' and 'his' have been used throughout for convenience only, though 'she' and 'her' apply equally in most cases.

Chapter 1
What Franchising Means

Forms of franchising

We have referred in the introduction to business format franchising. This is the form of franchising operated by such well-known names as Wimpy, Prontaprint and Body Shop and is in fact what people generally now mean by the word. There are, however, other forms of franchising and it is important to be clear about the distinctions between them. The term franchise covers a wide variety of arrangements under which the owner of a product, a process, a service or even just a name having certain connotations (eg that of a sportsman) licenses another to make or use something in exchange for some form of payment. This can be either direct, in the form of a fee and/or a royalty, or indirect in the shape of an obligation to buy a service or product in which the licence holder has some kind of commercial interest. An example of the latter with which most people are familiar is the 'tied' pub, where the licensee has to obtain his supplies from a particular brewery. This type of arrangement, by the way, has been around for some 150 years, so franchising in the UK has a history stretching back a long way before the Wimpy bar.

Let us look at the various types of relationship between licensee and licensor which are also described as franchises but which, though having a good deal in common with the business format franchise, are also quite different from it.

1. A distributorship for a particular product, such as a make of car. This is also sometimes referred to as an *agency,* but there is a fundamental difference between these two concepts. An agent acts on behalf of a principal. Even though he is not employed by him, and even though he may have an agency for the products and services of more than one principal, what the agent does, says or represents to third parties is binding on the principal in question, as if they were employer and employee. A distributorship, however, is an arrangement where both parties are legally independent, as vendor and purchaser, except that the purchaser, in exchange for certain exclusive territorial rights, backed up by the vendor's advertising, promotion and, possibly, training of his staff, will be expected to hold adequate stock and maintain his premises in a way that reflects well on the vendor's product or service.

2. A licence to manufacture a certain product within a certain territory and over a given period of time, have access to any secret process this involves and use its brand name in exchange for a royalty on sales.

This arrangement resembles a distributorship. Licensor and licensee are independent of each other, except that the licensor will no doubt insist that the licensee complies with certain specifications as regards content and quality in order to preserve the good name of his product. This arrangement is often found in industry and two well-known examples have been the Rank Organisation's licence to produce the photocopying devices pioneered by the Xerox Corporation and the licences granted by Pilkington's for their revolutionary plate glass manufacturing process.

3. The use of a celebrity name to enhance the sales appeal of a product and guarantee, at least by implication, its quality.

The most common example is the endorsement, by a sports personality, of equipment associated with his activity and bearing his name, in return for a royalty payment by the manufacturer.

The realisation that a 'personality' can sell things bearing his name came about principally through the exposure of sports in the media. In the thirties there were some attempts to capitalise on movie stars' names in a similar way – an early poster associating Ronald Reagan with a brand of cigarettes has been much reprinted since he became prominent in another sphere – but sportsmen and women have been more ready, and perhaps better organised, to cash in on the advertising spin-off from the media coverage they get. A name can be franchised, at least for a while, to validate a product, particularly if there appears to be a direct connection between them: Arnold Palmer golf clubs, for instance.

4. The use of a trade mark. Here a widely recognised product is exploited commercially for a fee and subject to certain licensing conditions, rather than the name of an individual. A recent instance with which many readers will be familiar was Rubik's cube, always shown with the symbol TM beside it.

Although all these forms of franchising continue to flourish, it could be said that business format franchising has emerged as the dominant and certainly the most rapidly expanding mode. This is because it meets the commercial needs of the present time in the same way as some other forms of operation developed in response to conditions at that time. Looking back into the history of franchising for a moment, it is interesting to note that distributorship franchises were first applied to Singer Sewing machines after the American Civil War, when the USA emerged as a vast market, but when communications were too poor across great distances to make centralised distribution effective.

The concept was picked up by the motor car industry, though the problem there was somewhat different; not so much, at that time, of finding a mass market, but more one of establishing outlets to provide display space, back-up service and, of course, to buy the actual cars. Plainly the manufacturers could not afford to set up distribution outlets and finance stock as well as make the cars.

The success of such forms of franchise encouraged numerous imitators from the twenties to the fifties, during which time the trend was to rationalise small, locally-based manufacture into national and even multi-national entities. This did, however, cause problems of sales and distribution. Local industries, aware of local market conditions, were shown in many cases to have been rather more successful in this respect than 'faceless corporations' located a long way distant. The answer was to re-create, in some way, the virtues of local industry by franchised distribution and licences. From the

19

point of view of the franchisor, these arrangements turned out to have other advantages as well over the costly alternative of keeping total control by setting up national networks of salesmen and warehouses to cover a region – and in the post-war period, overseas countries. The franchisee was usually more dedicated to the interests of the franchisor, in whose success he stood to share, than many a salaried employee would have been. This was true even when the franchisee was also trading in goods and services other than those for which he held a franchise – indeed distributorship franchises were often arrangements which placed no great obligation on the franchisor and gave a corresponding amount of freedom to the franchisee.

Business format franchising

Business format franchising incorporates elements from all these earlier ideas and combines them in a way that is particularly suited to current circumstances and economic conditions. Its main features are:

1. It is a licence for a specific period of time to trade in a defined geographic area under the franchisor's name and to use any associated trade mark or logo.
2. What is franchised is an activity, usually some form of service, which has already been tried and tested to produce a formula of operating that has been found to work elsewhere.
3. The franchisor provides the entire business concept of that formula (usually called the 'blueprint') for the conduct of operations. This must be followed by the franchisee. In fast food, for instance, the ingredients of any 'secret' recipes for the type of food being offered are strictly laid down, as are the specifications for the surroundings in which it is served.

   The blueprint is generally set out in an operating manual which is given to the franchisee when negotiations are completed.
4. The franchisor educates the franchisee in how to conduct the business according to the method laid down in the blueprint.
5. The franchisor also provides back-up services in order to ensure that the franchise operates successfully. This should certainly cover advertising and promotion of the franchise's name in general and may also cover promotion of the particular franchise in its locality. It can cover many other aspects: ongoing business advice including help in raising finance, market research into the viability of a particular location for trading purposes, assistance with negotiating leases and obtaining planning permissions, site development, the provision of building plans and specifications, a standard

accounting system – virtually anything connected with setting up a new business.

6. In exchange for the business blueprint and the services the franchisor provides, the franchisee is expected to make an initial investment in the business and to pay a weekly or monthly royalty to the franchisor thereafter, normally based on turnover. There may also be an obligation on the franchisee to buy some or all goods and equipment from sources nominated by the franchisor. When the franchisor benefits financially from such an arrangement, acting in effect in the role of a wholesaler, the royalty will be lower. In some cases in fact there may be none at all.

7. The participation of the franchisor in setting up the business does not mean that he owns it. It belongs to the franchisee and he is free to dispose of it, though he will probably have to give the franchisor first refusal and obtain his approval of the person the business is sold to, if the franchisor does not want to take it off his hands.

Definition of a franchise

A formal definition of a franchise is set out by the British Franchise Association, as follows:

> A contractual licence granted by one person (the franchisor) to another (the franchisee) which:
>
> a) permits or requires the franchisee to carry on during the period of the franchise a particular business under or using a specified name belonging to or associated with the franchisor; and
>
> b) entitles the franchisor to exercise continuing control during the period of the franchise over the manner in which the franchisee carries on the business which is the subject of the franchise; and
>
> c) obliges the franchisor to provide the franchisee with assistance in carrying on the business which is the subject of the franchise (in relation to the organisation of the franchisee's business, the training of staff, merchandising, management or otherwise); and
>
> d) requires the franchisee periodically during the period of the franchise to pay to the franchisors sums of money in consideration for the franchise or for goods or services provided by the franchisor to the franchisee; and
>
> e) which is not a transaction between a holding company and its subsidiary (as defined in Section 154 of the Companies Act 1948) or between subsidiaries of the same holding company or between an individual and a company controlled by him.

The last clause establishes the important distinction between a franchise and an agency; though this official definition is certainly useful it does not mention a number of aspects which are important from the point of view of the person taking up a franchise. It does not indicate that an initial fee is usually payable by the franchisee nor does it stress that the subject of the franchise should be a tried and tested commercial operation (though running a pilot scheme is a condition of membership of the BFA). It does not mention, further, that the business, once set up, is the property of the franchisee, nor does it warn him of the degree of control he may be subject to under clause b). Further, it gives no indication of the extent of the back-up services that the franchisee might reasonably expect to get for his money. In other words, the definition is not an adequate measure against which to check the franchise contract, a subject we shall deal with in more detail in Chapter 5.

The British Franchise Association expects its members to follow its code of practice, set out below:

1. The BFA's Code of Advertising Practice shall be based on that established by the Advertising Standards Association and shall be modified from time to time in accordance with alterations notified by the ASA.

   The BFA will subscribe fully to the ASA Code unless, on

some specific issue, it is resolved by a full meeting of the Council of the BFA that the ASA is acting against the best interests of the public and of franchising business in general on that specific issue, in this case the BFA will be required to formally notify the ASA, setting out the grounds for disagreement.

2. No member shall sell, offer for sale, or distribute any product or render any service, or promote the sale or distribution thereof, under any representation or condition (including the use of the name of a 'celebrity') which has the tendency, capacity, or effect of misleading or deceiving purchasers or prospective purchasers.

3. No member shall imitate the trade mark, trade name, corporate identity, slogan, or other mark or identification of another franchisor in any manner or form that would have the tendency or capacity to mislead or deceive.

4. Full and accurate written disclosure of all information material to the franchise relationship shall be given to prospective franchisees within a reasonable time prior to the execution of any binding document.

5. The franchise agreement shall set forth clearly the respective obligations and responsibilities of the parties and all other terms of the relationship, and be free from ambiguity.

6. The franchise agreement and all matters basic and material to the arrangement and relationship thereby created, shall be in writing and executed copies thereof given to the franchisee.

7. A franchisor shall select and accept only those franchisees who, upon reasonable investigation, possess the basic skills, education, personal qualities, and adequate capital to succeed. There shall be no discrimination based on race, colour, religion, national origin or sex.

8. A franchisor shall exercise reasonable surveillance over the activities of his franchisees to the end that the contractual obligations of both parties are observed and the public interest safeguarded.

9. Fairness shall characterise all dealings between a franchisor and its franchisees. A franchisor shall give notice to its franchisee of any contractual breach and grant reasonable time to remedy default.

10. A franchisor shall make every effort to resolve complaints, grievances and disputes with its franchisees with good faith and good will through fair and reasonable direct communication and negotiation.

The Ethics of Franchising

The BFA's code of practice is actually contained in a more far-reaching document, an explanatory guide available from the Association, entitled *The Ethics of Franchising*. It is intended to lay down ethical standards for members, but at the same time the BFA hopes that these standards will also be followed by non-members.

The BFA have laid down that franchisors should disclose the following subjects to franchisees in the literature they send them or that they should otherwise be prepared to commit themselves to stating them in writing:

● The business and financial position of the franchisor
● The personnel involved in the franchise company
● The franchise proposition
● The franchisees already operating
● The financial projections and the contract.

The document goes on to explain what is meant by 'fair dealing' and, perhaps most important of all, describes the arbitration procedures available in the case of a dispute between franchisors and franchisees. These can also be applied through the intermediacy of the

BFA when the franchisor is not a BFA member – but it should be stressed that arbitration can only be used to resolve a dispute if both parties agree to do so. Once they do and make an application to the BFA for an arbitrator's intervention, his findings when he has heard both sides of the case are legally binding under the Arbitration Act. You cannot, in other words, appeal against them in a court of law. However, arbitration is a lot cheaper than legal action.

The BFA is, of course, a franchisor organisation and in the main the code of ethics is aimed at member companies. However, its existence in itself gives some further protection to franchisees, irrespective of whether the franchisor with whom you are negotiating is a BFA member, because it sets standards to which any reputable franchise will be expected to adhere by the banks and the legal profession. Any franchisor who does not meet its requirements should be looked at with misgiving.

The practice of business format franchising

According to the 1986 Power Report on the UK franchising industry, the five largest fields of activity for franchising in terms of system numbers are: home improvement and maintenance; leisure products and services; fast food restaurants; clothing, fashion and personal accessories and equipment; professional and commercial services to business. The simplest form and usually the cheapest to acquire is a job franchise service which is run from home, a cleaning service, for instance, or a vehicle maintenance franchise such as Home Tune. Much the largest group of franchises, though, are those which entail acquiring premises and often a substantial investment in equipment in addition to the initial fee payable to the franchisor: fast food restaurants and print shops are two of the most visible and widespread franchises of this type. At the top end of the market are investment franchises like Holiday Inn, where the start-up costs can run well into six figures. A prime Wimpy bar franchise will now also run to over £250,000, as will some computer franchises. Overall the range of activities which can be franchised is very wide and some 65 have been identified in the USA, going from hotel ownership at the top end to a soft drink bottling franchise with the unlikely name of Cock 'n Bull Ltd at the other. The latter is an indication that not all American enterprises can be readily transplanted to the UK, (an important point to consider if the franchise is of foreign origin, incidentally), but there are at the moment at least 40 types of franchise in Britain, covering a variety of fields from fast food to dry cleaning.

The principles in each case are broadly the same and it might at this stage be useful to take a hypothetical example from the fast food area – one of the most active ones – to illustrate them from the point of view of both franchisee and franchisor.

A BASIC OPERATION

Let us use as an example a fast food operation offering slimmers' lunches. They already own a couple of outlets for which they have found a catchy name – Calorie Countdown – and for which they have established a standard image in terms of decor, layout, tableware and graphics. They have a gimmick; each dish at a counter service buffet has a calorie rating, and along with your bill you get a calorie count for what you have bought. They also have some recipes and dishes which they have pioneered. They are doing well at both outlets, have ironed out the start-up bugs and learnt a lot about the catering and accounting problems involved in running first one and then a second restaurant of this type.

The indications now are that there is a demand for a similar place on the other side of town. It's a tempting prospect, but there are two problems. One is that of control; their existing outlets are within walking distance of each other and so control is at present easy, but it will be a different matter with the third outlet which will be some distance away. How can they get someone motivated and experienced enough to run it without close supervision? The other problem is financial and administrative. Even if such a person is available – a member of their existing staff, for instance – do the

27

owners of Calorie Countdown have the capital to invest in another outlet and do they want to get involved in further wage bills and administrative overheads, even though the indications are that success is probable? If they are doubtful whether this is the right way to expand, the answer could be to franchise the Calorie Countdown business format.

As we have seen, this consists of a business concept that is both original and has been tested and found to work in practice (though in this case an adviser might feel that, since the firm in question is opening up its first franchise, this fact ought to be reflected in the financial arrangements), that has some secret recipe or process, that has a degree of standardisation in design terms and has acquired enough of a reputation with the public for a demand to arise from another location. Further, in terms of the definition of a business format franchise, the owners of Calorie Countdown would give an undertaking not to let anyone else trade under that name within an agreed radius, would pin-point a location for the franchise, help the franchisee to get permission from the planning and environmental health departments, possibly make a presentation to the bank for finance, get decorators, graphic designers and architects to have the new Calorie Countdown look as much like the original as possible and come to some agreement about the extent and nature of advertising. While this was going on, they would be training the franchisee to prepare food the Calorie Countdown way and teaching him about all the administrative matters he will have to deal with and advising him on procurement of equipment and supplies. Finally, all the operating instructions would be embodied in a manual and someone from the original Calorie Countdown would be on hand to keep an eye on the franchise in its opening weeks.

In exchange for all this, the franchisors of Calorie Countdown would expect the franchisee to pay them a start-up fee and some continuing form of payment, either by way of a royalty on sales or profits, or through an agreement to purchase food or equipment from them; or possibly some combination of all these factors.

What we have described is a very basic operation. The more sophisticated packages offer a wide range of services which include assistance from head office staff in negotiating site acquisition and development, celebrity openings, annual training sessions in the latest merchandising techniques, regular assistance with financial and administrative matters and/or formal procedures for dealing with these as well as on-demand 'trouble shooting' and so forth. The better established and stronger the franchisor, the more services he will offer in his package – but the more costly, in general, the franchise will be.

Chapter 2
Advantages and Disadvantages of Taking up a Franchise

The advantages and disadvantages of taking up a franchise depend to some extent on the content of the agreement but there is a core of balancing factors which are largely common because they relate to the nature of the kind of activity which franchising involves.

The franchisor

From the franchisor's point of view, the *advantages* are that he does not have any direct investment in an outlet bearing his name. The inventory and equipment are owned by the franchisee. Because of the shortage of prime sites, there is a growing trend for franchisors to acquire leases on behalf of franchisees or at any rate to stand as guarantors. Nevertheless the effect on the liquidity of the franchisor, in contrast to expansion by opening branches is enormous – though if he does his job properly there are heavy start-up costs in piloting the franchise and in setting up and maintaining training. Thereafter there are further costs in providing a continuing service to franchisees in such matters as research and development, promotion, administrative back-up and feedback and communication within the network. The expectation is that these costs will be offset by the fact that the franchisee, as the owner of the business, is more likely to be highly motivated than an employee and more responsive to local market needs and conditions; that the franchisor receives an income from the franchise; that he saves on personnel and administrative costs; and that, without direct financial involvement, he may in this way derive some of the benefits of expansion, inasmuch as franchising gives him economies of scale from centralised purchasing and, if he wishes it and it is feasible, some degree of centralised administrative facilities.

The *disadvantages* are that although the failure of an individual franchise may reflect badly on the franchise operation as a whole, all he can control is the format itself and he can only influence the running of individual operations by pulling the reins on this or that clause in the agreement – the broad terms of which we shall discuss shortly. In extreme cases he may terminate the agreement or at any rate not renew it, but he cannot throw the franchisee out as if he were an employee. He is therefore dependent on the willingness of the franchisee to observe the rules and play the game, while at the same time any failure to do so is equally and perhaps more damaging to the franchisor (and to other franchisees) than to the franchisee concerned because of its adverse effects on the franchise as a whole.

Another disadvantage sometimes turns out to lie in the curious mixture of dependence and independence that franchising produces. The franchisee is encouraged to think of himself as an independent business entity and to a large extent this is indeed the situation. Nevertheless he is operating the franchisor's business concept under a licence for which a fee is payable. There are cases where the franchisee identifies so closely with the particular business he is running that he ultimately resents the payment of the fee. The success is felt to be due to the franchisee's efforts, not to the franchise concept or to the franchisor. This is apt to be particularly so if the franchisor adopts a lower profile than he should, either in terms of direct help or in matters such as national advertising. Clearly, of course, the franchisee would be obliged to pay under the terms of the agreement, but a sour relationship is not good for either party, so it is up to the franchisor to maintain his part of the bargain both in letter and in spirit. Franchises are a matter of mutual interest and obligation.

The franchisee

From the point of view of the franchisee, also, there are advantages and disadvantages which might, perhaps, be most clearly expressed in the form of a list.

Advantages

- A business format or product which has already been market tested and, presumably, been found to work; consequently, major problems can be avoided in the start-up period.
- A recognised name of which the public is already aware and which has credibility with suppliers.
- Publicity, both direct in that the franchisor advertises his product or services, and indirect promotion through signage and other corporate image promotion in all the franchisor's outlets.
- Although taking up a franchise is not cheaper than starting on your own, it is considered that the percentage of expensive

errors made by individuals starting on their own is substantially reduced by adoption of a tested format.

- Direct and close assistance during the start-up period.
- A period of training on production and management aspects.
- A set of standard management, accounting, sales and stock control procedures incorporated in an operating manual.
- Better terms for centralised bulk purchase negotiated through the franchisor, though he may be looking to mark-ups in this area as a source of revenue from the franchisee.
- The benefit of the franchisor's research and development in improving the product.
- Feedback throughout the network on operating procedures and the facility to compare notes with other franchisees, both formally and informally.
- Design of the premises to an established scheme saves on interior design fees and may eliminate these altogether where the franchisor has a set of specifications.
- The benefit of the franchisor's advice on equipment selection and initial inventory levels, though this may not be impartial where the franchisor is also the supplier.
- Help with site selection, negotiating with planning officers and developers.
- Possibly, though not universally, access to the franchisors' legal and financial advisers.
- The protected or privileged rights to the franchise within a given area.
- Improved prospects of obtaining loan facilities from the bank.
- The backing of a known trading name when negotiating for good sites with letting agents or building owners.

Disadvantages

- Business format franchising is, of necessity, something of a cloning exercise. There is virtually no scope for individual initiative in matters of product, service or design. However, the franchisor will demand uniformly high standards of maintenance, appearance and packaging in whatever the franchise entails. These are usually monitored by regular inspections.
- The royalty (sometimes called a management fee) paid to the franchisor. This is usually based on gross turnover or on profits. The problem here is that if the franchisor is not pulling his weight or if the franchisee does not feel this to be the case,

31

the royalty can be a subject of bitter dispute. The franchisee may then feel justified in withholding all or part of it on the grounds of non-performance by the franchisor, but this is always a difficult matter to prove in the courts. Furthermore the franchisor's resources to conduct a long drawn-out case will usually be greater than the franchisee's.

- A further problem is that a high turnover does not necessarily imply a highly profitable operation. If the franchisor's income is wholly or partially based on turnover, he may try to push for this at the expense of profitability.

- The franchisee is not absolutely at liberty to sell the franchise even though he is in many respects operating the business independently. The sale has to be approved by the franchisor, who is also entitled to vet the vendor and charge the cost of any investigations made to the existing franchisee. Furthermore, although the business would be valued as a going concern in trading terms, the goodwill remains the property of the franchisor. Again, the franchisee may feel that, at least to some extent, the goodwill has been built up by his own efforts. The resale of a franchise, in other words, is a process rich in those grey areas which can lead to expensive litigation.

- Territory agreements may be difficult to enforce in practice. For instance, our hypothetical firm of Calorie Countdown may have the exclusive rights in the suburb in which it is located, but there is nothing to prevent the citizens of that suburb buying their slimmers' meals in some neighbouring Calorie Countdown outlet.

- The franchisee, as well as paying a royalty to the franchisor, may be obliged to buy goods and services from him as well – possibly at disadvantageous rates.

- Though the franchisor places all sorts of controls and obligations on the franchisee to maintain the quality of his image, the scope for doing the reverse is more limited. If the franchisor's product or service gets bad publicity, this is bound to affect the franchisee adversely, and there is very little he can do about it. Equally, the franchisor may engage in promotional activities – and involve the franchisee in them as well – which, though perfectly harmless are, from the point of view of a particular outlet, an irrelevant waste of time.

- The failure of a franchisor may leave the franchisee with a business which is not viable in isolation.

Mutual dependence

From this list of advantages and disadvantages to both parties a more detailed picture emerges of the business format franchise as a relationship of mutual dependence which allows each party to release his strength to mutual and, at best, equal advantage. The franchisor is able to expand without further investment and, though the return is obviously lower than from expansion by ownership, he does receive an income from the franchisee as well as getting both an outlet for his product and more muscle in negotiating the purchase of materials and equipment. The franchisee, on the other hand, is able to concentrate his entrepreneurial skills at the sharp end of sales and customer service, while the administrative headaches of setting up the business are mitigated by the uniform nature of the format. By the same token he is saved, through feedback to the franchisor of the accumulated experience of other franchisees, from making the errors to which businesses are prone in their earlier and most vulnerable stages. This relationship is expressed in agreements: the purchase agreement and the franchise agreement. But before considering these, it is necessary to evaluate the franchise as a whole.

A recent study by Professor Russell M Knight of the University of Western Ontario illustrates the close agreement between franchisees and franchisors on the advantages of franchising – though in general, franchisees were slightly less enthusiastic.

The advantages of franchising

	Franchisees in agreement %	Franchisors in agreement %
● You can make more money in a franchise than in an independent business	51	47
● A franchise is less risky than going it alone	78	88
● A franchise offers greater job satisfaction than salaried employment	95	82
● A franchise offers more independence than salaried employment	92	83
● A franchise offers a proven business formula	83	99
● A franchise offers the benefit of a known trade name	96	99
● You can develop a franchise more quickly than an independent business	92	86

Chapter 3
Evaluating the Franchise

Most franchisors have discovered that the hard sell is neither in their own interest nor that of the franchisee. Successful franchising is, as we have seen, a question of mutual dependence and a franchisee who finds or feels that he has been sold a pup is not likely to be a co-operative member of the franchise family. At the same time it must be said that, with the exception of the prohibition of pyramid selling* in the 1973 Fair Trading Act, very little specific legal protection is available to the franchisee. Basically, what protection there is, is embodied in the franchise agreement but that document is subject to omissions and commissions of wording which can make a great deal of difference to the deal which is being offered to the franchisee. It can also throw much light on the good intent or experience of the franchisor. A great many questions need to be asked about it by the intending franchisee and his advisers in order to put the provisions of the contract into context.

There are four areas, aspects of which may not be fully covered in the contract but which require close investigation and scrutiny.

1. The product or service offered.
2. The territory and the site.
3. The relationship between the franchisee and the franchisor.
4. The nature of the franchise package.

The product or service offered

It may be new or it may be already established. There is nothing wrong with a product or service being new, provided it has been tested and found to work, preferably for at least a couple of years in a location or community similar to that for which it is now being offered (as is a condition for membership of the British Franchise

---

*Pyramid selling is a concept in which franchisees are recruited to sell 'distributorships' while the actual product or service being distributed plays a secondary part and may, indeed, be quite unviable.

Association) and provided also that the franchisee is satisfied that it enjoys a good reputation among users and customers. It is also important, of course, that the franchisee is doing something that he wants to be associated with.

Equally, there is no automatic guarantee of success in dealing with an established product or service. The franchisee must check whether the market is growing, static or declining.

Whether the franchise relates to a new or established product or service, the franchisee needs to be satisfied that it has staying power (remember skateboards, the craze that was going to be with us forever?), to what extent the demand is seasonal (people in the UK are less addicted to ice cream in winter than in some other countries) and whether its appeal is to any extent confined to a specific age group or sector of the community.

It should have some unique feature like, for instance, the 'secret recipe' of the sauce for Kentucky Fried Chicken and preferably this should be protected by a patent or trade mark.

If its success is tied to a celebrity name, the franchisee will have to find out how active that celebrity is in promoting it and to judge how durable his fame is likely to be.

How competitive is the product or service in price and quality with similar ones on the market and, in particular, available in the franchisee's vicinity.

All these points have been painfully brought home by the well publicised failure in 1986 of one or two franchisors who were thought, even by the banks, to be soundly based. In each case, though, questions addressed to the actual franchisees would have shown that all was far from well. In other words, there is no substitute for first-hand investigation and research – not even expert hearsay.

The territory and the site

Though the franchisor should provide a map showing the exact extent of the territory, this is not in itself a guarantee of absolute protection. For one thing, under EEC competition laws the franchisor cannot prevent one franchisee trading in another's 'exclusive' territory, though he may decline to *license* a competitor within it; for instance, there is nothing to stop a print shop in one territory serving customers from the territory of another franchisee. There is very little that can be done about this, except to check where the nearest operator of the same franchise is located or planned to be located – and indeed where operators of franchises and other businesses offering a similar product or service are to be found. The franchisee should also check whether the agreement specifies any circumstances under which his territory could be reduced.

The rationale behind the territory assignment needs to be examined. Has the franchisor picked it out arbitrarily or has he conducted – as he should have done – market surveys to indicate that the franchise is likely to be viable in that territory? These should cover aspects like traffic flows, access, population mix by age and class, and so forth, and they should be made available to the franchisee.

The site

Narrowing the focus further, the franchisee should ask the same questions about the site itself. Expert advice on site selection is described as being one of the principal advantages business format franchising has to offer, but the franchisee should not allow himself to be 'blinded with science'. If he or his adviser has good reason to believe, in the light of personal knowledge of local conditions, that the site is a poor choice, then the franchisor must be pressed very hard to justify it and to demonstrate that it has the necessary qualities of visibility and accessibility to cars and pedestrians, and adequate frontage.

Access

How important each of these factors is obviously depends on what is being franchised. A take-away restaurant, for instance, would need to be accessible to both cars and pedestrians. Accessibility to cars would be less important for an ice cream parlour but fairly vital for a product franchise where customers might need to load up their purchases.

Tenure

The method of tenure of the premises is important. Either the franchisor or the franchisee can be in the 'driving seat'. Where the franchisor holds the freehold or the lease this does not in any way remove the franchisee's security as a tenant or a licensee during the term of the agreement, but when it comes to an end his situation is less favourable. As stated earlier it is becoming more common in franchises that are operated from business premises, especially on good commercial sites, for the lease to be controlled by the franchisor.

There are grounds on which the franchisor can reclaim the premises which have nothing to do with whether the franchise was conducted satisfactorily – in particular when the franchisor is also the landlord and wants to take over the premises himself. The franchisee is then entitled to be compensated for improvements he has made to the premises, though that provision is not without potential complications.

First, movable fixtures and fittings are not counted as improvements. The franchisee will have to dispose of them as best he can, unless he can persuade the franchisor to buy them back or some other franchisee to take them over.

Second, the franchise contract may require a continuous scheme of improvements in order to keep the place up to standard. How the franchisee is to be compensated for such work on termination of the agreement should be spelled out in it. Otherwise the franchisee may drag his feet over doing more than the prescribed minimum to keep the place spick and span.

Another obvious point to check is whether the rent is reasonable in relation to the neighbourhood. The difference between a lease and a licence is largely technical, except that in the case of a licence, the licensor is responsible for paying the rates.

Where the lease or licence is negotiated separately from the franchise agreement, it is obviously important to check that they both cover the same time span.

Ownership of the lease or freehold confers some clear benefits. In the case of the franchisor these are that ownership creates an asset for borrowing purposes and also makes it possible for him to terminate a franchise without losing a valuable site. From the point of view of the franchisee, it makes it possible for him to divert a good site to another purpose (should he not wish to carry on with the franchise), or derive an unambiguous benefit from the sale of the site if its value has improved due either to the franchisee's efforts or to planning changes.

The relationship between the franchisee and franchisor

Perhaps the most important single question to put to the franchisor is how long he has been in business in the UK, how many outlets he has established in that time, how successful they have been (and what the criteria for success are),* how many have been closed down, and for what reasons. Failing a track record in the UK, the question must be related to his operations elsewhere – in the USA or Europe, most probably. It would also be useful to know who the directors are and something of their qualifications, background, experience and nationality.

Foreign franchises

In the case of foreign-based franchises it is at least desirable that there should be a UK master licensee of proven status and experience. The cultural differences between consumer habits and trading customs are still powerful and foreign franchises generally need to be filtered through a process of adaptation before they are launched in another country. It is also on the cards that a franchisor's domestic market would take precedence if there was a problem over matters like supplies, unless there was a strong master licensee who could put pressure on headquarters staff.

Supplies

The success of the franchise, in terms of both profits and turnover, will be closely related to sources and costs of equipment, goods and services. These will be controlled, wholly or in part, by the franchisor. The franchisee needs to be sure that the prices are fair and competitive and that supply is likely to be trouble-free. There might, for instance, be question marks where goods have to be obtained from Third World countries with political problems. Some franchisors set a minimum ordering quantity for supplies and this has to be realistic in relation to the franchisee's resources and his expectations in terms of business volume. Ideally, though, the franchisee should not be too closely tied to the franchisor or the nominees as a main source since this obviously gives the franchisor a degree of leverage which is open to abuse. Indeed some good franchise agreements leave franchisees the option to buy elsewhere if goods from

---

*Financial information should be checked by an accountant.

sources suggested or even nominated by the franchisor are uncompetitive or unobtainable.

Standards of quality

The franchisee should establish such aspects of the relationship as what standards of quality are being set – and the cost implications of this – what opening hours have to be kept (again these may have implications in terms of staffing and overtime payments), and what the reporting procedures are for accounting purposes. Even though the franchisee is running his own business, the franchisor will want to check that royalties being paid accurately reflect the volume of business and he will also demand the right to enter and inspect the premises at will.

Future developments

The business format is not a constant. It may be amended from time to time and the franchisee will have to go along with the amendments. Therefore it is important to establish, as far as possible, what the franchisor's future plans are. Has he got any costly innovations up his sleeve? Is he planning any new franchises or other moves that may be in competition with the franchises he is now offering? Is he doing things which might stretch the financial and human resources of his existing operation to its detriment? In all of these cases, the franchisee might suffer.

Termination

The conditions under which the franchise can be terminated by either party, assigned or renewed should be clearly spelt out. There should be a satisfactory disputes procedure. Arbitration in such cases has become a popular alternative to litigation since the 1979 Arbitration Act, and the BFA are encouraging its use as a standard dispute practice by its members. They are also campaigning for its extension to non-members, who can refer to the BFA in such circumstances.

The franchise package

To a large extent the package determines and overlaps the nature of the franchisor/franchisee relationship, but it has characteristics of its own. Fees are most important here: not only how much, but the form in which they are paid. There will be an initial fee, a royalty on turnover and/or a mark-up on goods supplied for resale, but there can be considerable – and significant – differences in the amounts and the way they are collected. In general, the advice is to be very careful about franchises with a high initial fee and a low royalty (unless, of course, the franchisor receives part of his income in the form of a mark-up on goods supplied): the franchisor may be of the 'take your money and run' variety. Equally, low royalties may reflect a high mark-up on the tied supply of goods and services. The question then is whether the product being offered is competitive in price. A low initial fee is not necessarily favourable either – it may mask high royalties or hidden charges.

Another point to watch out for is whether the franchisor sets a minimum figure the franchisee must pay, irrespective of income from the franchise. If so, is the amount reasonable? Here again, the advice of an accountant would be invaluable.

Advertising

Related to the question of fees is that of advertising. Increasingly this is being shown as a separate and additional charge. The question then is whether it is dedicated to the franchise as a whole or to promoting individual outlets? In both cases the franchisee needs to be satisfied that the advertising is good and relevant, both as regards contents and medium. This question should also be asked where the franchisor imposes a specific advertising levy, separate from the royalty – a growing practice.

Local press, radio, tv and cinema advertising is most helpful to the franchisee. National campaigns are costly and the purpose behind them may be to sell franchises rather than to further the franchisee's particular business. Nevertheless some national advertising may be essential if a nationwide franchise chain is to be developed, with its knock-on benefits to individual franchisees. In the USA, for example, McDonalds, one of the world's largest franchisors, spends more on TV advertising than Kelloggs, and virtually the same as the Ford Motor Company.

Point of sale, counter and window advertising is also important in this latter respect and the agreement should state who pays for it. If the franchisor requires such advertising to be done, then it could represent a sizeable additional cost to the franchisee.

Training

Another area where who pays for what needs to be clarified is that of training. Indeed, since training is in itself a very important part of the package, the franchisee must know how much there will be and how long it will take. In America the concept of training is sometimes taken to ludicrous lengths – McDonald operate a Hamburger University and one suspects it is only partly meant as a joke, if at all.

However, training should cover such basic skills as operating methods, financial controls, the care and maintenance of equipment as well as instruction on how to carry out the various statutory requirements – employment legislation, calculating PAYE, VAT, and so forth – with which the owner of a business is expected to comply.

There is also the question of refresher courses, employee training and instruction in new methods. In each case the franchisee should be clear as to what extent training is compulsory or necessary, whether it is the subject of extra charges and how these are arrived at.

Apart from formal training and refresher courses, there ought also to be some procedure for when things go wrong. What happens if the franchisee falls ill? Can an emergency crew step in? And what happens if the franchisee runs into administrative or equipment trouble? Is help of sufficient calibre available, how quickly and at what cost?

Operating manual

The operating manual embodies the 'blueprint' of the business format franchise and some contracts state that its status is paramount over anything that is said in the agreement. The franchisee and his advisers must be sure that they fully understand the manual and that it covers all the situations they are likely to encounter in operating the franchise. It is also worth finding out how often it is updated and when the last update took place.

While many of these points will be covered in the contract or provided as general background by the franchisor, there are two important aspects which the franchisee will have to evaluate but which will not be part of the standard information package: what is known about the franchisor himself and the experience of other franchisees.

The franchisor

A good franchisor will ask the franchisee a lot of questions (often by way of a questionnaire sent with a response to an initial enquiry) about his qualifications to run a business: about experience, health, financial resources and so forth. Indeed, to some extent the more searching such questions are the better, because it indicates that the franchisor has a close interest in the good and successful conduct of each outlet. Equally, though, the franchisee should be ready with some questions of his own. Apart from those that come under the heading of franchisor/franchisee relationship, it is important to establish the following.

When was the company started? How long was it in operation with the product or service before it started franchising it? It is obviously important that the franchisor should have got the bugs out of the system before starting to franchise it and the period it takes to do this is not usually less than two or three years. Membership of the BFA is conditional on proper piloting, so if the franchisor is not a member, why not? If they are not members – and it is fair to point out that some important franchisors are not – it is essential that the scheme should have bank support, ie that reputable banks are willing to lend money to finance franchisees' start-up costs.

Apart from its record of growth in the past – which should preferably show steady rather than mushroom progress – what are the plans for the future? Very rapid expansion could cause administrative problems which would adversely affect individual franchises. This is particularly true when it comes to ensuring regular supplies of goods from the franchisor. Well conducted franchises in retailing and fast food have often adopted a policy of expanding only along viable lines of supply, for instance in a defined geographical area.

Unless the franchisor is a household name, it is worth asking your accountant or bank manager to check on his financial standing. The effect of the franchisor going out of business could completely undermine the operation of individual franchises; at best it would cause time-consuming legal and financial complications.

Again, unless the franchisor is a household name, the franchisee ought to find out whether the business history of the principals is related to the product or service they are franchising – or indeed whether it is in franchising at all. It is important to know not only the history of the franchise itself, but also of the principals. They may merely have bought into an established company without having adequate acquaintance themselves of what running a franchise involves. This danger is likely to increase as franchising grows in popularity.

Find out the size of the headquarters staff and whether or not they work full time. This could be an important factor if and when you need assistance. You should also make a point of seeing the franchisor's premises and form your own judgement about the appearance of the place, the quality of staff and so forth.

The fact that all of the franchisor's outlets are operating successfully and that few or none have been closed down may not tell the whole story. Find out if the franchisor is operating any outlets himself; in other words, how many are franchisor-owned. He may be keeping the best outlets to himself or re-purchasing the less successful ones in order to preserve a respectable track record.

The experience of other franchisees

The most reliable proof of the pudding is in its eating and you should certainly talk to other franchisees before committing yourself. They should be those who have been in business for at least a couple of years and the outlet they are operating should be similar to the one you are contemplating in terms of size and catchment area. The following questions need to be asked:

1. What total investment was required; not only the down payment to the franchisor, but additional costs in the way of equipment etc?
2. Were the franchisor's projections of costs and revenues reasonably accurate?
3. Did the franchisors live up to their promises regarding help with launching the business, training, promotional back-up?
4. Was the operating manual practical and easy to follow?
5. Is the product good enough? Are service and deliveries to the franchisee prompt and efficient?
6. When problems arise, how long does it take for trouble-shooters or franchisor's repair men or other services provided by the franchisor to materialise?
7. What disagreements have arisen with the franchisor, over what? Were they settled satisfactorily?
8. What proofs does the franchisor require of turnover and profitability? Are they reasonable and easy to comply with?
9. How much inspection does the franchisor impose on the conduct of the franchise? Is it reasonable?
10. What unexpected expenses have been incurred and for what reason?
11. How long did it take the business to reach break-even, including paying the franchisee the level of income he expected to get and a return on his investment?
12. If you could change anything in the contract with the wisdom of hindsight, what would it be?
13. Does the product have a steady and continuing sale or is it subject to seasonal, or even weekly or daily peaks and troughs?

This sort of information is best gleaned from a franchisee in whom you have no personal interest – in other words not from one whose franchise you are thinking of taking over, because he will tell you only the good things, not the bad ones. It is also important to talk to more than one franchisee, and not all of them should be names given to you by the franchisor. Equally, though, if the franchisor shows any reluctance over letting you talk to other franchisees, it could be taken as a bad sign. However, if you put together all the methods of evaluating a franchise shown in this chapter, it should enable you and your advisers to check whether the franchise bears out the franchisor's claims about its performance.

The financial viability

Presumably you are taking out a franchise in the hope of making money, or at least a reasonable living, in a way that is congenial to you. Chapter 4 deals with the personal factors; here we look at the financial aspects, and ask the question: When you are presented with a set of figures by your franchisor, what should you be looking for? This process is known as *interpretation of accounts* and breaks down into two areas:

How healthy is the franchisor's organisation as a whole?

How attractive is the particular franchise opportunity that you are being offered?

Some of the answers to the first question are provided in Chapter 8, but you may not actually start talking to a franchisor until some months after you read this book, and in the meantime he may have filed another set of annual accounts which you will need to inspect to see whether the trends are healthy.

Interpreting the franchisor's accounts

The first step is to find out whether the franchisor is operating as a limited company, and if so what its name is; it may not be the same as the trading name. For example, Kall-Kwik Printing is the trading name of KK Printing (UK) Limited. If the company will not give you a set of its audited accounts and you would like more information than is provided here or by the most recent accounts, you will need to get it from Companies House. Most of the larger franchises are limited companies; a few of the smaller and newer ones are sole traders or partnerships, in which case their accounts are not publicly available. However, you should still try to see them before you commit yourself to the franchise.

When you get your copy of the accounts you will find that there are two financial documents, the *profit and loss account* and the *balance sheet,* and a number of legal forms and records.

THE PROFIT AND LOSS ACCOUNT

This account shows the income generated and expenditure incurred by the company. Running down the table on page 49, the main elements are:

The date, an essential ingredient in every account. For the profit and loss account it is usually given as 'the year/month/week ended'. This tells you the interval of time covered by the record.

44

Sales turnover is the total income from customers for goods or services rendered.

Cost of sales. A common misconception is to believe that everything spent in the business has gone into 'making' the product. However, in calculating the 'cost of sales' only those costs directly concerned with making are considered. These will include the cost of all materials and the cost of manufacturing labour. It is calculated in this example by adding the opening stock to the purchases and deducting the closing stock. In a service business with no manufactured end product the same principles apply. So, for example, a travel agent's cost of sales would be the payments made to carriers (airlines). The money that is left after such payments is the gross profit.

Gross profit is arrived at by deducting the cost of sales from the sales turnover. This figure gives an indication of how efficient the business is at putting its product or service together. It also shows the maximum sum available to market and to administer the business.

Expenses is the general name given to the costs incurred in selling, marketing, administering, distributing and advertising the company's products or services. It will include the directors' remuneration which, if not listed separately as an expense, should be disclosed in a note. In conjunction with the dividend figure, it will tell you how much the proprietors are taking out of the business. Depreciation is the name given to the expense associated with using a fixed asset. So a piece of equipment costing £7000 with an expected life of seven years could be depreciated at the rate of £1000 per annum. From a cash point of view the full sum may be paid out on day one. But as far as an entry in the profit and loss account is concerned an expense called depreciation of £1000 is incurred, which effectively allocates some of the cost to the appropriate time period. For tax purposes depreciation is added back as it is not an allowable business expense. The tax allowance, insofar as there is one, is given on the capital expenditure.

Operating profit, or as it is sometimes called, trading profit, is the income left after expenses have been deducted.

Interest charges. Another major expense is the cost of borrowing money. By convention these interest charges are deducted leaving the *profit before tax*. Once *taxation* has been deducted (or allowed for), the total sum available to distribute to the shareholders is left. This is called the *profit after tax* and once *dividends* are paid out to shareholders, the residue, *retained profits*, are available to reinvest in the company. (In this simplified example the effects of tax and dividends are ignored.)

THE BALANCE SHEET

The balance sheet is the second essential financial statement and this shows the picture of a business at a particular moment in time. It shows where a business has got its money from and what it has done with that money. Like a photograph, it is only true at the moment it is taken. Look again at the table on page 49 to see the structure of this account.

The date. This is an essential record of when the financial picture was taken.

The layout. The balance sheet comprises two main sections. The 'What have we done with the money?' section is headed 'Fixed Assets'. The 'Where did we get the money from?' section is headed 'Financed by'. And surprise, surprise, they have to balance, as the things a business has done with its money must equal the sum of money invested in it.

Assets are the valuable resources owned by a business, which were acquired at a measurable money cost. There are really only three types of asset a business can hold.

Fixed assets include such items as premises, machinery and motor cars. These are assets that a business intends to keep over the longer term. They will be used to help make 'products' and eventually profits too, but they will not physically vanish in the short term (unless sold and replaced, like motor cars, for example).

Working capital is the money tied up in 'things' immediately involved in the business's products (or services), that will vanish in the short term. Stocks get sold and are replaced; debtors pay up, and creditors are paid; and cash circulates. The working capital is calculated by subtracting the current liabilities from the current assets. (Current is a term used to describe something that has a financial 'life' of up to a year – although you will always have debtors, hopefully they will be different.) This is the net sum of money that a business has to find to finance the working capital. In the balance sheet this is called the net current assets, but on most other occasions the term working capital is used.

Investments. Finally, a business can put money aside over the longer term, perhaps in local government bonds or as an investment in someone else's business venture. In the latter case this could be a prelude to a takeover or merger; in the former it could be a reserve for future capital investments. It is not shown in this example as it is a fairly rare phenomenon in this field.

The *Financed by* section shows where the business got its money from. Once again there are really only three sources of funds:

Share capital, sometimes called equity; if the business is not a limited company it will be called 'owner's capital introduced'. This is the money invested by the owner(s) or shareholders in the business. It can be put in at the start and increased at a later date. Shareholders are entitled to all the profits the business makes, after everyone else has been paid. They can reinvest that profit rather than take it out as dividends.

The profit (or loss) from previous years, ploughed back into the business is a second possible source of funds. Other terms frequently used to describe this source are 'retained earnings' and 'reserves'.

This latter term conjures up pictures of sums of cash stored away for a rainy day. It is important to remember that this is not necessarily so. The only cash in the business is that shown under that heading in the current assets. The reserves, like all other funds, are used to finance a business and are tied up in the fixed assets and working capital.

Loan capital is the final source of money open to a business. These long-term loans are from outside parties and could be in the form of a mortgage, hire purchase agreements or long-term loans from a bank. (An overdraft would be treated as a current liability and dealt with in the working capital equation.) The common feature of all such loans is that businesses have to pay interest on the money, and eventually have to repay the capital whether or not the business is successful. Conversely, if the business is a spectacular success the lenders, unlike the shareholders, will not share in those profits.

INTERPRETING THE ACCOUNTS

An understanding of financial reports is essential to anyone who wants to invest in acquiring and running a business, but simply knowing how these reports are constructed is not enough. To be effective, the businessman must be able to analyse and interpret that financial information.

The starting point for any useful analysis of a franchisor's accounts is some appreciation of what should be happening in a given situation. If, for example, you fill your car up with petrol until it flows out, you expect the fuel gauge to read full. If it does not you would think the gauge suspect. (If you had left someone else to fill up the car you might have other doubts as well.) This would also be true for any other car you may come across.

Ratios, the tools of analysis

All analysis of financial information requires comparisons and there are three yardsticks against which business performance can be measured.

First, you can see how well a franchisor is meeting a personal goal. For example, he may want to double the number of franchise outlets or add 25 per cent to profits. This activity is called budgeting, when comparisons would be made between actual results and the budget.

Second, you might want to see how well the franchisor is doing this year compared with last, comparing performances against a historical standard. This is the way in which growth in sales or profits is often measured.

Third, you may want to see how well the franchisor is doing compared with someone clsc's business, perhaps a competitor, or someone in a similar line of business elsewhere. This may provide useful pointers to where improvements can be made, or to new and more profitable business opportunities. For this type of analysis you need external information. Fortunately the UK has an unrivalled wealth of readily available financial data on companies and industries. The chief source of this information is Companies House, but summaries of this data are available in trade directories in the reference sections of most major libraries.

The main way in which all these business yardsticks are established is through the use of ratios. A ratio is simply something expressed as a proportion of something else, and it is intended to give an appreciation of what has happened. For example, a percentage is a particular type of ratio, where events are always compared with a base of 100.

What results are you looking for?
You should be looking for financial results in two areas that are vital to a business's chances of survival. The first result looked for is a satisfactory level of profit. If you had some personal cash that you wanted to invest you would shop around and look for an organisation that paid a good 'interest rate' for the risk you were prepared to take. Once you had decided on, say, building societies, you would research for the best interest rate for the term you were prepared to tie your money up for.

A business is in exactly the same position. It has to give a satisfactory return to shareholders – or the owner(s) – bearing in mind the risk they are taking. If your proposed venture is highly speculative and the profits are less than building society rates, your shareholders (yourself included) will not be happy.

Also they must make enough profit to allow the company to grow. If a business wants to expand it will need more working capital, and eventually more space or equipment. An important source of money for this is internally generated profits – reserves.

The second result looked for is for survival, and to survive the business must be financially sound. Clearly, all businesses are exposed to market risks; competitors, new products and price changes are all part of a healthy commercial environment.

The risks that you should be particularly concerned about are high financial risks. These include the danger of running out of cash, or of the franchises being so heavily borrowed that the interest charges weigh the business down.

Interpreting the Accounts*

The Profit and Loss Account for the year ended 31.12.87

The Balance Sheet at 31.12.87

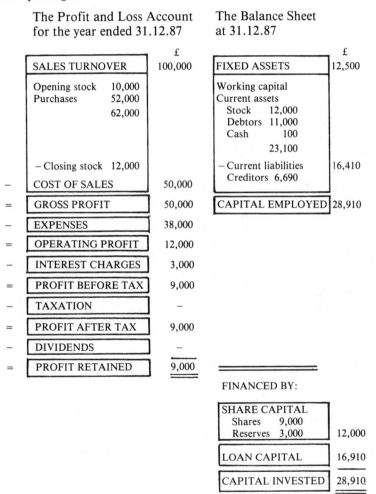

The Profit and Loss Account for the year ended 31.12.87

		£
SALES TURNOVER		100,000
Opening stock	10,000	
Purchases	52,000	
	62,000	
− Closing stock	12,000	
−	COST OF SALES	50,000
=	GROSS PROFIT	50,000
−	EXPENSES	38,000
=	OPERATING PROFIT	12,000
−	INTEREST CHARGES	3,000
=	PROFIT BEFORE TAX	9,000
−	TAXATION	−
=	PROFIT AFTER TAX	9,000
−	DIVIDENDS	−
=	PROFIT RETAINED	9,000

The Balance Sheet at 31.12.87

	£
FIXED ASSETS	12,500
Working capital	
Current assets	
Stock 12,000	
Debtors 11,000	
Cash 100	
23,100	
− Current liabilities	16,410
Creditors 6,690	
CAPITAL EMPLOYED	28,910

FINANCED BY:

		£
SHARE CAPITAL		
Shares	9,000	
Reserves	3,000	12,000
LOAN CAPITAL		16,910
CAPITAL INVESTED		28,910

*If you are relying on published accounts only, then you will not have access to all this information. You will, however, see: sales turnover, net profit before tax, tax paid; and certain items of expense such as: dividends, directors' pay, depreciation and leasing charges.

Factors that affect results

Look at the table opposite and you will see how the results of the business, as measured in the profit and loss account and the balance sheet, affect business performance.

The profitability of a business can be measured in two ways. Both are important and to a large extent interdependent. Return on Capital Employed (ROCE) relates the profit to the capital invested in the business. In the example here this ratio is calculated in this way.

$$\text{ROCE:} \qquad \frac{\text{Net profit}}{\text{Capital employed}} = \frac{9,000}{28,910} = 31\%$$

This is the fundamental performance ratio of any and every business and can be used to compare and contrast results. You could say of this result, for example, that it is more than three times greater than a building society's rate.

Profit margins relate various levels of profit to the level of sales activity. The first of these is the gross profit which is calculated by deducting the cost of sales from the sales and expressing the result as a percentage. In this example this is £100,000 (sales) − £50,000 (cost of sales) = £50,000 (gross profit); then £50,000 (gross profit) ÷ £100,000 (sales) = 50 per cent. This ratio gives an indication of how efficient a business is at 'producing'.

Operating profit is calculated by deducting the expenses from the gross profit. This figure is then divided by the sales and expressed as a percentage. For this example this ratio is 12 per cent (12,000 ÷ 100,000).

This tells you how well (or badly) the business is performing if you ignore all the factors outside your direct control. Those factors include interest rates and levels of corporation tax. Clearly, changes in these will affect your overall results, but the changes themselves are decided by people outside the business's control or influence.

Net profit is calculated by deducting the interest charges (and tax, if any) from the operating profit, and expressing it as a percentage of sales. For this example the ratio is 9 per cent (9,000 ÷ 100,000).

These ratios are useful when comparing one period's performance with another, or when comparing similar businesses. They are not universal, however, so comparing a fast print franchisor's profit margins with those of a fast food franchisor's would be meaningless.

How sound is the financial position?

Maintaining a sound financial position for most businesses seems to be focused on keeping away from overgearing or overtrading, the two rocks on which many founder. You have to be confident the franchisor is going to be around for long enough to deliver his end of the contract!

Overgearing

A business has access to two fundamentally different sorts of money. Equity, or owner's capital, including retained earnings (reserves), is money that is not a risk to the business. If no profits are made then the owner and other shareholders simply do not get a dividend. They may not be pleased, but in the short run there is little they can do about it. Loan capital, or debt capital as it is sometimes called, is money borrowed by the business from outside sources; it puts the business at financial risk and is also risky for the lenders. In return for taking that risk they expect an interest payment every year, irrespective of the performance of the business.

High gearing is the name given when a business has a high proportion of outside money to inside money. For a new business with no substantial historical profits to invest in future growth, borrowing money represents perhaps the only option.

Gearing

Capital structure	*No gearing*	*Average gearing* 1:1	*High gearing* 4:1
	£	£	£
Share capital	100,000	50,000	20,000
Loan capital		50,000	80,000
Total capital	100,000	100,000	100,000
Interest on loan at 12%	0	6,000	9,600
Profit before interest	9,000	9,000	9,000
Times interest earned	–	1.5X	0.94X

Look at this example. Our hypothetical business needs capital of £100,000 to make profits of £9000 (before interest charges). If all the money is provided by the owner (or shareholders) there is no gearing, as this relationship between share capital and loan capital is called. If the owner decided to borrow £50,000, the gearing ratio would be 1:1. If he decided to go for £80,000 of borrowed money his gearing ratio would rocket to 4:1. This may seem to him at the time to be his only option. But if he pursues this course he will become overgeared. His £9000 profits are not enough to cover the interest charges on the borrowing. Recent evidence from research into reasons for the failure of companies given loans under the government loan guarantee scheme shows that a start-up gearing greater than 4:1 is nearly always fatal.

As well as looking at gearing, you should study the business's capacity to pay interest. Do this by using a ratio called 'times interest earned'. This is calculated by dividing the profit before interest by the loan interest. There are no hard and fast rules on what this ratio should be, but much less than three times interest earned is unlikely to give lenders confidence.

Overtrading
Overtrading is the term used to describe a business which is expanding beyond its capacity to get additional working capital resources. As sales expand, the money tied up in stocks and customers' credit grows rapidly. Pressure also comes from suppliers who want payment for the ever-increasing supply of raw materials. The natural escape valve for pressures on working capital is an overdraft (or a substantial increase in the current one). Unfortunately, many small or expanding businesses do not have the financial controls to alert them to the dangers in time.

Here are the most important control ratios to monitor working capital:

The current ratio (a measure of liquidity)
A business's ability to meet its immediate liabilities can be estimated by relating its current assets to current liabilities. If for any reason current liabilities cannot be met, then the business is being exposed to an unnecessary level of financial risk. Suppliers may stop supplying or could even petition for bankruptcy if they are kept waiting too long for payments. In our example this ratio is:

$$\text{Current ratio} = \frac{\text{Current assets}}{\text{Current liabilities}} = \frac{23,100}{6,690} = 3.4$$

This shows current liabilities covered 3.4 times, and the ratio is usually expressed in the form 3.4:1. There is really only one rule about how high (or low) the current ratio should be. It should be as close to 1:1 as the safe conduct of the business will allow. This will not be the same for every type of business.

A shop buying in finished goods on credit and selling them for cash could run safely at 1.3:1 (Marks and Spencer's current ratio is usually 1.1:1.) A manufacturer with high raw material stocks to store and customers' credit to finance may need over 2:1. This is because the period between paying cash out for raw materials and receiving cash in from customers is usually longer in a manufacturing business than in retailing.

It is a bit like the oil dip-stick on a car. There is a band within which the oil level should be. Levels above or below that band pose different problems. So for most businesses, less than 1.2:1 would probably be cutting things a bit fine. Over 1.8:1 would mean too much cash was being tied up in such items as stocks and debtors.

An unnecessarily high amount of working capital will lower the rate of return on investment because it makes the bottom half of the sum bigger: ROCE = Profit ÷ (Fixed assets + Working capital).

Credit control
Any franchise that is not selling exclusively on a cash basis has to finance its customers with its own cash. This is particularly true if the

customers are big companies. A key ratio in this area is:

$$\text{Average collection period} = \frac{\text{Debtors}}{\text{Sales}} \times 365 \text{ (or days in period)}$$

For our example this sum is $\dfrac{11,000}{100,000} \times 365 = 40$ days.

This shows that on average customers are taking 40 days to pay up. This area has been comprehensively covered in the preceding chapter. If you want to know something of a particular company's credit record then Credit Ratings Ltd (51 City Road, London EC1Y 1AY; 01-251 6675) can help.

Stock control
Some franchisors such as fast food or printers will have to buy in raw materials and work on them to produce finished goods. They may have to keep track of three sorts of stock: raw materials, work in progress and finished goods. A retailing business will probably only be concerned with finished goods, and a service business may have no stock at all. A key ratio in this area is:

$$\text{Days' stock held} = \frac{\text{Stock}}{\text{Cost of sales}^*} \times 365 \text{ (or days in period)}$$

*Cost of sales is used because it accurately reflects the amount of stock. The sales figure includes other items such as a profit margin.

For our example the sum is $\dfrac{12,000}{50,000} \times 365 = 88$ days.

This shows that the business has enough stock in hand to last for 88 days. It is impossible to make any general rules about stock levels. Obviously a business has to carry enough stock to meet customers' demands or production requirements.

Credit taken from suppliers and others
Of course the credit world is not all one-sided. The franchisor, too, will be taking credit. It would be prudent to calculate how many days' credit, on average, are being taken from suppliers, a very similar sum to average collection period. The ratio is as follows:

$$\text{Average credit period} = \frac{\text{Creditors}}{\text{Purchases in period}} \times 365 \text{ (or days in period)}$$

Which for our example is $\dfrac{6,690}{52,000} \times 365 = 47$ days.

As a rough rule of thumb you should be looking for at least as much credit from suppliers as is given to customers. (In our example we are giving 40 days and taking 47.)

Cash control

The residual element in the control of working capital is cash or, if there is no cash left, the size of overdraft needed in a particular period.

Usually, the amount of cash available is finite and specific, as is the size of overdraft it can take. Stock levels, creditor and debtor policies and other working capital elements have to be decided with these limits in mind. This information is assembled in the cash flow forecast.

How attractive is the proposition you are considering?

At the very minimum you will expect the franchisor to give you a breakdown of the capital you will be expected to provide, and what it will be used to buy, and a projected profit and loss account, perhaps showing different results according to the level of sales achieved.

Two typical examples are Prontaprint from the instant print area, and Spud U Like from fast foods. As can be seen from a comparison of the two documents, Prontaprint have provided a far more detailed breakdown, and one that is far more helpful to the potential investor. It would be almost impossible for the franchisee to make any adjustments to the Spud U Like capital requirements without substantial further enquiries; whereas he or his professional advisers can immediately see where Prontaprint's estimates might be unduly optimistic or pessimistic. Moreover, Prontaprint specifically state that prices are exclusive of VAT, whereas Spud U Like leave the investor in the dark as to whether the total capital requirement is £28,650 plus the £800 mentioned in small print or whether VAT of up to £4300 (assuming all the equipment and shopfitting carried VAT) would also have to be financed.

It is, however, probably unfair to judge franchisors solely on the basis of information included in their publicity brochures; the franchisors have their business to protect and as they are dealing with individuals who have at least some entrepreneurial spirit, there is a risk of their costings being used by someone else to set up independently. This possibility cannot be eliminated, as anyone who is being asked to part with a fee should demand a detailed breakdown first, but it need not be made too available to the general public.

Assuming that the franchisor has got the start-up costs right, in many cases he is in a position to put the franchisee in touch with sources of finance (see also pages 103-12). If the franchisor has made arrangements with a bank for the provision of loans then there is some reassurance that the proposition has been examined and approved (or at least not rejected) by someone with some experience: an important point when the franchisor is not one of the old-established or household names.

Inventory & Capital Requirement for a Typical Basic Unit

		£
Equipment –		
Offset Machine (*see note 1*)	5,000	
Camera/Processor	1,625	
Guillotine	1,225	
Cash Register	475	
Electronic Composer	4,425	
Sundry Finishing	500	13,250
Building and furnishings (*see note 2*)		
Shopfitting		
Heating		
Electrical		
Decor		
Signs		
Office Stationery		
Furniture		
Carpets		8,000
Legal fees		1,000
Franchise 'package' fee –		
Property fees		
Architect fees		
Launch promotion		
Training		
Sundry corporate items, etc		5,600
Licence fee		3,900
Training course expenses (accommodation and travelling)		400
VAT (reclaimable)		3,415
Estimated total capital investment		35,565
Less finance leasing		13,250
Estimated initial capital requirement (*see note 3*)		22,315

VAT shown above is calculated against Equipment, Licence Fee and Franchise Package Fee. All other amounts shown are VAT exclusive. VAT is recoverable with first VAT return and can then become working capital.

Notes:
1. A reconditioned offset machine may be available at a reduced price.
2. Building costs are based on a shop unit not requiring major construction work. Undeveloped sites will involve a correspondingly higher outlay and a property premium may also be required.
3. Licensee's drawings during first year will be required in addition.

While every effort has been made to ensure that the information contained in this statement is accurate, it is intended only as a guide and will vary in each case according to the condition of shop, proposed geographic location and the individual circumstances.

October 1982

Capital Requirement Breakdown

Shopfitting	£25,000
Equipment	£11,000
Franchise fee	£2,500
	+ VAT
	To be paid on
	signing contract
	£38,000
	+ 2,875 VAT
	£41,375

We have taken a shop with a turnover of £2000 per week as an example. There is no such thing as an absolute average shop and this breakdown is only given as a guide. Prices quoted are correct at time of printing. Franchise fee includes on site opening assistance and training. There will be an opening publicity campaign which will cost in the region of £800.

©Spud U Like 1980

It is important to have a clear idea of the start-up costs and capital requirements of a franchise, if only because these are going to be a prime determinant of the franchise chosen.

LEASING

Leasing is another method of avoiding high initial capital expenditure, but at the cost of raising the overhead running costs and a certain loss of flexibility – leased assets cannot be used as security, nor can they be sold. It may not be possible to terminate the agreement without substantial penalties being incurred, which could be a disadvantage should the equipment be found to be unsuitable, or inferior to another available product. It does, however, provide 'off balance sheet finance' and the business may at first sight appear less highly geared than is operationally the case. *Gearing* is the ratio of a business's borrowings to its equity.

ANTICIPATED PROFITABILITY

This has to be the crucial area for examination. The potential franchisee wants to make, if not a fortune, at least a living. The downside of the increased security and reduction of risk that are the attractions of franchising also mean that the potential rewards are likely to be lower. In order to consider the problems of interpreting the predictions given by franchisors, it may be useful to consider a fictional example constructed from various brochures:

Gamesters Ltd

Capital outlay:	£
Shopfitting	12,000
Equipment	4,000
Stock	10,000
Franchise fee	3,000
Sundries	1,000
	30,000

Profit forecast:	£
Sales	52,000
Cost of sales (45%)	23,400
Gross margin	28,600

	£	£
Gross margin		28,600
Expenses:		
Franchise royalty (5%)	2,600	
Advertising fund (2%)	1,000	
Wages and NHI	11,000	
Rent, rates, insurance	5,000	
Light & heat	500	
Postage and telephone	400	
Motor and travel	700	
Accountancy	600	
Depreciation	1,500	23,340
Net profit		5,260

The franchisors stated that the sales of £1000 per week was a conservative estimate, and given that the business (selling and repairing computer games) would more than break even in the first year, the franchisee could expect a healthy return in subsequent years, if the growth in demand for electronic leisure goods continues.

The prospect looked reasonable, and the franchisee went ahead financing it as follows:

	£
Own capital	10,000
Loan from parents	10,000
Loan from bank	10,000
	30,000

plus £2000 of his own which provided his initial cash for working capital.

Towards the end of the first year, it became apparent that all was not well; he was running close to the limits of his overdraft facility despite achieving the predicted sales. The only two courses of action appeared to be either to run down his stocks, or to replace his skilled employee with a less able part-timer. Either of these would probably cause sales to deteriorate, and Gamesters would rapidly complain about the damage to their corporate image.

This sort of situation is often caused by a misunderstanding of the term 'break-even'. There are, in fact, three break-even points which should have been calculated in order to assess the financial viability of the business:

1. The operating break-even. The business *has* achieved the operating break-even, considering this as follows: Out of every pound's-worth of sales, 45p goes straight out on the immediate cost of goods sold, leaving 55p towards other expenses. The franchise royalty and the advertising fund, which vary directly with sales, take out another 7p, so the other, fixed, costs must be met out of the remaining 48p. These fixed costs total £19,700, so £19,700 ÷ 0.48 or £41,042 sales are required to break even.

2. The cash flow break-even. Unfortunately, the operating costs do not include all *cash outflows* from the business and as detailed, do not allow for bank interest or repayments of principal, nor do they allow for drawings for the franchisee and his family to live on. Assuming bank interest at 14 per cent and repayments averaging £2000 a year, £3400 is being added to the costs; and if a minimum living expense is estimated at £5000 then the break-even becomes £19,700 + £8500 ÷ 0.48 or £58,750, which is not being achieved. Even if depreciation is eliminated as not involving cash flow (though the assets will eventually have to be replaced) the break-even is still £55,625.

3. 'Desired return' break-even. This is a rather more nebulous concept, but in the present case the following would probably be taken into account:
   a) The figure should allow for some interest on the loan from his parents, which he would feel morally, if not legally obliged to pay – allow £1400 (as to the bank).
   b) Had he been able to invest his own capital, it would have earned interest; allow £12,000 at 10 per cent = £1200 (less tax at 30 per cent) = £840.
   c) Had he been working as an employee, he might have earned say, £9000 a year rather than the £5000 drawn. The extra income would therefore be approximately (depending on his precise tax position) £4000 less tax = £2800.

The desired return break-even therefore, would increase to £19,700 + £8500 + £5040 ÷ 0.48 which would require sales of £69,250 – an increase of 33 per cent on his current takings.

To keep things simple these figures do not allow for taxation on profits but, of course, depending on personal circumstances, tax may be due.

Looking at an actual forecast, again taking Prontaprint as one of the most detailed and realistic estimates, there are still some short-comings: John Smith (an actual individual, though not of that name) having some experience in printing and design, considered taking out a Prontaprint franchise, but eventually decided to go it alone. However, he found the predicted costings he had been given useful, and prepared his business plan on the basis of them. He obtained finance from the bank under the loan guarantee scheme. Now, after about 18 months' trading, he is in severe financial difficulties because of cash flow problems, and the business could fail in the next few months.

Doubtless Prontaprint would say that this merely proves that he should have had the strength of the franchise company behind him, but it is instructive to see where his costs differed from those predicted.

First, the cost of sales figure was too low. Recent increases in the price of paper especially meant that the £13,000 needed to be increased by 50 per cent to £19,500. Advertising was about £400, telephone £1,000, sundries £900. The rent, rates and insurance figure was underestimated by £3000 (the figure might have been adequate outside London, but not within; a central London location would have involved an even higher figure). Given that the capital requirements breakdown gave a leased assets figure of £11,000, the 'machine rentals' at £840 seems extremely low. On a four-year contract £2800 was regarded as realistic. On the other hand, £1500 was regarded as a more realistic figure for depreciation, given that the fixtures and fittings were estimated at £7000. Obviously, this would, to a large extent, depend on how quickly the franchise fees and licence fee were written off. This would not, however, affect the cash flow position.

If Prontaprint's figures are adjusted for these amounts, the profit of £8360 reduces to £1800; and this, it should be remembered, is an operating profit, not taking into account repayments of capital. It is not clear to what the interest figure refers, but if it is a bank loan, then the repayments would presumably be fairly substantial. Nor has anything been allowed for living expenses. So, allowing new fixed overheads of £30,700 and a lower contribution rate of 62.5p operating break-even would represent sales of £49,120, and cash flow break-even correspondingly higher, depending on loan repayments and personal circumstances.

Projected Operating Statement for an Established Shop

	£	%	£	%	£	%
Weekly average sales	1500		2000		3000	
Sales	78000	100	104000	100	156000	100
Royalty 5% Marketing services fund-5% (see note 1)	7800	10	10400	10	15600	10
Cost of sales	19500	25	26000	25	34000	25
Gross profit	50700	65	67600	65	101400	65
Overheads						
Wages	16000	20	20800	20	32200	20
Advertising	750		900		1600	
Free beverages and music	300		400		700	
Heat and light	1100		1300		1900	
Postage and stationery	350		450		650	
Motor and travel	1100		1200		1800	
Repairs and renewals	1900		2400		3000	
Telephones	700		800		1100	
Sundry expenses	750		1000		1500	
Rent, rates and insurance	7800		7800		7800	
Interest (HP)	1320		1320		1820	
Machine rentals	840		1560		2800	
Depreciation	3040		3040		3700	
Bank charges	150		350		400	
Accountancy fees	750		900		1200	
Total overheads	36850	47	44220	43	62070	40
Net profit (see note 2)	13850	18	23380	22	39330	25

Notes:
1. Marketing services fund is guaranteed to be spent entirely on advertising and marketing services to promote and develop the service in accordance with clause 7(a) (ii) of the licence agreement.

2. These figures should not be construed as representations of profits of any specific franchise nor as any assurance that a new franchise will in fact make a profit.

© Prontaprint Limited   October 1982

Had he been a franchisee he would also have had to pay the royalty and marketing fees of £5200, which would have turned his profit into a loss of £3400 and his operating break-even sales would have been £58,500.

Whether the franchisee could avoid this would depend on the franchisor's policies – is he allowed to raise prices, or are they fixed? Can he open for longer trading hours? Can he stock sidelines of higher mark-up goods? All these questions need to be answered before signing the contract.

Taking over an existing franchise outlet

Whether you are considering taking over an existing franchise outlet, or a new one, many of the points you should consider are exactly the same. However, the existence of another party, the vendor, introduces some complications but makes certain problems less worrying.

If there is an existing outlet for sale, then you have the reassurance that the franchise organisation has some proven value; you do not have to take the same risks as with a new franchise, where all you may be able to rely on is the franchisor's pilot operation. All the same, all the questions that arise as to the viability of the franchisor's organisation, and the terms of the franchise contract should still be considered just as carefully.

The main difference from taking up a new outlet is the availability of more information. Instead of the franchisor presenting you with a set of 'typical' start-up costs and a projected profit and loss account for a 'typical' unit, there will be a definite cost, the purchase price, and definite accounts.

The first point that you should ascertain is why the vendors are selling. No one willingly sells the proverbial 'little gold mine'. You do not want to purchase a business which is being sold because the owners cannot make a living out of it, unless you have good reason to think that you could do better. This may, in fact, be the case. For example, someone might take out a franchise of a 24-hour plumbing or drain clearing service after being made redundant from a nine-to-five office job and discover, after trying to adjust for a year or so, that he simply cannot cope with the type of work, or the erratic hours, and decide to get out. He has made a mistake as to the type of business he should have been in, but that does not mean there is necessarily anything wrong with the franchise itself, as long as you are convinced that you will not make the same mistake.

Where the reasons for sale are given as being personal, you should try to check up on the facts. The death of the proprietor is probably the most convincing personal reason; explanations such as illness, wish to move to be nearer relatives etc should be viewed, not necessarily with scepticism, but certainly as possibly not being the whole truth. If there are employees, a talk to them may help verify the reasons given.

Assuming that the franchise outlet has been in existence for some time, you should expect to be given at least three years' accounts. Once you start to go back beyond three years, then the information becomes rather of academic interest, given changing conditions. You now have to decide how much reliance to place on the accounts you are given. At this point consultation with an accountant will probably be advisable. If the vendors were operating as a limited company, then you should demand to see the audited accounts; but as these disclose only minimum information (they do not, for example, require so necessary a figure as the gross margin to be disclosed), you will also require the detailed accounts that the management uses.

If the vendor was a sole trader or a partnership then there will not be 'audited' accounts. There will, however, be accounts prepared for the proprietors, if only in order to agree the tax liability with the Inland Revenue. Here you should be quite clear about the function of the accountant. Except when he is auditing the statutory accounts of a limited company, when his duties are laid down by law, he is acting for his client and on his instructions. Most accounts prepared for sole traders and partnerships have a qualification such as 'these accounts were prepared from books and records presented to us, and information given to us by the client, and are in accordance therewith. We have not carried out an audit'. In other words, if the vendor has misled the accountant the accounts will be wrong, and the accountant will accept no responsibility.

You should make a distinction between the possibility that the accounts are definitely misleading or even fraudulent, and the probability that they will show a somewhat pessimistic view. As stated above, most sole trader and partnership year-end accounts are prepared for presentation to the Inland Revenue, and there is therefore a tendency to depress the profit figures in order to minimise the tax liability. You should not, however, accept from the vendor a grossly different figure based on this fact. If his accountant holds a reputable qualification there are requirements of professional ethics from his professional body that mean there are limits to how far he can deviate from what he knows to be the case; he certainly cannot falsify information, though there is some latitude in obscuring it. If the accountant is unqualified, these restraints do not necessarily apply, but even so, no accountant who has a regard for his professional reputation is likely to be willing to endanger it for one client.

Assuming that you have decided the accounts are reliable, you should look for a trend to increasing profits; certainly a turnover figure and a profit figure which increase at least greater than inflation. When looking at the profit figure you should see whether any amounts have been taken out by way of management salary by the vendors, as what you are interested in is the total profit available to you. You should also compare the figures with the franchisor's 'typical' figures and investigate any material differences. You should also consider how your own costs might differ; for example, if you intended to employ more people your wage costs would rise. You should also consider the employees that you will be taking over; they might not be the ones you would have chosen, but you might find it difficult to get rid of them.

Finally, you should bear in mind that the vendor probably wants to sell to you at least as much as you want to buy from him; unlike the deal with the franchisor, there is likely to be considerable leeway for negotiation on the price he is asking.

This could also be true where an already established business is turning branches into franchised outlets – a practice which many observers think is likely to grow. However, skilled professional advice on the accounts and a good deal of research into the viability of the site is essential – plus your own personal judgement of the situation. Why is such a switch being made? You have to be realistic about the fact that a franchisor of this kind is unlikely to franchise his most profitable branches. If the trade is not there, franchising is unlikely to change the situation. The potential for good profits by cutting costs and better management must be evident.

Occasionally, an established business, having made the decision to grow via the franchising route, will sell off some, or all of their existing outlets. A recent example is Holland & Barrett. By 1984 they had 150 company-owned outlets but their market research indicated that the UK could support around 2000 health food shops by 1990. To maintain their 20 per cent share of this market they would need a further 300 or so outlets. With three manufacturing subsidiaries to finance in this rapidly expanding market, Holland & Barrett opted for franchising as a way forward in the retail market. As a consequence a number of 'quality' outlets were put on to the market.

When considering buying an existing outlet a prospective buyer should question the parent company's management closely on their strategy, and on their commitment to franchising. Holland & Barrett's boss, Ken Mullarkey believes, 'there are some clear reasons why our form of retailing lends itself more to franchising than some others. There is a strong element of personal service – it isn't a supermarket operation. People come in asking for advice on what products they should buy to achieve a particular aim – like healthy ways of losing weight for instance.'

Chapter 4
Evaluating Yourself

Suitability for self-employment

No less important than evaluating the franchise and the organisation behind it is the question of evaluating your own suitability for self-employment. This is not just a question of financial resources, nor is a desire for independence, however passionately felt, enough in itself. Even a willingness to work hard, important though that is as a first step, is no more than one of several qualities you will need to make a success of setting up in business on your own. In fact one of the problems of self-employment is that few people realise just how much work is involved. They may pride themselves on never having been clock watchers as employees of someone else, but that usually means working long hours when they were called on to do so – once or twice a month perhaps, or even a couple of times a week. To a self-employed person long hours are normal, and the 'normal' working day of others the exception.

One reason for this is that working for yourself is not just a matter of doing the one job. People launching out on their own after years of working for others tend to forget what a warm, comfortable place the organisation is. 'Someone' looks after the PAYE and VAT returns, 'someone' does the paperwork, orders supplies, chases up goods that have failed to arrive, checks that the right instructions have been given to the right people and that they have been carried out. Maybe you will be or have been that 'someone' for one or other of these jobs as an employee, but as 'head cook and bottlewasher' in your own firm you will be that 'someone' for each and every one of these tasks. Even on days when you would have taken time off for sickness had you been employed, you will probably have to turn up to check on things, so good health is as important in self-employment as a healthy bank balance.

Family support

The healthy bank balance is not something you will achieve quickly. With the exception of a very few lucky people, most of those who

have opted for self-employment report that the price of independence is a high one and that, for the hours worked, the money is worse than they were making as an employee, at least during the first two or three years. For this reason it is important to have an understanding family behind you, if you have a family at all. They may not see very much of you for a while. You will find it difficult to take holidays, and the weekends which you may previously have spent taking them out in the car or cutting the hedge, are now more likely to be devoted to poring over the accounts or making up the order book. In fact it helps enormously if you can persuade members of your family to take part in the business. Apart from the psychological advantages of the fact that they might better understand the pressures you are under, there are tax advantages to employing your wife in the business. Assuming she has no other source of income, she is then eligible for a tax-free allowance on the first £2425 of her earnings. These days, when so many young people are out of work, there may also be other members of the family who are very glad of the chance of a job.

Leadership and discipline

This is another important aspect of self-employment in which many people have little experience. It is notoriously difficult to keep young people in order at home and it becomes no easier in a work situation – though probably considerably more important. Successful franchising depends heavily on maintaining standards of appearance, cleanliness and time-keeping. The failure to do so is taken as a breach of contract and can eventually lead to its cancellation by the franchisor. Operating a franchise means leading by example and being fairly tough on discipline. That does not mean standing over the staff with a whip, but it does entail a readiness to take unpopular decisions, including sacking staff if all else fails.

Personal characteristics

Most important of all, perhaps, is that you should evaluate whether you are actually going to enjoy the work. Career consultants have come to the conclusion that no matter how you test people, whatever ways you measure aptitudes and put together lists of personal characteristics that are required for specific types of jobs, success or failure largely depends on whether they like what they are doing. In addition to checking out the franchise itself and whether it lives up to the franchisor's performance promises, it is absolutely vital that it should be something you actually want to do. If you don't like dealing with the public, or hate cooking, a fast food franchise is not for you. If the product is not something you would actually want for yourself, the franchise is probably not for you either. Quite apart from that, some personal charcteristics might indicate that, although self-employment is a good idea for you, the particular form of it which franchising offers is not. Franchising does entail a good deal of uniformity in operating methods and presentation of the product, and if you are a person who does not take kindly to having his work inspected and who likes to take a very independent line, you may find yourself on a collision course before long. Perhaps the best way of discovering whether you are cut out to be a franchisee is to follow that old training officer's learning method of 'sitting next to Nellie'; in other words, having a spell working in the sort of franchise you are thinking of taking on to see whether it really suits you. Even if you do it for no pay, it could be worth hundreds of pounds in terms of experience.

A recent study of the personal franchisee characteristics required for success, carried out by Professor Russell M Knight of the University of Western Ontario, concluded that franchisees and franchisors had a large measure of agreement on what made for success.

They disagreed only in rating management ability and creativity – a point that may provide some clues as to what franchisors are really looking for in a franchisee.

Personal Franchisee Characteristics Required for Success

	Franchisee %			Franchisor %		
	Very important	Important	Not important	Very important	Important	Not important
● Previous management experience in same industry	0	20	80	2	14	84
● Previous own business experience	12	46	42	16	47	37
● Management ability	84	15	1	66	31	3
● Desire to succeed	90	10	0	93	7	0
● Willingness to work hard	92	8	0	93	6	1
● Creativity	26	56	18	12	44	44
● Strong people skills	63	32	5	64	34	2
● Financial backing	71	27	2	67	27	6
● Support from family	52	28	20	46	32	22

(Study size: 148 franchisors and 105 franchisees replied to questionnaire with follow-up interviews to 25 members of each group.)

Questionnaire

In the meantime, here are some questions to ask yourself which have a good deal of bearing on your general suitability for self-employment as a franchisee:

1. Do you like dealing with the general public, or are you shy and reserved?

2. Do you work well on your own initiative, or do you find you perform better when others tell you what to do?

3. In the sort of situations that running a business is likely to involve, do you lead or follow?

4. Are you a good organiser and administrator?

5. Are there some tasks which you hate doing, either because you find them boring or because you are no good at them, but which might nevertheless be involved in running your own business?

6. Can you work very long hours for long periods of time or do you tire easily?

7. Is your health good?

8. Can you be sure of moral and maybe physical support from your family?

·9. Are you easily discouraged by setbacks or do you see things through regardless?

10. Do you make decisions readily? Are they good ones?

11. Can you be tough with people when you have to be?

12. Are you good at listening to advice and even criticism, or are you touchy and impatient about it?

Chapter 5

The Franchise Contract

The obligations of the franchisee and the franchisor, all the rules and limitations governing the way the business is conducted, as well as the conditions under which it may be terminated by either party, are incorporated in the franchise agreement. It goes almost without saying, therefore, that every line of this document ought to be scrutinised very carefully before the franchisee commits himself to its contents by signing it. Indeed, it is essential that he should go through it with a solicitor, having first made a note of any points which he wishes to query, either because he does not understand them or because he disagrees with the conditions they impose.

The general advice of those experienced in franchise matters is to beware of the franchisor who is prepared to haggle to any substantial extent over the terms of the contract. If a clause was not reasonable in the first instance, why was it there at all, having regard to the fact that trust between franchisor and franchisee is essential if the deal is to work? If that trust does not exist, the possibility is that there may be future differences over meanings of the fine print. Once the agreement is signed it becomes much more difficult to argue over what has been contracted. Thus the general recommendation is that, unless there is a broad measure of agreement over terms, and their meaning is clear and acceptable to both parties, it is better not to go ahead at all.

All contracts, naturally, are somewhat different as between companies and the type of franchise involved, but they also have quite a number of features in common. An example of one agreement is given on pages 76-94, but in fact a franchise sometimes involves signing two agreements: a purchase agreement and the franchise agreement itself.

The purchase agreement

This is a fairly short document which simply states that, subject to the franchisor finding a suitable site, the franchisee will enter into the contract set out in the franchise agreement – provided, of course, that the prospective franchisee has read and approved that document within a reasonable time. Given that condition, a sum is paid to the franchisor's solicitors as part of the initial fee. This gives the franchisor the go-ahead with his search for a suitable site, which includes not only investigating its commercial viability but also finding out whether consents and planning permission would be available for its intended use. If no suitable site is found in a given time, the deposit is returned to the prospective franchisee; but if he rejects the site or changes his mind in the interim, then the deposit is forfeited.

The franchise agreement

This is a much longer document. Not necessarily in this order, it covers:

1. The nature and name of the activity being franchised.
2. The franchise territory.
3. The term of the franchise.
4. The franchise fee and royalty.
5. What the franchisor agrees to do.
6. What the franchisee undertakes to do.
7. The conditions under which the franchisee may sell or assign the business.
8. The conditions under which the franchisee may terminate the franchise and what his obligations are in that case.
9. The terms and obligations of the franchisor in similar circumstances.

The nature and name of the activity being franchised

This is simply a standard set of clauses which describes the franchise and warrants that the franchisor has a right to it and its associated trade marks, methods, recipes, specifications and whatever else is involved. The franchisee should, of course, be aware that the franchisor cannot guarantee protection from competition by similar products that are not franchised or which are part of some other franchise.

The franchise territory

The franchise will normally be a protected or privileged right to operate in a certain territory, best shown on an actual map. The problem is that this is hard to enforce fully because there is virtually nothing that can be done to prevent a franchisee from a neighbouring territory trading in yours, even though he may not be allowed a physical presence there. The questions to ask, therefore, are:

1. How close is the nearest outlet of the same franchise and how many such franchises are located in that general area?
2. Can the territory be reduced by the franchisor, and if so under what conditions?
3. Who has chosen the territory? If the franchisor has made the choice, on what basis was it made? Has there, for instance, been an independent market survey and has it vindicated the franchisor's claims for the territory's viability?

The term of the franchise

This is the duration over which the franchise runs. The franchisee should have an option to renew the franchise at the end of this period without further payment and for a similar length of time, though he may be asked to give warning of his intent to do so before then. No further start-up fee should be payable and the terms of the extension of the franchise should be similar to those under which he is operating at present, or at any rate, no less favourable than those under which new franchises are being offered. Other points are:

1. The franchise usually runs for at least five years, but the point to watch is that it lasts long enough for you to get the start-up costs back. Remember that you may be involved in considerable investment in equipment as well as the franchisor's initial fee.
2. Complications can arise over leased premises. Does the lease run for the same length of time as the franchise? If you have a 10-year lease and a seven-year franchise, what restrictions are being placed on you from trading at the same premises in another capacity?
3. If the premises are part of the franchise deal, you should check whether you have any obligations to make repairs at the end of the term. The costs involved could be considerable.

The franchise fee and royalty

The clauses under this heading set out when the initial payment is due and how much it will be. Equally important, it establishes the royalties due to the franchisor – the percentage, how it is calculated, whether advertising is treated separately, how often it is paid and what proofs the franchisor requires that the amount remitted to him is correct. There are obviously many things to watch out for here and the advice of an accountant and a solicitor might well be opportune.

1. A low royalty rate is not necessarily a favourable sign, particularly when it is combined with a high start-up fee. It could mean that back-up and services from the franchisor will

not be adequate. It could even mean that he is interested in nothing much more than taking your start-up fee and running with it!

2. Since the royalty is usually based on sales turnover rather than profits, the franchisor may press to increase volume at the cost of profitability. The two are by no means necessarily the same.

3. Ideally there should be a royalty rate reducing as volumes grow. It is also a good thing if the start-up fee is payable in two instalments – eg part on signature of the contract, the rest when you commence business.

4. A low royalty rate may also be balanced by the franchisor putting an excessive mark-up on goods and services which the franchisee is obliged to buy. It is important to find out whether such 'hidden extras' operate.

5. The conditions of the franchise may allow you to sell other goods and services – for instance, you may have a deep freeze from which you can supply non-franchised food and drink. In that case you should establish whether royalties are due on all takings or only on those relating to the franchise.

6. It is also important to ensure that where royalties are paid on sales, these are net of VAT.

7. Where relevant, the agreement must state whether royalties are paid on amounts invoiced, or only on those actually paid for.

8. When the franchisor generally undertakes to devote a proportion of the fees to advertising, the question arises, what proportion? And is it devoted to promoting the franchise as a whole, or your particular one? Or a mixture of both, and if so, in what proportion? When a separate percentage is charged for advertising, you will also need to be reassured on these points.

9. If interest is due on late payments, is the rate reasonable?

10. If a minimum monthly payment is laid down, is it a fair figure?

What the franchisor agrees to do

The question of advertising may well be covered under this heading, but it is plainly an important issue since, to a large extent, the 'established name' which is an essential part of the business format, is promoted in this way. Other aspects that should be included under this section of the agreement are:

1. Training. What is offered? Who pays for it? How long does it go on for? If training is a prerequisite for the franchisee and/or his staff, who pays for it and what happens if either of

them fails? If staff need to be trained, the same question has to be asked.
2. Site selection and layout. Is assistance provided? If so, at what additional cost?
3. Specifications for premises and equipment. The franchisor will probably lay down certain quality controls in providing this service as well as demanding uniformity with other franchises in the group.
4. The provision of promotional and other advertising material. The question that arises here as well as in 3. is the extent to which this is useful in your particular franchise, assuming it has to be paid for. One of the main points of friction between franchisor and franchisee is when the latter is committed to acquiring point of sale material or bits of 'styling' or equipment which he may not feel he needs or does not like.
5. The operating manual. As stated earlier, it is important that this document should be intelligible.
6. Where the franchisor supplies goods and/or services to the franchisee, these should be fairly priced. It is equally important that, should there be any delays and hold-ups in supply, the franchisee should be free to purchase elsewhere.
7. Normally the franchisor should provide assistance during the opening period and also pledge himself to provide back-up, support and help, as and when it is needed over a wide range of matters – trouble with the product or its preparation, staff training, book-keeping, negotiations with local authorities etc.

What the franchisee undertakes to do

Essentially the franchisee undertakes to observe the franchisor's conditions and requirements, so the question to consider is whether these are fair and reasonable.

1. They may include a clause prohibiting the franchisee from trading in anybody else's products or getting supplies from other sources. What happens if there are unreasonable delays?
2. If selling prices are set by the franchisor, do they provide an adequate margin and are they competitive with similar goods and services obtainable in the area?
3. Are the obligations placed on the franchisee as regards standards of equipment, decor, and participation in national or regional sales promotion or training exercises fair, or do they constitute a hidden cost?
4. Are the operating procedures contained in the manual simple to follow and practical or are they complex and burdensome?
5. Are there any unreasonable conditions which would prevent you carrying on some other trade for any period of time should

you wish to discontinue the franchise at the end of the term, or indeed before then?

6. Are there any unreasonable conditions which would prevent you from getting the best price for the franchise should you want to sell it?

The conditions under which the franchisee may sell or assign the business

The extent to which you are free to sell or assign the business at its market value (preferably assessed independently) is a measure of the freedom or control you have over it. If you cannot sell except to the franchisor, or unreasonable obstacles are placed in the way of your disposing of it to a third party, its value will be greatly diminished and in extreme circumstances the effort you have put into building up the business might be negated completely.

Most franchise agreements will lay down, first, that you will give the franchisor first refusal in the event of your wishing to sell or assign the franchise; second, that any third party you want to sell to has to be approved by the franchisor. It is natural that he should want to impose that condition, since he would want to be sure that the new franchisee is acceptable to him and that he is a fit person, financially and in every other respect, to run the operation.

Problems would occur, however, if the franchisor were to demand an excessive start-up or transfer fee from the new franchisee, or high royalties. At best, it would reduce the amount he would pay you for the franchise. At worst, an unscrupulous franchisor could effectively block any disposal, except on his terms. It is important the question of transfer is covered in a way acceptable to you, even if at the moment it is far from your intention to dispose of the franchise. Sadly, the question of death or disability cannot be ignored altogether.

The conditions under which the franchisee may terminate the franchise

There is no sense in holding someone to a franchise against his will, but the agreement should specify that the franchisee can terminate it before the set date. Apart from such considerations as illness, it could be that the business fails to make a sufficient income for its owner or simply that he does not like that kind of work.

Often a minimum period of time is laid down before the agreement can be terminated before the due date from causes within the control of the franchisee and he may also have to give notice of intent in writing in such cases. The starting-up fee will, of course, be forfeited but the point to watch is that there are no other financial penalties; for instance, an obligation to compensate the franchisor for loss of income should it prove impossible to find another buyer for the business.

Another potential problem is stock in trade and equipment. If you cannot sell them on the open market upon termination, will the franchisor buy back from you and if so, on what terms?

The conditions under which the franchisor may terminate the franchise

The obvious reason for the franchisor to terminate an agreement before its end would be if the franchisee failed to comply with its conditions; which makes it doubly important that you, as franchisee, should read this document carefully and satisfy yourself that you understand it and are able to comply with it. However, specific circumstances for termination should be set out in the agreement – beware of any that conceal them in the fine print. There should also be a period of grace in which you are given the chance to put right any faults the franchisor has pointed out to you.

He may, however, spell out circumstances which he regards as so serious a breach of the agreement as to justify termination without notice: consistent failure to report sales if the franchise royalty is based on percentage (as it usually is); failure to stay open for business over a prolonged period; trading in goods which are not part of the franchise without the franchisor's permission; acts which are prejudicial to the good name of the franchisor – all these are examples of what might reasonably be called material breaches of contract.

Conditions which you should question, however, and which have been known to appear in agreements, are:

1. A requirement, as a condition of the agreement, to purchase minimum quantities of goods or services from the franchisor or some source nominated by him.
2. A stipulation that certain sales quotas are reached (unless you are absolutely certain that these are feasible).
3. An open-ended obligation to commit yourself to expenditure on goods or services or equipment, ie one that is not related to a realistic level of profitability.
4. Anything described as a 'material' breach of the agreement which in your opinion or that of your advisers is in fact a trivial one.
5. Any clause which places a penalty on you other than the franchisor's legal costs in case of a dispute and the loss of the franchise itself should a premature termination be enforced. In other words, anything you have paid for should remain your property and you should be free to dispose of it at whatever

price you can get for it, unless the franchisor agrees to buy it back at market rates.

While no reputable franchisor is out to gain an unfair advantage over you in the agreement, it is vital to bear in mind that since he and his advisers have drawn it up, it will tend to favour him rather than you as the franchisee. Do not assume, therefore, that the benefit of the doubt will be on your side, and sign nothing (not even a contract with a 'cooling off period') until you have thoroughly understood it, had any provisions that are not clear explained by *your* advisers, and thought about the implications of every clause in it.

Typical franchise agreement

The following franchise agreement has been reproduced with the kind permission of Kall-Kwik Printing (UK) Limited, a full member of the British Franchise Association. Kall-Kwik Printing is now one of the leading UK franchisors.

KALL-KWIK PRINTING (UK) LTD
FRANCHISE AGREEMENT

Franchisor: **Kall-Kwik Printing (UK) Limited**

Franchisee:

Address:

Location:
(or such other premises replacing the same in accordance with Clause 2 hereof).

Centre Number:

Franchise Fee: thousand pounds
                        (£   ) (not including VAT)

Date of Agreement:

Commencement/
Opening Date:

The Mark:	The legend 'KALL-KWIK PRINTING' and 'KALL-KWIK PRINT COPY and DESIGN' and the logos associated with the name and any additional or substitute marks which the Franchisor shall deem suitable during the Term.
The Know-How	The operational systems and methods of the Franchisor derived from Kwik-Kopy Corporation of Houston, Texas, USA and divulged to the Franchisee from time to time during the Term.
The Permitted Name:	The permitted business name of the Franchisee shall be KALL-KWIK PRINTING CENTRE NUMBER _____ or such substitute permitted business name as the Franchisor shall deem suitable during the Term.
The Business:	To commence and undertake the business of instant print copying and ancillary services in the style and manner stipulated by the Franchisor using the Mark and the Know-How under the Permitted Name.
The Operations Manual:	The written system of and regulations for the operation of the Business issued and amended by the Franchisor from time to time during the Term incorporating the Know-How.
The Term:	From the Commencement/Opening Date until 8th October 2008 or sooner determination in accordance with the terms hereof.
The Continuing Fees:	Six per cent (6%) of gross sales of the Business.
The Promotional Contribution:	Four per cent (4%) of gross sales of the Business as a contribution to the advertising and promotional budget of the Franchisor to promote and expand the Mark for the benefit of all Franchisees of the Franchisor throughout the United Kingdom.
Signatories:	
Signed for and on behalf of	_____ Authorised Signatory of the Franchise Limited Company

Signed by _____

Signed by _____

Signed for and on
behalf of KALL-
KWIK PRINTING
(UK) LIMITED   _____
                              Authorised Signatory

WHEREAS (1) The Franchisor warrants that it is authorised by the beneficial owner of the Mark and Know-How to enter into this Agreement.

(2) The Franchisor operates through its franchise outlets (hereinafter called 'the Trade Name') a business of Instant Print and Copying Shops according to a plan or system (hereinafter called 'the Method') comprising the use of the Mark Trade Name and other insignia including trade marks logos designs and other identifying materials methods of advertising and publicity, patents know-how trade secrets and the style and character of furnishings and fittings and appliances and standard operational procedures set out in the Operation Manual protected by the law of copyright or by the registration of trade marks or designs or by patent or otherwise.

(3) The Franchisee wishes to obtain a Franchise from the Franchisor for the right to use the Permitted Name and the Know-How to operate the Business including all those matters referred to in Recital 2 above and to obtain the continuing assistance of the Franchisor in the on-going running of the Business and the Franchisor is willing to grant such a Franchise to the Franchisee on the terms and conditions as set out in this Agreement.

THIS AGREEMENT WITNESSETH as follows:

1.00   GRANT OF FRANCHISE

1.01   **Franchise Grant.** IN CONSIDERATION of the Franchise Fee paid by the Franchisee to the Franchisor (receipt of which is hereby acknowledged) and in consideration of the mutual agreements covenants and undertakings herein contained the Franchisor hereby grants a Franchise to the Franchisee the right to operate the Business at the Location (the 'Centre' which expression shall mean where the context so requires either or both of the Business and the Location) with the right to use in connection therewith the Mark the Know-How and the Permitted Name during the Term.

1.02   **Trade Mark Use.** The Franchisor reserves the absolute and express right to control all uses of the Mark by the Franchisee for all purposes: the Franchisee is not permitted to use the Mark or any derivation of the same in the corporate name (if any) of the Franchisee or other legal entity except the Permitted Name during the Term shall be the sole trading name used by the Franchisee and during the Term shall not be varied in any way without the prior written consent of the Franchisor.

2.00 LOCATION OF KALL-KWIK CENTRE

2.01 Approval of Location of Centre. The Franchisor approves the site of the Centre as an acceptable site for a Kall-Kwik Centre.

2.02 Relocation of Centre. If during the Term relocation of the Centre is deemed mutually desirable by the Franchisor and the Franchisee or is required as a result of the expiration or other termination of the lease, the Franchisor will select a new location for the Centre which shall be reasonably acceptable to the Franchisee. The Franchisor shall not be responsible for any expenses or losses of the Franchisee as a result of or incidental to or arising out of any relocation of the Centre.

2.03 Lease of Premises for the Centre. If the Franchisor takes a lease or assignment of a lease of the premises for the Centre the Franchisee shall execute an Underlease in the Franchisor's standard from which will provide interalia that default by the Franchisee under such Underlease or the termination thereof or default under this Agreement or the termination hereof shall entitle the Franchisor at its discretion to terminate the other document. If the Franchisee shall take a lease or an assignment of a lease or any other legal estate in the premises for the Centre in the Franchisee's own name then the Franchisee shall enter into a Deed of Option in the Franchisor's standard form granting the Franchisor the first right to take at Market Value (to be determined in accordance with the provision set out in Clause 11 below) the premises for the Centre, in the event that the Franchisee wishes to assign or sublet them, merge surrender or share or part with possession or occupation or otherwise transfer or dispose of the legal interest in any way to any assignee, sub-lessee, licensee or other occupier who will not be using the Centre for the Business. Any lease renewals or new lease obtained during the Term whether of the original premises for the Centre or new premises obtained in accordance with this Clause shall be subject to the terms of this sub-clause.

2.04 The Franchisee must obtain the written approval of the Franchisor to the terms and conditions of any lease to be granted or assigned to the Franchisee.

3.0 OBLIGATIONS OF FRANCHISOR

3.01 Training at the Cost of the Franchisee. To provide training in the conduct of the Business for the Franchisee (or in the case of a corporate Franchisee one of its directors) and one initial employee at a time and place to be chosen by the Franchisor provided that Clause 4.10 below (Non-disclosure) has been complied with.

3.02 Eligibility for Training. Only a Franchisee of the Franchisor or an employee of a Franchisee shall be eligible to receive training under the terms of this Agreement.

3.03 Time of Training. Initial training will be made available to the Franchisee after execution of this Agreement. Training shall be completed within ninety (90) days of the date of this Agreement.

3.04 Training of Additional Persons. If the Franchisee requires additional training for himself or requires additional training for any employees at any mutually agreeable time after the initial training such training shall be made available by the Franchisor at the cost of the Franchisee.

3.05   Equipment. The Franchisor will arrange the supply of the initial equipment package and advice and assist the Franchisee in the requisition of all materials stock and equipment necessary for the Centre, the Franchisee being liable and responsible for the costs of all materials stock and equipment.

3.06   Decor. The Franchisor will provide the Franchisee with the designs of and advice for the fitting and decoration of the Centre and installation of equipment in the Centre. The Franchisee must obtain the prior written approval of the Franchisor to any alterations additions and conversions.

3.07   Marketing. The Franchisor will undertake a marketing and promotional programme for the Mark in the United Kingdom by such methods as it considers appropriate using the Promotional Contribution provided for below.

3.08   Expenditure. Upon written request the Franchisor will submit to the Franchisee an account of the total expenditure on advertising marketing and promotional matters in each of the Franchisor's financial years throughout the Term. In the event that the Franchisor expends sums on marketing and promotional matters in excess of the total of the Promotional Contribution from all its franchisees in any year the Franchisor shall be entitled to recoup from the total of the Promotional Contribution of all such franchisees in any subsequent years the amount of any such excess.

3.09   Manuals. The Franchisor will issue to the Franchisee such Manuals for equipment supplies sales service advertising marketing promotion and such other matters related to the Business as the Franchisor deems appropriate, and ownership of any Manuals shall remain in the Franchisor and no right of reproduction in any form whatsoever of such Manuals is granted to the Franchisee.

3.10   Continuing Advice. The Franchisor will provide the Franchisee with continuing advice and consultation concerning the conduct of the Business throughout the Term as the Franchisor considers reasonable.

3.11   Records. The Franchisor will provide the Franchisee with sales reports and accounts forms to assist the Franchisee in maintaining accurate financial records.

3.12   Franchise Services Directory. The Franchisor will use best endeavours to provide all those services as set out in the Franchise Services Directory.

4.00   OBLIGATIONS OF FRANCHISEE

The Franchisee covenants with the Franchisor as follows:

4.01   Training. Not to commence the Business until the Franchisee (or in the case of a corporate Franchisee one director of the Franchisee) and one senior employee have received training from and have been approved as competent by the Franchisor.

4.02   Training of Personnel. To provide such training for his personnel as may be necessary to meet the qualification levels set by the Franchisor from time to time.

4.03 Attendance. To devote his full time energies and attention to the Business (and in the case of a corporate Franchisee to ensure that at least one director complies with the attention provisions of this Clause) and to procure the greatest volume of turnover for the Centre consistent with good service to his customers and the standards quality and methods stipulated in the Operations Manual.

4.04 Reports. To make such reports and keep such records concerning the Centre as the Franchisor shall from time to time require and to use all forms designated by the Franchisor to complete and process such forms in a manner satisfactory to the Franchisor and to forward all records and forms to the Franchisor at such times and in such manner as the Franchisor shall from time to time require and if requested to supply to the Franchisor copies of all Bank Statements relating to the Business, copies of VAT returns, and till rolls.

4.05 Payment of Fees. To pay punctually any and all sums or amounts due to the Franchisor (or any other persons company body or authority) under this Agreement or under any document connected with the Franchise hereby created.

4.06 Payment of Debts and Performance of Obligations Guaranteed by Franchisor. To pay punctually any and all sums or amounts owing by the Franchisee the payment of which has been guaranteed in any manner by the Franchisor and to perform duly and punctually any and all obligations of the Franchisee the performance of which has been guaranteed in any manner by the Franchisor.

4.07 Payment of Trade Accounts. To pay promptly all suppliers of the Franchisee and the Franchisee shall notify the Franchisor immediately of the Franchisee's inability to honour any such obligations.

4.08 Payment of Rent and Compliance with Lease. To pay promptly the rent and other payments due under the lease for the Centre as such payments become due, time being of the essence. The Franchisee will not breach or default in the performance of any terms or conditions of such lease.

4.09 Trade Secrets. To keep confidential the Know-How or any other systems or methods used in the Business as divulged to the Franchisee by the Franchisor and not to reveal to any employee of the Franchisee any such information except that which is necessary for the proper conduct of the duties of the employee in the Business and to keep all such information in a secure place at the Centre accessible only to the Franchisee (or its directors in the case of a corporate Franchisee).

4.10 Non-disclosure. Not to employ any person in the Business until such person has signed a non-disclosure undertaking in the form approved by the Franchisor from time to time.

4.11 Insurance. To keep in force a comprehensive employers and public liability policy approved by the Franchisor in respect of the Centre together with all risks insurance for the full replacement value of all equipment and stock of the Centre and loss of profits which shall include provision for the payment of the Continuing Fees and Promotional Contribution in the event of the cessation of the Business for a period of twelve months and to furnish the Franchisor with a copy of such policy and in each year of the Term to supply to the Franchisor a premium payment certificate if so required by the Franchisor PROVIDED THAT if the Franchisee fails to comply with this sub-Clause the Franchisor may obtain such insurance and keep the same in force and effect and the Franchisee shall pay to the Franchisor on demand all premiums and other costs and expenses incurred by the Franchisor.

4.12 Notification to Public. To display a notice in a prominent position at the Location clearly indicating that the Franchisee is operating an independent business under licence from the Franchisor and is not a partner agent or employee of the Franchisor.

4.13 Promote Goodwill. Constantly to protect and promote the goodwill attached to the Mark and to hold any additional goodwill generated by the Franchisee for the Mark or the Permitted Name as bare trustee for the Franchisor.

4.14 Special Promotions. To co-operate with the Franchisor and other Franchisees of the Franchisor in any advertising campaign sales promotion programme or other special activity in which the Franchisor may engage or specify including the display of services advertising and the distribution of special novelties promotional literature and the like.

4.15 Conduct. To conduct himself and to ensure that his employees conduct themselves in such a manner as not to discredit or denigrate the reputation of the Business or the Permitted Name. Any behaviour amounting (in the opinon of the Franchisor) to misconduct if not promptly abated shall be a cause for termination of the Franchise in accordance with Clause 8.01 hereof.

4.16 Compliance. To use best endeavours to comply with the systems and methods as set out in the Operations Manual, Marketing Manuals and any other Manuals relating to the operation of the Business issued by the Franchisor from time to time.

4.17 Access. To permit the Franchisor or its agents full free and unrestricted access and right of entry to the Centre for any purpose whatsoever under or pursuant to this Agreement including but not limited to checking ensuring or enforcing compliance by the Franchisee with any of his obligations hereunder whether during the Term or after its expiration or sooner determination.

4.18 Staff Standards. The Franchisee shall keep the Centre staffed with sufficient number of competent employees so as to enable the Franchisee to operate the Centre efficiently in accordance with the highest trade standards and in accordance with the standards from time to time prescribed by the Franchisor and if reasonably required by the Franchisor, to arrange staff to undergo training specified by the Franchisor.

4.19 Premises. To take possession of the Centre and open for business immediately the centre is ready to open and to keep the centre open for business during normal business hours or otherwise as prescribed from time to time by the Franchisor.

4.20 To keep the premises in a good state of internal repairs and decoration and to keep the premises clean and tidy and up to the reasonable demands and requirements of the Franchisor and to keep the premises internally lit and all illuminated signs lit until at least midnight of every day.

5.00 OPERATION OF KALL-KWIK CENTRE

5.01 **Business Name of Franchisee.** The business name of the Franchisee shall be the Permitted Name and no other name.

5.02 **Independent Contractor and Business**

5.02.1 The Franchisee is and shall in all events be an independent contractor and nothing herein contained shall be construed as constituting the Franchisee as agent partner employee or representative of the Franchisor for any purpose whatsoever.

5.02.2 The Franchisee acknowledges that there is no authority granted to him under this Agreement or otherwise to incur any obligations liabilities or responsibilities on behalf of the Franchisor or to bind the Franchisor by any representations or warranties or otherwise howsoever, and the Franchisee agrees not to lead anyone to believe that the Franchisee has such authority.

5.03 **Infringement Indemnity.** To indemnify the Franchisor from any alleged unauthorised use of any patent trade mark or copyright (other than the Mark) by the Franchisee or any claim by any third party in respect of the Business or the conduct or neglect of the Franchisee or any infringement of any relevant regulations.

5.04 **Prices.** The Franchisee is free to establish prices for goods or services offered in the course of the Business at the Franchisee's sole discretion but having regard always to the Franchisor's price estimating methods and commercial viability.

5.05 **No Unsuitable Display.** The Franchisee shall ensure that the Mark is not used or displayed on any materials or products which are illegal pornographic or offensive or are critical or derogatory of any nation government religion religious body whether or not the same are associated with the Mark nor associate the Mark or the Business in any way with any political or religious movement or beliefs nor to print or distribute any materials which would denigrate the goodwill of the Mark.

5.06 **No Other Business.** Not without prior written approval of the Franchisor to permit any other business venture to operate or trade at the Centre nor without such approval to extend the scope or range of the Business at the Centre and if the Franchisor approves any such sharing or extension to procure that the gross sales of the same shall be subject to this Agreement and to pay the Continuing Fees and Promotional Contribution.

5.07 **Audit.** The Franchisee grants to the Franchisor the right at all reasonable times for the Franchisor or authorized representative to entre the Centre to make an examination and/or audit of all the Franchisee's financial books and records including those records referred to in Clause 4.04 hereof (together with a right to make copies thereof) which can be made either by an employee of the Franchisor or by an independent contractor employed by the Franchisor for such purpose such examination and/or audit to be at the Franchisor's sole expense except as provided below. Should the Franchisee fail to make a Sales Report to the Franchisor within thirty (30) days from the date when such Sales Report becomes due the Franchisor may examine and/or audit the Centre to determine Gross Sales and any Continuing Fees or other fees due and may charge the expenses of such examination and/or audit to the Franchisee. Furthermore should any examination and/or audit by the Franchisor of the Centre establish the Franchisee's failure to report sales or pay any royalty or fees by at least 1% of that which should have been reported or paid the Franchisor may charge the Franchisee the expense of the examination and/or audit in addition to all other payments or charges which may be due.

5.08　**Credit Sales.** Extension of credit is the sole responsibility and risk of the Franchisee and the Continuing Fees and Promotional Contribution shall be due and payable on credit sale to the same extent as if such business had been by cash sale.

6.00　FRANCHISE FEES

6.01　**Initial Payment.** The Franchisee shall pay to the Franchisor upon execution of this Agreement the Franchise Fee.

6.02　**Further Payments.** The Franchisee shall during the Term make payments to the Franchisor as follows:

6.02.1　**Dates.** To pay the Continuing Fees and the Promotional Contribution without deduction or set-off to the Franchisor or as it directs once every week every Tuesday in respect of the Business during the immediately preceding week, except that the Franchisor may waive this condition from time to time and direct and grant permission to the Franchisee to make payments monthly on or before the seventh day of each calendar month during the Term in respect of the Business during the immediately preceding calendar month, time being strictly of the essence in respect of either weekly or monthly payments.

6.02.2　**Calculations.** The Continuing Fees and the Promotional Contribution shall be calculated on the gross sales of the Centre during each calendar month or week of the Term (and for any period less than a complete calendar month or week) and gross sales shall include:

(i) all credit sales of whatever nature whether or not the Franchisee has received payment of the outstanding accounts by the Payment Date relevant to the period when such credit sales were made

(ii) all cash sales made but not invoiced by the Franchisee in such period

(iii) all goods sold or delivered and services performed by the Franchisee during such period which are unpaid and not invoiced on the relevant Payment Date.

(iv) all goods sold services performed and business dealings whatsoever (other than purchases) made or conducted on or from the Centre but shall execute any Value Added Tax or any other tax or duty replacing the same during the Term.

6.02.3　**Tax Contingency.** Whenever applicable to pay to the Franchisor Value Added Tax or any tax or duty replacing the same during the term charged or calculated on the amount of the Franchise Fee the Continuing Fees and the Promotional Contribution.

6.03　**Gross Sales Report.** On each of the Payment Dates to furnish the Franchisor with complete and accurate statements in the form approved by the Franchisor of the gross sales of the Centre since the last Payment Date and if the Franchisee shall fail to supply the Gross Sales Report within thirty (30) days of the Payment Date the Franchisor may estimate the gross sales of the Centre by taking an average of the last six monthly figures supplied by the Franchisee. If the Franchisor makes such an estimate it will notify the Franchisee in writing of the amount of such estimate and the amount of the Continuing Fees and Promotional Contribution shall upon receipt of such notice become immediately due and payable in such estimated figure. When the true amount of the gross sales is known the Franchisee will immediately pay to the Franchisor any balance outstanding together with interest thereon or in the event that the estimated figure is greater than the true figure the Franchisor will forthwith credit the Franchisee's account with the amount of any such excess but no interest shall be due and payable to the Franchisee in any event.

6.04   **Interest.** All sums due to the Franchisor under this Agreement which are not paid on the due date (without prejudice to the rights of the Franchisor and the condition that the Continuing Fees and Promotional Contribution are paid time being of the essence) shall bear interest from day to day at the annual ratge of 6% above the current Barclays Bank Plc daily interest rate with a minimum of 12% per annum.

6.05   The Franchisee shall have trading accounts and records audited once a year during the term and by a qualified auditor and submit a certified copy of the whole of such audited accounts to the Franchisor within three months of the end of each such year.

7.00   ASSIGNMENT AND TRANSFER

7.01   **Assignment by Franchisor.** The Franchisor may assign charge or otherwise deal with this Agreement in any way and its rights hereunder shall inure to the benefit of its successors and assigns PROVIDED THAT any such successors and assigns shall agree in writing to assume all of the Franchisor's obligations hereunder and PROVIDED FURTHER THAT any such assignment shall be made in good faith by the Franchisor. Such assignment shall discharge the Franchisor from any further obligations hereunder.

7.02.1   The Franchise hereby granted is personal and is granted to the individual Franchisee named in the particulars. Under no circumstances may the Franchisee grant a sub-franchise. The franchisee may transfer his interest in the Franchise and sell his interest in the Centre to another individual, partnership or limited company provided that the Franchisee and prospective transferee make prior written application to the Franchisor and receive written approval from the Franchisor for such transfer. The Franchisor will not unreasonably withhold its approval to such transfer provided that the transferee agrees to enter into the Franchisor's standard form of Franchise Agreement at the time in force such transfer is effected, and establishes to the satisfaction of the Franchisor that he is a respectable and responsible person with the personal capacity and financial ability to perform the obligations of a franchisee under the Franchise Agreement. Furthermore it shall be a condition of any such approval to transfer that the prospective transferee at his own cost shall satisfactorily take and complete the training then required by the Franchisor of all new Franchisees prior to the prospective transferee commencing the Business. The Franchisee shall pay to the Franchisor a reasonable transfer fee to be determined by the Franchisor to cover all costs and expenses of and incidental to such transfer. Any such transfer by the Franchisee under this sub-clause shall be considered a termination in respect of the Franchise for the purpose of Clause 8.0 hereof.

7.02.2 **Death of Sole Franchisee.** On the death of a sole Franchisee his personal representatives shall have six calendar months from the date of such death to notify the Franchisor of their decision:

(i) to continue the Business whereupon such personal representatives shall be deemed to be proposed assignees of the Business and the conditions set out in Clause 7.02.1 shall apply.

(ii) to assign the Business to any of the heirs of the Franchisee or to a third party whereupon the conditions set out in Clause 7.02.1 shall apply.

(iii) to terminate the Franchise Agreement and discontinue the running of the Business provided always that the personal representatives comply with the provisions and procedures set out in Clauses 9.02, 9.03, 9.04, 9.05, 9.06 below.

7.02.3 **Death of Joint Franchisee.** On the death of one of several Franchisees the survivor or survivors shall succeed in all respects to the rights of the deceased Franchisee under this Agreement.

7.02.4 **Sales Agent.** At the request of the Franchisee or his personal representatives as the case may be the Franchisor may act as a non-exclusive sales agent for the sale of the Business and in such event shall be paid a reasonable fee and its expenses of the same.

7.03 **Incorporation.** The Franchisee shall be free to incorporate and thereafter carry on the Business through any limited company owned by the Franchisee provided that the written permission of the Franchisor is first obtained and the limited company executes all agreements then required by the Franchisor for a corporate Franchisee. The Franchisee shall remain jointly and severally liable with the limited company in respect of all obligations on the part of the Franchisee contained in this Agreement and shall continue personally to supervise the Centre. Any such limited company shall be subject to all the restrictions on transferability herein contained together with a restriction on the dealing in, or sale of, or transfer or charge of the shares in the said limited company without the prior written approval of the Franchisor. A note of this restriction shall be lodged with the Register of shares and shareholding. The Franchisor shall have the right to inspect the Statutory Books of the said limited company. The Franchisee shall not be entitled to use the Permitted Name or any derivation thereof in its corporate name.

7.04 In the event that the Franchisee is in breach of the above clause 7.03 by trading at the Centre by or through a limited company without having first obtained the written permission of the Franchisor pursuant to the provisions of Clause 7.03, this breach shall in no way affect the Franchisor's right to hold the limited company jointly and severally liable with the Franchisee and jointly and severally responsible for all the obligations and conditions referred to in this Agreement. Any such action by the Franchisor shall be entirely without prejudice and in no way affect or waive the aforementioned breach by the Franchisee of Clause 7.03 and shall not affect the Franchisor's rights in respect of that breach.

7.05 **Ownership of Corporation.** Prior to incorporation or any transfer of the Franchise to a limited company the names and addresses of the proposed shareholders and directors together with the amount and percentages of the issued share capital owned or to be owned by each shall be submitted to the Franchisor in writing and the Franchisor shall have the absolute right to accept or reject the presence of any such shareholder or director before any such transfer is made. Consideration given by the Franchisor to the acceptance of the proposed corporate Franchisee shall be the same as that given to any other new Franchisee. All Directors appointed from time to time shall be required to agree in writing to be bound by the Franchise Agreement as if they were parties thereto.

7.06 **Change in Corporate Ownership.** As (in the case of a corporate Franchisee) this Franchise has been granted to the Franchisee by the Franchisor in reliance upon the quality of the directors and shareholders of the Franchisee the Franchisee will not permit any transfer or other dealing with its shares nor any change in its directors without the prior written approval of the Franchisor which shall not be unreasonably withheld in the circumstances set out in Clause 7.02.1.

7.07 **Invalid Transfer.** No transfer or assignment of the Franchisee's interest in the Franchise or the Centre shall be effective until approved in writing by the Franchisor and until the transferree has executed all agreements required by the Franchisor.

8.00 TERMINATION BY FRANCHISOR

8.01 **For Cause.** The Franchisor shall have the right in its absolute discretion to terminate this Agreement for cause (which shall include but not be limited to a breach by the Franchisee of any obligation covenant or duty contained herein and which shall include any breach of covenants conditions and stipulations in any Lease or Underlease of the Centre) by giving written notice to the Franchisee not less than thirty (30) days prior to the date of termination and stating the reason for termination. Any such notice shall state whether the cause for termination may be remedied and if so what corrective measures are acceptable to the Franchisor.

8.02 **Correctable Cause.** If the notice of termination states that the cause for termination may be remedied then the Franchisee shall have the right to remedy the same in a manner acceptable to the Franchisor within thirty (30) days following the date of the notice and if all such causes are remedied to the satisfaction of the Franchisor within thirty (30) days then the Franchisor shall withdraw such notice.

8.03 **Repeated Cause for Termination.** Commencing with a second notice of termination for a correctable cause the Franchisor may notify the Franchisee because of a repeated cause for termination that a subsequent repeat of a given cause in the following twelve (12) month period shall be sufficient cause for a final termination which shall not be remediable.

8.04 **Insolvency.** If the Franchisee enters into liquidation or bankruptcy or suffers a receiver to be appointed or makes a composition with any creditors the Franchisor may at its sole discretion at any time thereafter terminate this Agreement on notice with immediate effect AND

8.04.1 No creditor agent employee representative or trustee of the Franchisee shall have the right to dispose of any of the equipment or materials at the Centre or to continue the Business without the prior written consent of the Franchisor.

8.04.2 Until payment of all moneys due to the Franchisor from the Franchisee on any account the Franchisor shall have a lien on any of the stock and equipment fixtures and fittings and all other items connected with the Centre not then disposed of by the Franchisee and also on any moneys received by the Franchisee in respect of the Centre.

8.05 **Low Sales Termination.** The Franchisor may at its sole discretion determine this Agreement in the event that substantial turnover arising from the Business at the Centre is not achieved within eighteen (18) months of the date of the Agreement or for a continuous period of six (6) months at any time thereafter during the Term Provided that the Franchisor shall have the right (but not the duty) to appoint management personnel to supervise the Business at the expense of the Business in the event of any such failure to achieve substantial turnover to assist the Franchisee to increase sales.

8.06 **Management During Period of Notice.** At any time after the service of Notice of termination the Franchisor shall have the right (but not the duty) to appoint management personnel to supervise and manage the Premises at the expense of the Business.

8.07 **Termination of Lease Centre.** The Franchisor shall have the right in its absolute discretion to terminate this Agreement immediately upon the termination (by effluxion of time or determination for any other reason whatsoever) of the lease of the Centre unless within one (1) month following the effective date of such termination written agreement has been reached between the Franchisee and his competent Landlord within the meaning of the Landlord Tenant Act 1954 to obtain a new lease of the Centre or written agreement has been reached between the Franchisor and the new Franchisee for relocation of the Centre.

8.08 This Agreement shall be mutually terminated in the event of a transfer of the Franchise pursuant to and in accordance with Clause 7.02.1.

9.00 TERMINATION BY FRANCHISEE.

The Franchisee may terminate this Agreement at any time after the expiration of thirty-six (36) months from the commencement/opening data in the following manner:

9.01 Firstly the Franchisee confirms in writing their undertaking to continue to comply with Clause 12 of this Agreement.

9.02 Secondly serving upon the Franchisor written notice of the Franchisee's intention to surrender or assign the leasehold interest in the Centre to the Franchisor, requiring the Franchisor to give written notice of agreement to accept such surrender or assignment of lease within two calendar months of the date of the service of such notice or alternatively requiring the Franchisor to give written notice of intention not to accept such surrender or assignment of lease within two calendar months of the date of the service of the Franchisee's notice.

9.03   In the event that the·Franchisor gives written notice of agreement to accept such surrender or assignment of lease the current edition of the then National Conditions of Sale shall apply to such agreement insofar as the same are not varied by the terms herein contained.

9.04   Thirdly and upon receipt of the Franchisor's Notice the Franchisee may not give less than six (6) calendar months prior written notice referred to in Clause 9.02 above to the Franchisor to terminate this Agreement.

9.05   In the event that the Franchisor serves notice agreeing to accept surrender or assignment of leasehold interest the provisions as set out in Clause 11 below shall apply. In the event that the Franchisor serves notice states their intention not to accept surrender or assignment of the Franchisee's leasehold interest to a third party PROVIDED THAT such assignment will contain an express prohibition against use of the Centre by third party in any business competitive with the Business or the Mark of the Business of the Franchisor for a period of five years from the date of such assignment.

9.06   The date of the legal completion of the assignment or surrender to the Franchisor as referred to in Clause 9.02 above shall be the date of the expiration of the Franchisee's notice of termination.

10.00   RIGHTS AND OBLIGATIONS UPON TERMINATION
Upon termination of this Agreement for any reason.

10.01   **Payment of Debts to Franchisor.** The Franchisee will immediately pay to the Franchisor all sums or amounts due to the Franchisor up to the date of termination

10.02   **Payment of Business Debts.** The Franchisee will immediately pay all debts and liabilities of the Centre giving first priority to those guaranteed by the Franchisor.

10.03   **Cease Representation.** The Franchisee will immediately cease to represent himself as a Franchisee of the Franchisor and will discontinue use of the Mark and Permitted Name and cease to operate the Business.

10.04   **Franchisor's Agency.** The Franchisor may at its sole option sell as an agent of the Franchisee all or any part of the Business including tangible and intangible assets at a price agreed upon between the Franchisor and the Franchisee. If no price can be agreed upon, the Franchisor shall have the discretionary right for a period of six (6) calendar months following the termination of this Agreement to operate the Business as the Franchisee's agent. If no such bona fide offer to purchase is received within such six (6) month period acceptable to the Franchisee, then the Franchisor may thereafter liquidate the Business and apply the proceeds firstly to pay all of its reasonable costs and expenses as agent for the Franchisee second to satisfy the creditors of the Franchisee and then to pay over any balance remaining the Franchisee.

10.05 **Telephone/Telex/Fax.** The Franchisee shall use his best endeavours to procure a transfer of the telephone telex and Fax number(s) of the Centre to such person as the Franchisor directs and shall indemnify the Franchisor against any cost or claim arising from such transfer.

10.06 **Premises.** The Franchisee shall deliver up and surrender possession of the Centre to the Franchisor on the termination date and do everything the Franchisor or other lessor of the Centre may require to enable the Centre to be used by the Franchisor (in such manner as it thinks fit) or by any other person nominated by the Franchisor. Notwithstanding anything herein contained it is understood and agreed that in the event of the expiration or termination of this Agreement at any time of any reason, the Franchisee shall continue to be responsible for any and all payments connected with the lease to which the Centre is subject and the Franchisee hereby indemnifies the Franchisor against any and all claims with respect thereto up to and including the date of such surrender transfer or assignment and in connection with such surrender transfer or assignment.

10.07 **Stationery and other material relating to the Centre.** The Franchisee shall destroy all stationery used in the Business and return to the Franchisor all publicity promotional and marketing material issued by the Franchisor to the Franchisee or printed by the Franchisee and to return to the Franchisor the Operations Manual, Marketing Manuals and any other Manuals provided by the Franchisor from time to time in good condition and without having made any copies of the same and not to divulge to any third party any information concerning the Centre or the Know-How or any other systems or methods of the Franchisor used in the Business.

10.08 **Set-off.** Notwithstanding anything herein contained or implied the Franchisor shall not be obliged to pay or account to the Franchisee for any money which would otherwise be payable or owing by it to the Franchisee under or pursuant to this Agreement unless and until the Franchisee has paid satisfied or discharged all moneys debts or liabilities due or owing to the Franchisor and has satisfied all his other obligations to the Franchisor and the Franchisee hereby irrevocably authorises the Franchisor to deduct from any moneys otherwise payable by the Franchisor to the Franchisee hereunder or pursuant to this Agreement any moneys or the amount of any debts or liabilities due or owing or to become due or owing by the Franchisee to the Franchisor and to retain any moneys or amounts so deducted for its own absolute benefit.

11.00 ASSIGNMENT OR SURRENDER OF LEASEHOLD INTEREST UPON TERMINATION

11.01 In the event of the termination of this Agreement by either Franchisee or Franchisor the Franchisee shall execute and deliver such documents that may be necessary to assign to the Franchisor the benefit of the Franchisee's leasehold interest in the Centre and any fixtures and fittings therein required by the Franchisor.

11.02   If the Franchisee fails or refuses to execute such Deeds of Surrender, Assignment or other documents the Franchisor by or through any duly authorised officer or agent of the Franchisor shall have the right for and on behalf of the Franchisee to execute such Deed of Surrender, Assignment or other document. The Franchisee hereby grants to the Franchisor irrevocable right power and authority to execute on the Franchisee's behalf and in his name instead such Deeds and Documents as may be necessary in order to effect such an Assignment Surrender or Transfer.

11.03   The Franchisor shall pay to the Franchisee in consideration of such Assignment Surrender or Transfer an amount equal to market value of such leasehold interest (excluding the value of any goodwill appertaining thereto) together with the market value of any fixtures and fittings as aforesaid. Such market value shall be determined either by an agreement between Franchisor and Franchisee or failing which within 28 days after the date of such Assignment Surrender or Transfer at the joint expense of Franchisor and Franchisee by a valuer to be mutually agreed by the Franchisor and Franchisee or in default of agreement to be nominated on the application of either party by the President for the time being of the Royal Institution of Chartered Surveyors such valuer whether agreed or nominated as aforesaid shall act as an expert and not as an arbitrator and shall afford to each party an opportunity to make representations to him and his decision shall be binding on both.

11.04   The Franchisor shall within 30 days of such determination of the valuation referred to in Clause 11.03 above as aforesaid pay to the Franchisee the amount of such market value together with such interest thereon at 3% over Barclays Bank Plc base rate from time to time prevailing from date of such Assignment Surrender Transfer to the date of payment subject however to the right of the Franchisor to set off any sums due under this Agreement to the Franchisor.

11.05   The edition of National Conditions of Sale current at the date of such Assignment Surrender or Transfer shall apply to the Franchisors right hereunder so far as the same are not varied by or inconsistent with the terms of this Agreement.

12.00   RESTRICTIONS ON FRANCHISE

12.01   **No Competition.** Without Prejudice to Clause 5.05 hereof during the Term and for a period of eighteen months after any termination of this Agreement

12.01.1   not to engage directly or indirectly (whether as a director shareholder partner proprietor employee official agent or otherwise) in any business competitive with the Business or the Mark or the business of the Franchisor at the Centre.

12.01.2   not to engage directly or indirectly (whether as a director shareholder partner proprietor employee official agent or otherwise) in any business competitive with the Business or the Mark or the business of the Franchisor within a   metre radius of any Kall-Kwik Centre

12.01.2 and 12.01.3 to be agreed, completed and initialled by the Parties

91

12.01.3   not to engage directly or indirectly (whether as a director shareholder partner proprietor employee official agent or otherwise) in any business competitive with the Business or the Mark or the business of the Franchisor at or within a   metre radius of the Centre.

12.01.4   At any time after termination of this Agreement not to interfere with solicit or entice any of the customers of former customers of the Business or customers of any Franchisee of the Franchisor with the intent that any of them cease to patronise the Business or the Business of the Franchisor or any Business of a Franchisee of the Franchisor or direct their custom elsewhere.

12.02   **Confidential Information.** Except for the purposes of this Agreement during the Term and at any time thereafter the Franchisee will not disclose use or make copies of or reproduce in any form whatsoever the Operations Manual or any other Manuals issued to the Franchisee by the Franchisor or other confidential information including but not limited to confidential information concerning pricing methodology and structures advertising marketing sales promotions accounting systems business methods or procedures equipment or product studies evaluations or maintenance systems of operation and all other copyright material.

13.00 MISCELLANEOUS CLAUSES

13.01   **Grant back.** The Franchisor and Franchisee will notify each other of any improvements in the methods or equipment described in the Operations Manual or employed in the Business free of charge and the Franchisee shall permit the Franchisor to incorporate any such improvements notified by the Franchisee in the Operations Manual for the benefit of the Franchisor and all of its Franchisees.

13.02   **Headings.** All headings contained in this Agreement are for reference purposes only and shall not affect in any way the meaning or interpretation of this Agreement.

13.03   **Proper Law.** English Law shall apply to this Agreement and the English Courts shall have sole jurisdiction.

13.05   **Notices.** Any notice to be served on either party by the other shall be sent by pre-paid recorded delivery or registered post to the repsective addresses as stated above and shall be deemed to have been received the day after posting and each party shall notify the other of any change of address within forty-eight hours of such change.

13.06   **Severance.** If any provision of this Agreement or any part thereof is declared invalid by any tribunal or court of competent jurisdiction such declaration shall not affect the validity of this Agreement and the remainder of this Agreement shall remain in full force and effect according to the terms of the remaining provisions or parts of provisions hereof.

13.07   **Force Majeure.** Both parties shall be released from their respective obligations in the event of national emergency war prohibitive governmental regulations or if any other cause beyond the control of the parties shall render the performance of this Agreement impossible whereupon

13.07.1   all the Continuing Fees and the Promotional Contribution due shall be paid immediately.

13.07.2   the Franchisee shall forthwith cease the Business PROVIDED THAT this clause shall only have effect at the discretion of the Franchisor except when such event renders performance impossible for a continuous period of twelve (12) calendar months.

13.08   **Prior Obligations.** The expiration of termination of the Agreement shall not relieve either party of their respective obligations prior thereto to impair or prejudice their respective rights against the other.

13.09   **Receipt.** The receipt of moneys by the Franchisor shall not prevent either party questioning the correctness of any statement in respect of those moneys.

13.10   **Other Licences.** The Franchisor may grant a licence to any entity in the United Kingdom to manufacture any product for use in connection with the Business or displaying the Mark or for any other purposes without liability to the Franchisee.

13.11   **Other Franchisees.** The Franchisor may grant such other rights licences or franchises to any other entity in respect of the Mark in the British Isles as it decides without any liability to the Franchisee.

13.12   **Terminology.** All terms and words used in this Agreement regardless of the number and gender in which they are used shall be deemed and construed to include any other singular or plural and any other gender masculine feminine or neuter as the context or sense of this Agreement or any section paragraph or clause herein may require as if such words had been fully and properly written in the appropriate number or gender and words importing persons shall include companies and vice versa.

13.13   **Cumulative Rights and Remedies.** All rights and remedies herein conferred upon or reserved to the parties shall be cumulative and concurrent and shall be in addition to every other right or remedy given to the parties herein or at law or in equity or by statute and are not intended to be exclusive of any other right or remedy. This termination or expiration of this Agreement shall not deprive either party of any of its rights or remedies against the other.

13.14   **Joint and Several Liability.** Any covenant undertaking or agreement given or entered into by two or more persons shall be deemed to have been given or entered into by them jointly and by each of them severally so as to bind them jointly and each of them severally and each of their Legal personal representative successors and assigns.

14.00   ENTIRE AGREEMENT

14.01   This Agreement contains all the terms and conditions agreed upon by the parties hereto with reference to the subject matter hereof. No other Agreements oral or otherwise, shall be deemed to exist or to bind any of the parties hereto, and all prior agreements and understandings are superseded. No officer or employee or agent of the Franchisor has any authority to make any representation undertaking warranty agreement or promise either oral or in writing not contained in this Agreement and the Franchisee agrees that he has executed this Agreement without reliance upon any such. This Agreement shall not be binding upon the Franchisor until executed by an authorised officer thereof (as distinct from an employee or sales representative thereof). This Agreement cannot be modified or changed except by written instrument signed by all of the parties hereto.

14.02 **Financial Information.** All or any financial information relating to the operation of the Franchise including but without prejudice to the generality of the foregoing forecasts budgets and performance ratios cash flow projections provided to the Franchisee by or on behalf of the Franchisor or any employee or agent of the Franchisor whether before the signing hereof or during the continuation of this Agreement shall be provided in good faith that such information is for the guidance only of the Franchisee and in no way shall be treated by the Franchisee as a warranty representation or guarantee. The Franchisee hereby acknowledges that such financial information is not to be relied upon by him without first obtaining his own independent verification thereof.

14.03 The Franchisor acknowledges that in giving advice to the Franchisee in establishing his business whether before the signing of or during the continuance of this Agreement including but without prejudice to the generality of the foregoing any financial advice, market research advice, site selection advice, recommended equipment and materials, and the assessment of the suitability of the Franchisee, the Franchisor is basing its advice and recommendation on experience actually obtained in practice and is not giving any guarantees representations or warranties beyond the expression of the view that its advice and guidance are based upon its previous experience in its dealings with its Franchisees. The Franchisee acknowledges that he has been advised by the Franchisor and that he must decide on the basis of his own judgement of what he has been told by the Franchisor or such other Franchisees whether or not to enter into this Agreement.

14.04 The Franchisee acknowledges that no representations warranties inducements guarantees or promises made by the Franchisor or representatives of the Franchisor have been relied upon save such as may have been notified by the Franchisor in writing annexed to this Agreement.

14.05 **Survival of Liability.** The covenants and agreements herein which are intended by their nature to survive the cancellation termination or expiry of this Agreement shall continue in force following such cancellation termination or expiry for however long as may be required to give effect thereto.

IF FRANCHISING PRESENTS TOO MANY OBSTACLES,

PRESS FOR ACTION.

When it comes to franchising, NatWest have an excellent track record.

Not only can we offer you financial backing, but also extensive experience of the franchise world.

We were the first bank to appoint a Franchise Manager.

NatWest
The Action Bank

And over the last three years we have lent over £30 million to franchisees.

In fact, NatWest can offer you more information on franchising than any other bank.

So, to get in the running, contact your local branch.

Chapter 6
Financing a Franchise

How much will you need?

Starting any business involves financial risks. One serious cause of new business failure is underestimating exactly how much money is needed to get the business going.

This is not surprising when you consider that for most people, starting up is often a once in a lifetime event. Even for the few with experience, their subsequent ventures are rarely both in the same business field and on the same scale as their first. It is all too easy to miscalculate how much premises will cost to convert for your purposes, or exactly how much output you will get from a piece of second-hand machinery.

A further serious cause of financial failure is being too optimistic about your market. This in turn can lead to expecting too much cash in too soon and so underestimating how much working capital you will need to finance stocks, debtors and other overheads. Even when business picks up, young enterprises are often undercapitalised and so unable to fund the growth in sales. In bankers' language they are over trading.

The main financial advantage that a franchisor can provide for a franchisee is an accurate prediction of both fixed and working capital requirements. After all, the franchisors have launched tens and often hundreds of 'new' businesses. Their expertise in the field of 'launch' experience in a particular business area should be second to none.

It is perhaps worth mentioning at this stage one dichotomy presented by the franchisors' experience at launching outlets (or the lack of it). The well-established and often large franchise organisations use their very success as an argument for franchisees to 'buy in'. However, the entrepreneurial instinct of the potential franchisee will lead him to look for market gaps, innovations, new ideas and potential winners. This will encourage him to look at franchisors who may not have the base of experience needed to make good predictions about franchisees' capital needs.

DOES YOUR BANK
YOUR HOPES, FEARS

Most bank managers are very good at managing bank

But when it comes to helping a prospective franchise

they are not always so helpful.

At the Midland Bank we have a Franchise Unit to

advise our managers and offer general guidance to assist

potential franchisees with the evaluation of a franchise.

Once the choice of franchise has been made, wheth

you are setting up a new business or expanding an

existing one, you will need finance to assist with the

IANAGER SHARE
ND ASPIRATIONS?

chase of premises and equipment, as well as the
-to-day running of the business. Within Midland Bank
up we can provide the necessary finance in the form
t suited to your needs through a wide range of financial

ices. For a franchisee or franchisor information pack
e to: The Franchise Manager, Midland Bank plc,
d Office, Poultry, London EC2P 2BX.

 MIDLAND BUSINESS BANKING

One new fast food franchise that opened recently in Paris will serve as a warning. The franchisors' experience was based on a relatively new building which had many of the facilities required for a food operation already installed. It was also in a thriving Paris area with a good mix of residential and office property nearby. The franchisor sold his first franchise package after only a few months' operation in this pilot unit. His franchisee's premises, though filling all the basic requirements, were an old and ill-equipped building in an exclusively commercial area. Immediately it became apparent that the estimates for alterations and kitchen equipment were hopelessly wrong, and within a few weeks it was clear that his working capital projections were equally over-optimistic. This meant that instead of £30,000 start-up capital, the first franchisee found he needed £60,000. The franchisor was unable to help but fortunately the franchisee managed to raise it by the skin of his teeth, and so survived. But he is certainly not now rich, except perhaps in experience.

This all makes it extremely important to know as much as possible about the financial structure of the franchisor. We have tried to give you some clues both in Chapter 3 and in the information provided on each franchisor in Chapter 8.

Buying a franchise can cost as much as £300,000. A Holiday Inn franchise would be more again. Even within the same organisation, costs of outlets can vary considerably depending on size and location. Some offer different types of franchise within the same business, also with considerable differences in cost. The tables on franchise opportunities ranked by investment level (page 296) give you some idea of what is involved.

A further clue to the likely cost of taking up a franchise is provided in a research report 'Franchising in Great Britain – The Industry the Market'. The findings indicate that newly appointed franchisees have to find an average of £26,000 – just under £5000 for the franchise fee and £21,000 for equipment and fittings. Recurring annual payments to the franchisor total nearly £9900, two-thirds of this being a 5½ per cent royalty on turnover, and two-thirds of the balance being a 4½ per cent mark-up on supplies.

Specimen start-up costs of a small retail franchise

The 'cost' of buying a franchise is made up of a number of elements. A look at the table on page 102 will give you a good idea of the immediate costs, based on 600 square feet of suitable premises.

Franchise Finance

Like most banks, we can supply you with all the franchise finance you need. But The Royal Bank of Scotland can do more than just that.

Our franchise units have a great deal of experience and can offer you a whole range of advisory services should you need them.

And we won't just be there at the start of any franchise venture – we believe in supporting and continuing the business relationship. So if you're thinking about franchising call either Ron Campbell on 031 556 8555, or Alan Auld on 01 833 2121 them at the addresses below.

MONEY IS THE LAST THING WE'LL OFFER.

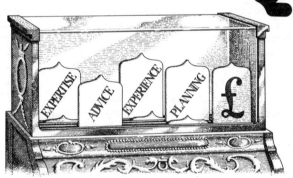

IT ALL POINTS TO THE ROYAL BANK OF SCOTLAND

The Royal Bank of Scotland plc

Registered office: 36 St Andrew Square, Edinburgh EH2 2YB. Registered in Scotland No. 90312.

Ron Campbell, Franchise Manager, The Royal Bank of Scotland plc, Head Office, 42 St Andrew Square, Edinburgh EH2 2YE.

Alan Auld, Franchise Manager, The Royal Bank of Scotland plc, Regent's House, PO Box 348, 42 Islington High Street, London N1 8XL.

Inventory and capital requirement guide

Building		
– Shopfitting		
– Heating		
– Electrical		
– Decor		
– Signs		
– Displays	£5,000*	
Furnishings		
– Office desks		
– Tables		
– Carpets	£1,000*	
Licence fee	£4,000*	
Franchise package fee		
– Training		
– Launch pack		
– Initial stationery	£3,000*	
Vehicle (approximately)	£6,000*	
Stock	£4,000*	
Working capital	£7,000	
Property negotiations	£1,000*	
Legal fees	£1,000*	
Total		£32,000
VAT (on items marked *)		£ 3,750
Total capital requirement		£35,750
Less finance		£17,000
Net capital requirement		£18,750

These are the 'start-up' costs of launching the franchise and providing for the first few months of operation. The building and furnishing costs are reasonably self-explanatory. The licence fee is a form of 'goodwill' in that the rights to use the franchisor's name are being conferred on the franchisee. The franchise package fee in this case includes training, help with the launch and some initial

stationery. (The licence and fee are more fully discussed in Chapter 5.) The vehicle cost is to some extent a matter of choice. You may decide that a Range Rover is essential for reasons of personal prestige rather than unhospitable terrain. As such it is not a 'true' cost of the franchise, though it may nevertheless be an acceptable business cost for tax purposes.

The other costs will be looked at more closely shortly.

So the total 'start-up' cost of this franchise is £35,750 and the franchisor expects to be able to arrange finance for nearly half of that. While you must take on a commitment for the full amount, you have only to produce £18,750 in cash. You will, of course, have to service the £17,000 borrowed with the franchisor's help in the normal way by paying interest and repaying the capital over a period of time.

How can you finance a franchise?

Financing a new franchise, while no easier than finding funds for any new venture, is at last attracting some heavyweight contenders.

Before considering possible sources of finance, we must first look at what we want to do with the money. By that we don't mean

103

refurbishing property or buying a vehicle or getting in start-up stock. Financial institutions tend to look at money as being either fixed or working capital. *Fixed capital* is money tied up in things the business intends to keep over longer periods of time, such as property, equipment, vehicles etc. *Working capital* is the money used to finance the day-to-day operations. The stock for example, and any money required to finance your customers until they pay up, are elements of working capital, as are all other running costs and overheads.

Type of capital	Business needs	Financing method
Fixed capital	Acquiring or altering a property. Buying equipment, such as cookers, ovens, photocopiers, or vehicles. The franchise fee and other 'start-up' package costs such as training.	Your own capital Term loans Hire purchase Leasing Sale and leaseback Venture capital Government loan guarantee scheme Mortgage loan
Working capital	Raw materials or finished goods; money to finance debtors; dealing with seasonal peaks and troughs, expansion or unexpected short-term problems; paying royalties.	Your own capital Bank overdrafts Factoring Trade credit Government loan guarantee scheme

Your own capital

Obviously the first place to start is to find out exactly how much you have to invest in the franchise. You may not have much in ready cash, but you may have valuable assets that can be converted into cash, or other borrowing. The difference between your assets and liabilities is your 'net worth'. This is the maximum security that you can offer for any money borrowed, and hopefully the calculations below will yield a pleasant surprise.

YOUR NET WORTH

Assets		Liabilities	
Cash in hand and in bank,	£	Overdraft	£
Building society, National Savings		Mortgage	£
or other deposits	£	Other loans	£
Stocks and shares	£	Hire purchase	£
Current redemption value of		Tax due, including	
insurance policies	£	capital gains	£
Value of home	£	Credit cards due	£
Any other property	£	Garage, local shop	
Motor car(s) etc	£	accounts due	£
Jewellery, paintings and other		Any other financial	
marketable valuables	£	obligations	£
Any money due to you	£		
Value of your existing business	£		
Total assets	£	Total liabilities	£

Net worth = Total Assets − Total Liabilities. £

External funds

To most of us borrowing money is synonymous with a visit to our local bank manager. Though not the only sources of finance the banks are a good starting point.

There are over a dozen clearing banks, as the High Street bankers are usually called, and they are in serious competition with each other for new business. It is as well to remember that a bank manager is judged on the quantity and quality of his lending and not on the deposits he takes. If he cannot 'successfully' lend, he can't make a profit himself.

For most satisfactory new business propositions the clearing bankers would normally be happy to match £1 for £1 the money put up by the 'owner', ie 1:1 gearing. Perhaps as an indication of how favourably the banks view ethical business format franchising, they will extend this ratio to two-thirds bank funding to one-third owner's cash, for approved franchise proposals.

They will also recommend a 'package' of funds – part term loan, part overdraft and perhaps part government loan guarantee – that best suits the type of franchise you are interested in (details of these types of financing are given below). For example, if the franchise you are considering is a service, requiring few physical assets, serving cash customers and expecting to break even in the first year, then you may be advised to take a small term loan and a larger overdraft facility. This will most closely match the funds to your needs, minimising interest charges without upsetting the long-term security of the business.

The converse relationship between loan capital and overdraft may be prudent if you are considering a 'capital intensive' franchise, such as a major fast food outlet.

One last point on the clearing banks. Normally your financial relationship with your bank is your business. If North American trends in franchise funding are anything to go by, this may be a thing of the past. There, and in some cases here, banks ask franchisees to sign a release, when they advance a funding package. This allows the bank to tell the franchisor if you are exceeding your financial limits.

At least five major banks and two other financial institutions have identified franchising as an important market for them to be in. As well as lending over £150 million to franchisees they have appointed managers and special departments responsible for looking after the franchise area. These suppliers of finance for franchising are listed in Chapter 12.

These banks can offer both general and specific advice to assist potential franchisees in evaluating a franchise from their considerable data base of market and financial information on franchise organisations. For the established franchisee, the banks can provide financial packages tailored to individual needs.

The banks offer a wide range of services in their own right. Through wholly- or partially-owned subsidiaries, they cover virtually every aspect of the financial market. For franchisees their services include overdrafts, term loans, factoring, leasing and the government loan guarantee scheme. As well as providing funds, the clearing banks have considerable expertise in the areas of tax, insurance and financial advice generally.

Overdrafts

Bank overdrafts are the most common type of short-term finance. They are simple to arrange; you just talk to your local bank manager. They are flexible, with no minimum level. Sums of money can be drawn or repaid within the total amount agreed. They are relatively cheap, with interest paid only on the outstanding daily balance. Of course interest rates can fluctuate, so what seemed a small sum of money one year can prove crippling if interest rates jump suddenly. Normally you do not repay the 'capital': you simply renew or alter the overdraft facility from time to time. However, overdrafts are theoretically repayable on demand, so you should not use short-term overdraft money to finance long-term needs, such as buying a lease, or some plant and equipment.

Term loans

These are rather more formal than a simple overdraft and cover periods of up to three, three to ten and ten to twenty years respectively. They are usually secured against an existing fixed asset or one to be acquired, or are guaranteed personally by the directors (proprietors). This may involve you in some costs for legal fees and arrangement or consultants' fees, so it may be a little more expensive than an overdraft, but unless you default on the interest charges you can be reasonably confident of having the use of the money throughout the whole term of the borrowing. The interest rates on the loan can either be fixed for the term or variable with the prevailing interest rate. A fixed rate is to some extent a gamble, which may work in your favour, depending on how interest rates move over the term of the loan. So, if general interest rates rise you win, and if they fall you lose. A variable rate means that you do not take that risk. There is another benefit to a fixed rate of interest. It should make planning ahead a little easier with a fixed financial commitment, unlike a variable overdraft rate, in which a sudden rise can have disastrous consequences.

107

The banks are becoming quite venturesome in their competition for new and small business accounts. One major clearer is producing a scheme which involves the bank taking a share option. Loans ranging from £25,000 to £200,000 (quite adequate for most franchisees' purposes) will be unsecured for up to ten years. Repayments arrangements would be flexible.

The key innovation is that the loan will be subordinated to other creditors, with the bank repaid before the shareholders but after all the other creditors if the company failed. In return for this risk they are likely to want an option on up to 25 per cent of the company's capital.

Government loan guarantee for small business

Government loan guarantees for small businesses were introduced in March 1981 for an initial period of three years and were extended in the 1984 and later Budgets, so it is now set to run until the end of the decade, at least. To be eligible for this loan, your proposition must have been looked at by an approved bank and considered viable, but should not be a proposition that the bank itself would normally approve. You can be a sole trader, partnership or limited company wanting funds to start up or expand. The bank simply passes your application on to the Department of Trade and Industry, using an approved format.

This is an elementary business plan, which asks for some details of the directors, the business, its cash needs and profit performance, or projection of the business. There are no formal rules on size, number of employees or assets, but large businesses and their subsidiaries are definitely excluded from the scheme. The other main exclusions are in the fields of agriculture, horticulture, banking, commission agents, education, forestry (except tree-harvesting and saw-milling), house and estate agents, insurance, medical and veterinary, night clubs and licensed clubs, pubs and property, and travel agencies.

The loans can be for up to £75,000 and repayable over two to seven years. It may be possible to delay paying the capital element for up to two years from the start of the loan, but monthly or quarterly repayments of interest will have to be made from the outset. The loan itself, however, is likely to be expensive.

Once approved by the Department of Trade, the bank lends you the money at bank rate plus 4 or 5 per cent and the government guarantees the bank 70 per cent of its money if you fail to pay. In return for this the government charges you a 2.5 per cent 'insurance' premium on the 70 per cent of the loan it has taken on risk. Borrowers would be expected to pledge all available business assets as a security for the loan, but they would not necessarily be excluded from the scheme if there were no available assets. Also on the plus side, directors will not normally be asked to give personal guarantees on security, an undertaking that may be required for other forms of borrowing.

The rule certainly seems to be to ask for as much as you need, plus a good margin of safety. Going back for a second bite too soon is definitely frowned upon. You do not have to take all the money at once. At the discretion of your bank manager, you can take the money in up to four slices, but each slice must be 25 per cent or more.

There are now 30 banks operating the scheme, and 16,000 loans worth over £500 million have been made. The average loan has been fairly constant at £33,000. A number of franchisees have received funds under this scheme including such household names as Prontaprint.

Factoring

This is only available to a franchise that invoices other business customers for its services. ServiceMaster, for example, who clean carpets and upholstery, have both domestic and commercial clients. So it may be possible to factor the commercial invoices.

Factoring is an arrangement which allows you to receive up to 80 per cent of the cash due from your customers more quickly than they would normally pay. The factoring company buys your trade debts and provides a debtor accounting and administration service. In other words, it takes over the day-to-day work of invoicing and sending out reminders and statements. This can be a particularly helpful service to a small expanding business. It allows the management to concentrate on growing the business, with the factoring company providing expert guidance on credit control, 100 per cent protection against bad debts, and improved cash flow.

You will, of course, have to pay for factoring services. Having the cash before your customers pay will cost you a little more than normal overdraft rates. The factoring service will cost between 0.5 and 3.5 per cent of the turnover, depending on volume of work, the number of debtors, average invoice amount and other related factors. You can get up to 80 per cent of the value of your invoice in advance, with the remainder paid when your customer settles up, less the various charges just mentioned.

If you sell direct to the public, if you sell complex and expensive capital equipment or expect progress payments on a long-term project, then factoring is not for you. If you are expanding more rapidly than other sources of finance will allow, this may be a useful service. All other things being equal, it should be possible to find a factor if your turnover exceeds £25,000 per annum, though the larger firm will look for around £100,000 as the economic cut-off point.

The Association of British Factors is at Moor House, London Wall, London EC2Y 5HE, tel: 01-638 4090, Secretary: Mr Michael Burke. ABF members charge between 0.75 and 2.5 per cent of gross turnover for the sales ledger package, and around bank overdraft rate for finance charges. They will advance about 80 per cent of the invoice price almost immediately the invoice is raised. They generally only consider customers with £100,000 per annum turnover, but may consider good cases from £50,000.

The Association of Invoice Factors, press office at 109/113 Royal Avenue, Belfast BT1 1FF, tel: 0232 224522, Mr A. M. Selig; also at Jordan House, 47 Brunswick Place, London N1 6EE, tel: 01-623 8462. This may be a better bet for small business. The members' average client has a turnover of £100,000 per annum, and they would be prepared to look at propositions from £1000 per month gross sales value. They advance 70 to 80 per cent of the value of the invoice, and charge between 0.5 and 3.5 per cent for maintaining the sales ledger. Between advancing you the money and getting it in from your client, their financing rate charges are similar to overdraft rates.

Leasing

This is a way of getting the use of vehicles, plant and equipment without paying the full cost at once. Operating leases are taken out where you will use the equipment for less than its full economic life – for example a car, photocopier, vending machine or kitchen equipment. The lessor takes the risk of the equipment becoming obsolete, and assumes responsibility for repairs, maintenance and insurance. As you, the lessee, are paying for this service, it is more expensive than a finance lease, where you lease the equipment for most of its economic life and maintain and insure it yourself. Leases can normally be extended, often for fairly nominal sums, in the latter years.

The obvious attraction of leasing is that no deposit is needed, leaving your working capital for more profitable use elsewhere. Also, the cost is known from the start, making forward planning more simple. There may even be some tax advantages over other forms of finance. However, there are some possible pitfalls, which only a close examination of the small print will reveal. So do take professional advice before taking out a lease.

Information is obtainable from: The Equipment Leasing Association, 18 Upper Grosvenor Street, London W1X 9PD, tel: 01-491 2783.

HIRE PURCHASE

This differs from leasing in that you have the option at the start to become the owner of the equipment after a series of payments have been made. The interest is usually fixed and often more expensive than a bank loan. However, manufacturers (notably car makers) often subsidise this interest, so it pays to shop around both for sources of hire purchase finance and manufacturers of equipment.

The Finance Houses Association, address and telephone number as for The Equipment Leasing Association, can provide you with a short list of companies to approach.

Mortgage loan

This operates in the same way as an ordinary mortgage. The money borrowed is used to buy the freehold on the business premises. That then acts as the main security for the loan with regular repayments made up of interest charges and principal, paid to the lender.

The main suppliers are the insurance companies and pension funds, who generally prefer to deal in sums above £50,000. Some of the smaller companies will lend as little as £5000, particularly if the borrower is a policy-holder. As well as the regular payments, a charge of about 2 per cent will be made to cover the survey, valuation and legal work in drawing up agreements.

Sale and leaseback

This involves selling the freehold of a property owned by a business to a financial institution, which agrees to grant you a lease on the premises.

The lender will want to be sure that you can afford the lease, so a profit track record will probably be needed, and all expenses involved in the negotiations are met by the borrower. The borrower then has the use of the value of the asset in immediate cash to plough into the business.

The tax aspects of sale and leaseback are complex and work more in the favour of some types of business than others, so professional advice is essential before entering into any arrangement.

As with other forms of finance, it is a competitive market and a few 'quotes' are worth getting.

Trade credit

Once you have established creditworthiness, it may be possible to take advantage of trade credit extended by suppliers. This usually takes the form of allowing you anything from seven days to three months from receiving the goods, before you have to pay for them. However, if your franchisor is your main source of supply, you may have very little flexibility in this area.

Even if you have a choice, you will have to weigh carefully the benefit of taking this credit against the cost of losing any cash discounts offered. For example, if you are offered a 2.5 per cent discount for cash settlement, then this is a saving of £25.00 for every £1000 of purchase. If the alternative is to take six weeks' credit, then the saving is the cost of borrowing that sum from, say, your bank on overdraft. So if your bank interest rate is 16 per cent per annum, that is equivalent to 0.31 per cent per week. Six weeks would save you 1.85 per cent. On £1000 of purchase you would save only £18.50 of bank interest. This means that the cash discount is more attractive. However, you may not have the cash or overdraft facility, so your choice is restricted.

Venture capital

This is the start-up capital usually associated with businesses involved in technological and technical innovation. The sums involved are usually up to £100,000 over periods of five years or more. With this capital usually comes management expertise, often in the form of a board member from the financial institution. So you would have to be able to work with him, and probably give a personal guarantee for the sums involved. The Bank of England's publication, *Money for Business* or the BBC's *Small Business Guide* are two useful and comprehensive guides to venture capital sources.

Improving your chance of getting external finance

Not having enough ready cash to finance buying a franchise will force you to look to one or more of these external sources of finance for the balance of your funds. At first glance this may appear to be a disadvantage. Nothing could be further from the truth. A hard critical look at your business proposal by an outsider is exactly what you need. To have a serious chance of raising money you will have to marshal all the facts about the franchise proposal yourself, and understand them well enough to communicate clearly to a third party. Simply having a good 'net worth' is unlikely to be sufficient in itself to secure a loan. This examination by an outside professional will certainly prompt you to ask your prospective franchisor some very searching questions.

The National Westminster Bank have produced a very useful check list to help you get your loan proposal together. Not every heading is appropriate to a franchise proposal but the great majority are. Working your way through this check list will certainly improve your knowledge and understanding of the franchise proposal itself; and it will improve your chances of reaching a satisfactory outcome to your search for funds.

Check list   ©National Westminster Bank plc

About you

○ Very brief synopsis for your own banker, detailed for approach to others: age, education, experience.
○ Personal means eg property, liabilities eg guarantees. Other business connections.
○ For a type of business new to you, or start-up situation, outline experience, ability and factors leading up to your decision.

Your business

○ Brief details of: when established, purpose then and now, how the business has evolved, main factors contributing to progress.
○ Reputation, current structure and organisation. Internal accounting system.
○ Past three years audited accounts if available, and latest position.
○ Up-to-date profit and loss figures, including details of withdrawals.
○ Up-to-date liquid figures, ie debtors, creditors, stock, bank balance etc.
○ Borrowing history and existing commitments, eg HP, leasing loans. Bankers.
○ Description of major assets, and any changes.

Your key personnel

○ Age, qualifications, experience, competence, of directorate/senior management. Directors' bankers.
○ Emergency situation, someone to run the business in your absence.
○ List of principal shareholders/relationships.

Your purpose

○ Explain fully your business plan, the use to which the money will be put, eg expansion, diversification, start-up.
○ Describe the practical aspects involved and the how and when of implementation.
○ Diagrams, sketches, photographs etc are usually helpful, eg property purchase and conversion to your use.
○ Consider: planning permission, legal restrictions, government policy.
○ Contingency plans for set backs: reliability of supplies/raw materials/alternative sources, other factors outside your control, eg weather.

○ Relevance to existing operations, opportunity for shared overheads, disruption of current business.
○ Personnel: are more staff required, availability of specialist skills/training? Management ability for expanded/different operation?

Your market

○ Estimated demand, short- and long-term. External verification of market forecasts, eg from trade associations, market research publications.
○ Competition, who from, likely developments.
○ Describe your competitive advantages, eg quality, uniqueness, pricing (justify) location – local/national.
○ Marketing included in costings?
○ If new, or technology based or highly specialised business – detail and perspective necessary.
NB A banker does not need to know how it works (though he may be interested), just that it does, is reliable, and has good sales prospects.

Your profit

○ Demonstrate how profits will be made, include detailed breakdown of costings, timing, projected sales, orders already held.
○ Profit projections should attempt to cover the period of a loan, however sketchy.
○ For capital investment – profit appraisal. Capital allowances, eg new small workshop scheme.
○ Everything included in costings, eg tax, stamp duty, legal fees, bank interest?

The amount

○ State precisely the amounts and type of finance required and when it will be needed. Is type of finance correct, eg overdraft to finance working capital, term loan for capital expenditure?
○ Is the amount requested sufficient, eg increased working capital requirements/margin for unforeseen circumstances?
○ Detail the amount and form of your contribution to the total cost.
○ Justify all figures – cash flow forecast for next 12 months: show maximum range. All outgoings considered, eg net VAT, holiday pay, bank interest and repayments, personal drawings.

Repayment

○ Relate projected profitability and cash flow to expected repayments. Justify fully the term requested: is it long enough?
○ How quickly will the business generate cash? Is a repayment 'holiday' necessary and what turnover needs to be achieved to break-even?
○ Consider the worst situation, feasibility of contingency plans, irretrievable losses.
○ Interest rate – effect of variation in base rate.

Security

○ What assets are/will be available as security?
○ Are any assets already used for security elsewhere?
○ Independent/realistic valuation of assets offered. Leasehold considerations, any unusual features/saleability. Support for guarantees.
○ Agreement of other interested parties/realistic awareness of loss of asset.
○ Insurance: life, property, business.

Even if the first financial institution you approach turns you down, don't despair. Ask why and profit by their explanation. Sometimes would-be borrowers have had different answers from different branches of the same bank.

What help can you expect from your franchisor in raising money?

A few years ago you could have expected your franchisors to do little to help you raise finance.

The past few years have seen a dramatic reversal. Indeed, it is probably true to say that if a franchisor cannot put his potential franchisees in contact with a financial institution for at least some of the money needed, there is something very suspicious about the franchise proposition.

For the lender of money, the business format franchise provides almost unparalleled security.

Any request for funds poses two problems for the lender. Is there a market for the product or service the business is going to offer? Is the person thinking of setting up the business suitable and appropriately skilled for the job? Normally the lender has to use his own unaided judgement to answer these questions, but with a franchise the position is much clearer. In most cases there are enough Body Shop or Dyno-Rod outlets to establish the market viability of the product or service and the franchisors themselves will both vet and train the franchisee. These factors can alter the balance of risk in the lender's favour.

Many franchisors have now established close relationships with financial institutions, and can provide a comprehensive financial package for potential franchisees. One example is the scheme prepared by Barclays Bank for Pip (UK) Ltd. This is set out in the table below. Pip's financial package, however, can and does extend to other sources of finance, including the National Westminster Bank, and other major clearing banks.

The Barclays Bank scheme for franchise holders of Pip (UK) Ltd

How we can help you succeed as a franchisee

You are considering the purchase of a franchise from Pip (UK) and you may have encountered a number of problems.

Where, for example, is the finance for the franchise package to come from?

How are you going to afford the fittings, equipment and stock you'll undoubtedly need?

And what about the insurance for the business?

In fact, while it is vital that you choose a sound franchise operation in the first place, it is equally important to find a reliable and comprehensive package of financial advice and assistance.

This is where Barclays can help you. Because with our considerable experience in assisting franchisees, we know the opportunities and advantages that exist in the right franchise operation, but also understand the problems to be faced and the importance of a speedy response to your financial requirements.

This is why our experienced franchise marketing manager has, in conjunction with Pip (UK), outlined a package of financial services that suit Pip's print franchise operation. The bank will further advise on tailoring this scheme to your individual needs.

Naturally, we will treat all the information you supply in the strictest confidence.

And work with you to make sure that the opportunity open to you is speedily and profitably exploited.

Finance for machinery, premises, shopfittings, equipment, purchases and working capital

As a new Pip franchisee, you will be involved in some major capital expenditure and will probably need working capital to see you through the early stage of the development of your business. Purchasing 'fixed assets', business premises, equipment etc may involve large and immediate payments, with the return in your investment coming over a number of years. Our loan scheme for Pip franchise holders takes account of all these requirements and is designed to help you not just in the early stages of operating your franchise but in the longer term.

Your application will be dealt with swiftly as we will usually be quite happy with receiving a copy of your Pip application form which can be the basis of our assessment of your individual position.

We require that you are able to show us that your business meets certain performance and financial standards and we can accept Pip's help in providing you with this information.

Usually a deposit of one-third of the total will be required but the amount financed can sometimes be unsecured, although a slightly higher interest rate will be charged.

For the first year or two, a capital repayment 'holiday' will be acceptable. During this period, interest only needs to be paid, thus helping considerably with your cash flow.

Capital can be repaid over a period of up to five years. In certain circumstances this can be a longer period. Naturally early repayment of all or part of the outstanding loan can be made without premium.

Insurance
Barclays Insurance Services Company Ltd offer a wide range of insurance services. They have investigated the requirements of a typical Pip location for insurance and through them we can arrange an excellent package covering risks such as fire, flood and storm damage as well as machinery breakdowns, consequential loss of profits and claims of negligence brought against you. In addition, specialist advice is available on life assurance and pension schemes for the self-employed.

Other services
There are many other ways that Barclays can be of help to you, and we will be pleased to discuss other areas of interest.

© Barclays Bank plc

First National Securities Ltd

The banks have tended to direct their attention to the more established franchise outlets, and also to larger borrowing requirements.

While not neglecting this area, First National Securities have selected a different category of franchisor to focus on. FNS have investigated some 75 franchisors and have agreed a funding package with some 50 of them. These are the ones they have satisfied themselves that offer the franchisee a realistic investment proposal. They include both established and new franchisors. Many of them require relatively small amounts of start-up capital, say £5000-£7000, sums that may not attract much attention from the clearing banks. They are also willing to support completely new franchise ventures if they can pass their own vetting procedure, and the franchisor's directors have a good track record. (Incidentally, 20 franchisors did not meet First National's standards.)

Information from: First National Securities Limited, Television House, Mount Street, Manchester M2 5NB, tel: 061-834 1107.

LET US READ THE SMALL PRINT.

(It could save you a lifetime's savings)

ROYDS BARFIELD SOLICITORS
2 Crane Court, London EC4A 2BL
Tel: 01-583 2222. Tx: 28198. Fax: 01-583 2034

Woolwich House, 43 George Street, Croydon CR9 1EY. Tel: 01-680 2050
18 Crown Lane, Morden SM4 5BS. Tel: 01-542 1067

The Consumer Credit Act

When this Act came into force in May 1985 banks were forced to review their policy on lending to lower priced franchises. The effect has been to cause several of the banks to raise their minimum lending figure to £15,001 because of a technical legal liability to the lender on loans under £15,000 to sole traders and partnerships.

Business Expansion Scheme (BES)

The BES was introduced in the UK in 1983 to replace the Business Start-Up Scheme launched two years earlier.

The scheme is aimed at UK tax payers who are not connected with the business they are going to invest in. They cannot be paid directors or employees of the business, nor can they own more than 30 per cent of the shares. The investor gets tax relief on up to £40,000 invested in any one year. The minimum investment is £500, and the funds must be left in for at least five years. The effect of this scheme is that a top rate tax payer could be putting as little as £2500 of his own money into a business in return for a £10,000 share, the balance being effectively paid by the Inland Revenue.

The 1986 Budget made companies in such areas as nursing homes, exclusively property based ventures, restaurants and vintage wine trades ineligible for BES funding, but that still leaves a sizeable number of eligible areas. Your solicitor, accountant or bank manager should be able to put you in touch with interested individuals.

118

Chapter 7
Legal and Tax Considerations

The legal form of the business

Introduction

Well before you start trading you will need to consider in what legal form you wish to run your business. For a potential franchisee there are only three likely possibilities, as certain structures such as workers' co-operatives are unlikely to be appropriate. These three possibilities are:

1. Sole trader
2. Partnership
3. Limited liability company

Each of these forms has certain advantages and some drawbacks which should be considered before you make a decision.

Sole trader

The sole trader is the original form of entrepreneur. You put in your own money as the risk capital, you take all business decisions, and you take all the profits. The drawback to this independence is that you also have to suffer any losses in their entirety.

If you are a sole trader there is no legal distinction between you and your business – your business is merely one of your assets, just as your house or car is. It follows from this that if your business should fail the creditors have a right, not only to the assets of the business, but also to your personal assets, subject only to the provisions of the Bankruptcy Acts which allow you to keep only a few absolutely basic essentials for yourself and your family. In other words, if the business goes down, everything you own – house, car, jewellery, furniture, savings – can be seized and sold to pay off the creditors.

To a certain extent it is possible to avoid these consequences by ensuring that your private assets are the legal property of your wife or husband rather than yourself. The creditors have a claim only against your assets, not against your spouse's. Before you decide that this is the answer to any possible problems you should consider the following:

(a) you cannot pass over the property when you realise you are running into trouble. The transfer must be made at least two years before, and while you are still solvent (ie able to meet your debts as they fall due). As most business failures occur in the early years this probably means making the transfer before you take out the franchise.

(b) in order to be effective, the transfer must be absolute – you cannot retain an interest in or control those assets. Therefore you have no power to dictate what your spouse does with them, and must consider carefully the degree of trust you place in your husband or wife and the stability of your marital relationship. You may have to decide whether you have more faith in your spouse or your own business acumen!

In return for the drawbacks, you have the pleasure of being entirely your own boss, subject only to your agreement with your franchisor, and you have very few legal formalities with which to comply, compared with a limited company. In fact, apart from regulations particular to your business (eg fire and health regulations for a fast food franchise), you may only encounter problems in keeping the records required for the Customs and Excise and for your accountant to negotiate your liability to tax with the Inland Revenue.

Partnerships

Partnerships are effectively collections of sole traders and as such share the legal problems attached to personal liability. Two points in particular merit attention:

1. Your partner may make a business mistake, perhaps by signing a disastrous contract, without your knowledge or consent. If this happens, the business as a whole can still fail, and your personal assets taken to pay the creditors even though the failure was no fault of yours.

2. If your partner goes bankrupt in his personal capacity – for example, in his private life he may have a tendency to fast women and slow horses – his share of the partnership is one of his assets, and his creditors will want to realise the cash from this. Obviously, you as a private individual are not liable for his private debts, but the requirement to buy him out of the partnership or to find someone to buy his share could prove fatal to the business.

The major advantages of partnerships are:

(a) By pooling resources you will have more capital.
(b) You have someone with whom to discuss problems and strategies.
(c) Your home life may be easier as there will not be the same pressure on you to be there all the time – you can split responsibilities.
(d) You can contribute different personalities, experience and talents.
(e) It will be less of a disaster if you are ill.

Most of these advantages do not have the same force if your prospective partner is your spouse. When considering whether to take in your spouse as a partner, or merely have them helping (paid or otherwise), you should consider these points:

● While you are starting up it may help your peace of mind to know that you have a spouse in steady employment outside the business, so you are assured of at least a basic income.
● If your spouse is a partner in the business you cannot protect your assets by transferring them into his or her name.
● You should keep firmly in mind that one in three marriages now ends in divorce. Although statistics are not available, it

is probable that the proportion is even higher among owners of newly started businesses because of the additional strains. If your spouse is a partner, you cannot get rid of them easily, and few people would relish the thought of having to run a business in partnership with someone they were in the process of divorcing! In most cases it is better to have your spouse as an employee. (See also the comments on taxation on page 126.)

Assuming that you have decided that a partnership is right for you, the legal requirements are dealt with in the Partnership Act, 1890. In contrast to modern protective legislation, this Act, framed in the spirit of Victorian self-help, assumes that competent businessmen should know what they are doing, and merely provides a framework of an agreement which applies *in the absence of agreement to the contrary*. Any of the arrangements can be varied according to the wishes of the partners. The main provisions are:

● All partners contribute capital equally.
● All partners share profits and losses equally.
● No partner shall have interest paid on his capital.
● No partner shall be paid a salary.
● All partners have an equal say in the management of the business.

These provisions may suit you perfectly well, but it is likely that you will want to vary some of them. In any case you would be well advised to get a *partnership agreement* drawn up in writing by a solicitor, because even though you can have a perfectly legal agreement established verbally or just based on how you have been conducting the business, there is always the problem of evidence in the event of an argument.

At the beginning of a partnership (like a marriage) there is usually a 'honeymoon' period when you are in agreement, full of enthusiasm and tending to brush aside any problems. It would, however, be foolhardy to assume that these will not arise and perhaps prove difficult to resolve without some bitterness. Therefore you should get eveything in writing while you are still on speaking terms. The main reason for using a solicitor is that he will almost certainly suggest problems and eventualities that you had not considered. For example, suppose two people decide to start up in a franchise outlet. One is in his late fifties, has taken early retirement and is using the lump sum he received on retirement plus the proceeds of an insurance policy as capital. He wants a profitable home for his money, and an interest that will keep him occupied at a fairly leisurely pace until retirement. The other is in his mid-twenties, has no capital to speak of, but does have boundless energy, enthusiasm and some experience in the line of business. As one is contributing all the capital, but the

other is doing most of the work, they might decide to split the profits evenly. If the capital contributed was £50,000 and the profits £15,000 one is getting 15 per cent on his capital and the other is getting a modest but livable wage of £7500, both of which seem quite reasonable.

But what happens if the business is very successful due to the hard work of the younger partner and profits go up to £40,000? The working partner is getting only £20,000 but the investor has a return on capital of 40 per cent. Is the split still fair? Perhaps, perhaps not; but there is the possibility of a major argument unless such contingencies have been provided for in advance.

A possibility to guard against is *accidentally* finding yourself in partnership with someone. Because there is no necessity for a partnership agreement to be in writing, or for any legal formalities, you may find yourself in a situation where you are held to be in partnership even though that was not the original intention. For example, if an employee (your spouse, perhaps) commonly negotiated with full authority, signed cheques, and was paid according to the level of profits he might well be held to be in partnership, particularly if his name appeared on the firm's stationery. None of these things would be decisive in itself, but in combination they might lead any person dealing with the business to reasonably suppose himself to be dealing with a partner.

Limited liability companies

As the name suggests, in this form of business your liability is limited to the amount you contribute by way of share capital. The essential point to realise is that the company is a separate legal entity – it has a legal personality which is quite distinct from that of the shareholders. It follows from this that if the business should fail, the creditors can only have a right to the assets of the business; they cannot demand any more from the shareholders than the amount of share capital they have contracted to take up – if they have already paid that in full then there is no further recourse.

Only in exceptional circumstances will this 'veil of incorporation' be lifted – for example, if a director, knowing that the company is insolvent, knowingly and wilfully continues to trade despite the fact that there is no possibility of paying the debts he is contracting, he is guilty of fraudulent trading and could be held personally liable. This protection of the shareholders places the creditors in a vulnerable position. Major providers of capital such as banks can demand personal guarantees from the directors, but ordinary trade creditors cannot. The law, therefore, requires all limited companies to file accounts annually at Companies House, where they can be inspected by any member of the public and copies on microfiche obtained on payment of £2.

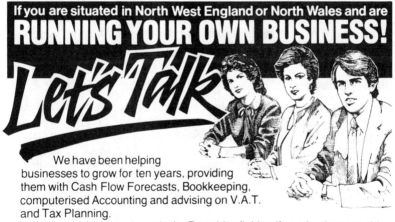

However the Insolvency Bill 1985, brought into effect the notion that limited liability is a privilege rather than a right. Under these new rules, incompetent as well as fraudulent directors may incur a measure of personal liability for debts incurred in the face of looming insolvency.

The Institute of Directors is launching a personal insurance scheme to protect UK company directors against successful claims brought under this Bill. Premium costs are between £225 and £1000 a year for cover up to a maximum of £100,000.

This requirement involves much more expense than a sole trader or partnership will incur. Setting up the company will cost about £125 if an 'off-the-shelf' company is bought from a firm specialising in this service and the filing fee is £20 a year, but the main expense will be the audit fee. The accounts must be audited by a chartered accountant or certified accountant – no one else may sign an audit certificate. You can certainly prepare the accounts yourself, or pay an unqualified book-keeper to do so, but the accountants are required by statute to satisfy themselves, using their professional judgement, that the accounts show 'a true and fair view' of the business. Neither you nor they have any power to vary this duty. Given the level of professional competence required, even the very smallest of companies will be likely to pay about £400 a year in audit fees and for anything larger £500-£1000 would be more realistic. You should realise that an accountant's function as an auditor is quite distinct from any other duties for which you may also pay – negotiating with the Inland Revenue, for example, and most accountants will quote you separate fees for accountancy as opposed to audit work.

Basic tax issues

Important as the question of the legal form of the business may be, many of the questions of liability arise only in the case of business failure. Taking a more optimistic viewpoint, tax considerations are more important when the business is making a profit.

It must be emphasised that taxation is an extremely complicated area, and one that changes very rapidly, so this section can give only a very broad outline of the main considerations.

The basis of taxation

Business profits (whether sole traders/partnerships or limited companies) are taxed according to the rules of Schedule D Case I or II. (I relates to profits from a trade, II to income from a profession or vocation – there are no important differences.) Your taxable profit is computed by taking your profit according to the accounts and adjusting it. The adjustment is necessary because the normal rules

for preparing a set of accounts are not the same as those in tax law, which means that your *accounting* profit will often bear very little relation to your *taxable* profit. An accountant's help is vital here if you do not wish to pay more tax than you legally must.

You are allowed to set an expense against your income if it is:

1. Incurred *wholly and exclusively* for the purposes of trade.
2. Properly charged against income (not, for example, purchase of a property lease, which is capital).
3. Not specifically disallowed by statute (for example, you cannot set entertainment of customers – except overseas customers – against your tax, although it is a perfectly legitimate accounting expense).

It is beyond the scope of this book to detail all the expenses which are and are not allowable; good, clear summaries can be found in the books mentioned in the bibliography. The following points should, however, be noted carefully:

(a) If you do some of your work at home you can normally set a proportion of your rent, rates, light, heat and telephone bills etc against your business income.

(b) If your wife cannot work outside the home (perhaps because there are young children) she can be an employee and be paid up to £2335 a year (1987/8) which will be deducted from your profits but will not be taxable on her. It is necessary to convince the Inspector of Taxes that she does actually do work for the business to this value, and that it is paid to her.

(c) If you are a sole trader or partnership your tax is assessed effectively a year in arrears, except in the first two or three years, when the profits earned in the first year or eighteen months determine the liability. For this reason it is vital that your taxable profits in this first period should be as low as legally possible (a loss is preferable) as this will affect your tax payable for three years.
Note: this does *not* apply to limited companies.

(d) Choose your *accounting date* carefully. Deciding when your business started trading is rarely a clear-cut decision. Often business expenses were incurred months and even years before the first cash came in. Left to their own devices, most people prepare their first accounts for a 12-month period, based either on the calendar or tax year. They mistakenly think that administrative tidiness or convenience are the only factors to consider. That is not so. There is an opportunity to influence the timing of cash flow in the business's favour. This sort of advantage can often mean the difference between success and failure in the first year. Look at the two cases below:

Business A decides on 31 March 1983 as the end of its first financial year. Half of the tax on the profits is due on 1 January 1984 and the balance on 1 July 1984, so tax is paid an average of 12 months after the profits have been made. (31 March 1983 to 1 January 1984 = 9 months; 31 March 1983 to 1 July 1984 = 15 months; (9 + 15) ÷ 2 = 12 months.)

Business B, however, decides to have 30 April 1983 as the end of its first financial year, as this is now after the end of the Inland Revenue's tax year, which ended on 5 April 1983, so tax is not due until 1985. Half is paid on 1 January 1985 and the balance on 1 July 1985. This means an average of 23 months elapses before tax is paid, giving an extra 11 months' interest-free credit.

This cash flow benefit is created by the simple expedient of choosing the best first year end for a particular business.

This example is something of an over-simplification and other factors will come into play. It will not, for example, apply to new limited companies who all have to pay tax a flat nine months after their year end, whatever that date is, but it does serve to illustrate the potential benefits to be gained by using professional advice.

(e) The biggest difference in treatment between sole traders and limited companies as far as tax is concerned relates to the treatment of *losses*. If you are a sole trader (or partnership) your income from the business is just one of your sources of income, and is added to any other income you and your wife may have. Similarly, as it is your aggregate income which is important, any business losses can be set against your other income. So if your wife earns £8000 a year as a teacher and has had PAYE deducted of (say) £1800, and your business makes a loss of £4000, then assuming you have no other income, the two will be netted off and you will have a joint income of only £4000 against which you will set the married man's allowance and the wife's earned income relief so you will be able to reclaim most of the PAYE. The relief in the opening years is even more generous – if you make a tax loss in any of the first four years of the business you may reclaim some or all of the tax you or your spouse has paid in the preceding three years. Neither of these loss reliefs applies to limited companies; a limited company is a separate legal person, so the profits belong to the company, the company has its own tax liability, and most importantly, the losses are 'locked into' the company; you cannot set company losses against your own other income. This is the other side of the coin of limited liability – if you wish to take advantage of the protection provided for your personal assets by operating the business through a separate legal entity, you cannot also treat that entity's losses as your own and benefit from them.

(f) If you are a limited company you will take remuneration as director's remuneration. As you are technically an employee of your company, tax should be paid under PAYE, and also National Insurance Class I contributions are due – both employer's (the company) and employee's (yourself). This can prove very much more expensive than the Classes 2 and 4 paid by a sole trader.

(g) Unless you take out the entire profits as director's remuneration, the balance will be taxed at *corporation tax* rate of 30 per cent on profits up to £100,000 rising to 50 per cent on profits over £500,000. The rate of corporation tax is fixed annually by Parliament in the Finance Act for the preceding financial year.

(h) The 1984 Budget announced the phasing out of capital allowance set-offs and, from 3 March 1986, all expenditure on plant and machinery thereafter qualifies for writing down allowances on a 25 per cent reducing balance basis. Therefore, the attractions of buying capital equipment outright have diminished and it may therefore make more sense in some circumstances to lease (the cost of leasing can be set against tax).

(i) Do not let the tax tail wag the commercial dog! In other words, you are in business primarily to make profits, not to avoid paying tax. Your primary concern should be with the business; do not make decisions purely to save tax.

Purely from a tax point of view, most businesses are better off starting as sole traders or partnerships and considering incorporation when taxable profits exceed £15,000 each approximately (depending on your personal circumstances). It is much simpler to start off as a sole trader or partnership and to incorporate when necessary than to try to do the procedure in reverse.

Despite the tax advantages to being a sole trader, particularly at low levels of profit, you may feel that the protection of your private assets by operating as a limited company is well worth the tax disadvantages – much depends on your personal circumstances and your attitude to taking risks.

Finally, it should be realised that in revenue law the onus of disclosure and proof is on the *taxpayer*. In criminal law you are innocent until proved guilty, but for tax purposes you are liable until you prove otherwise. Moreover, it is your responsibility to notify the Inland Revenue of taxable income, not for the Inspector to ask (though he eventually will). Remember, *ignorance of the law is no excuse.*

(j) The position on *leased assets* is somewhat different. You do not own the asset, the lessor does. He, therefore, is entitled to claim the writing down allowances and this benefit to him is reflected in the lower rental figure that he can then charge. Whether outright purchase or leasing is beneficial will depend on the individual business and the anticipated profits. If finance is not available, however, there may be no choice but to lease. One point to note is that if there is an option to purchase the asset after a certain period, the Inland Revenue may not regard the transaction as a genuine leasing arrangement, but as a form of credit sale. Again, this is not necessarily a disadvantage; it all depends on the pattern of profits and professional advice should be sought.

Employing people

Franchising has the feature, somewhat unusual in business start-up situations, that in many cases – certainly where retailing and fast

131

food are concerned – it is necessary to begin looking for staff at a fairly early stage. This will bring the owners into sharp contact with a number of problem areas with which they may previously have been mercifully unfamiliar. Apart from the difficulty of finding Mr or Ms Right – a task which even experienced personnel people admit in their more candid moments is something of a lottery – a mass of legislation has been enacted in recent years which, it is thought by some, has favoured the rights of employees at the expense of employers. The aim of this legislation has been mainly to protect the workforces of larger companies from arbitrary hiring and firing, as well as to take account of the special problems of racial minorities at work and the changes in public opinion about women's rights. However it also touches even the smallest employer in almost equal measure to large ones and it covers most part-time as well as full-time employees.

Franchisees are likely to be particularly affected, not only because they often employ workers who fall into all these categories, but because the rules of the franchise may impose conditions which have a great deal of bearing on the employer-employee relationship, and which are actually laid down by the franchisor: for instance the way employees who come into contact with the public are expected to dress. Even though such rules may have been imposed by the franchisor, when it comes to a dispute involving unfair dismissal, the franchisee cannot hide behind the terms of the franchise. Unfair dismissal, though, is only one of several issues involved. Whole books could be and have been written about the legal technicalities, but all we can do here is to draw the reader's attention to some of the major pitfalls to avoid when employing people.

The contract of employment

The contract of employment statement which has to be issued in writing to every employee who is going to work for you for 16 hours or more per week within 13 weeks of joining is in fact not a pitfall, but a rather sensible document which clarifies right from the outset what the terms of employment are. From the employer's point of view, the necessity of drafting a contract of employment statement should concentrate the mind wonderfully on issues about which it is all too easy to be sloppy at the expense of subsequent aggravation, such as hours of work, holidays and, above all, exactly what it is the employee is supposed to be doing. The following points have to be covered in the contract, and you must say if you have not covered one or other of them:

The rate of pay and how it is calculated
Whether it is paid weekly or monthly

The normal hours of work and the terms and conditions
relating to them
Holidays and holiday pay
Provision for sick pay
Pension and pension schemes
Notice required by both parties
The job title
Any disciplinary rules relating to the job
Grievance procedures.

If there is any change in any of these terms, the employee has to be notified of this fact in writing, within a month of the change having taken place.

Unfair dismissal

Probably the area of legislation which is easiest and most commonly fallen foul of is that relating to unfair dismissal, though it has been amended in favour of employers by the present government. The latest changes mean effectively that unfair dismissal cases can now only be brought by those who have been continuously employed in the business for more than two years.

The problem that an employer taking over a business has to watch out for is that, under the Transfer of Undertakings Act, contracts of employment entered into by his predecessor also apply to the relationship between the new owner and his employees; the employment 'clock', in other words, is not restarted when there is a change of ownership. This is particularly relevant because 'constructive' dismissal – radically altering the conditions of employment in terms that are disadvantageous to the employee – is equivalent to 'unfair' dismissal and can also be a cause for legal action before an industrial tribunal.

All this does not, of course, mean that you cannot sack an unsatisfactory employee. You must, however, bear in mind that the grounds for doing so should be demonstrably 'reasonable' in the event that an employee takes the matter to an industrial tribunal.

What is meant by this vague sounding concept is set out in a Code of Practice which has been issued alongside the actual legislation. The Code of Practice does not have the force of law, but to what extent it has been observed is taken into account in arriving at a judgement where a case does go to law. In the context of action taken by an employer against an employee the Code of Practice stipulates that this has to be taken against a background of disciplinary rules and procedures which are known and accepted by all concerned. It may sound very cold blooded, when taking staff on, to tell them of the conditions which render them liable to dismissal but the best way to ensure that they know the rules is to give them a copy, in writing, when they join and invite them to query anything they feel unhappy about or do not understand. It need not be a formidable or off-putting legal document, but it should indicate what action you, or anyone entitled to act on your behalf, would feel obliged to take in case of a breach of discipline. The Code of Practice, however, discourages employers from dismissing staff in case of a 'first offence' unless it was one of gross misconduct. It also asks them to ensure that no disciplinary action is taken until all the circumstances have been fully investigated.

Curiously enough, criminal offences outside employment are not regarded as adequate grounds for automatic dismissal, even where the nature of the offence may cast some doubt on the general honesty of the person concerned: shop-lifting, for instance. You have to be able to show first that it directly disqualifies them from doing their job or makes it impossible for other employees to work with them. Trade union officials also have a fairly charmed life. No matter how eagerly you may long to get rid of one of your staff, the Code of Practice advises against taking disciplinary action against them, other than an oral warning, until you have discussed the matter with a more senior union official. Indeed even where the person concerned has nothing to do with a union, it never does to be too hasty. The course of action recommended by experienced personnel people as likely to count in your favour, should a case be brought against you, is to issue a sequence of written warnings to the individual concerned, stating his inadequacies, telling him what he has to do to put them right, and spelling out the consequences if he fails to do so.

It goes without saying that the strict rules imposed by franchisors about the conduct of the franchise make unfair dismissal a potential minefield. A course of disciplinary action may be imposed on you of which you have to bear the consequences, even though you are not the instigator. For this reason, setting out the disciplinary procedures in writing as soon as you start employing people is most important. It would also be a good idea to show this document to the franchisor, so that he does not impose conduct on you which an industrial tribunal might eventually regard as unreasonable.

The trouble with all this legislation is that it leaves grey the area where most dismissal problems occur: that of competence. It is relatively easy to discipline an employee who regularly turns up late for work, but what about the much more common case of those whose work performance is simply not up to standard? The waitress who cannot cope, or the operative whose path is strewn with customer complaints and problems? Very often such employees can claim the whole thing is someone else's fault: the waitress blames the kitchen, the workman pleads that he cannot get used to the materials supplied to him as part of the conditions of the franchise. Very often there is enough truth in such claims to make dismissal on grounds of incompetence extremely difficult once the employee has been with you for 104 weeks. Quite frankly, though, if someone was incompetent you should have spotted the fact and dismissed them while you were able to do so without penalty. If you feel any doubt about the matter because they are not working directly under your supervision, ask the person who is their immediate superior for a report before the fatal two-year period is up. After that you really have to do your homework very carefully before dismissing someone. The inexperienced employer may unwittingly contribute to a judgement of the tribunal going against him by such steps as including the person concerned in a general salary rise before informing him he is not up to the job.

The biggest problem of all with franchises, though, occurs when a franchise is taken over as a going concern. Any employees around the place are regarded as having been in continuous employment from the time they joined, not from the time you appeared on the scene. If your predecessor's standards were less exacting than yours, you could be in for a lot of trouble once you start trying to change things in a way that affects jobs.

There are also some instances where you may be regarded as having dismissed someone unfairly even if they have worked for less than the statutory continuous period. One you have to be careful about is dismissal on medical grounds.

No reasonable employer would dismiss anyone in such circumstances if he could help it, but if you get stuck with someone who is persistently off sick and is able to provide satisfactory medical evidence, you would have to show proof that the absences were of such a nature as to cause disruption to your business before you could discharge him. Even more tricky is the case of employees who are engaged in public duties, such as being on the local council. You have to give them reasonable time off to attend those duties, though not necessarily with pay.

We have used the word 'he' of employees in some places (in the interests of brevity, not for sexist reasons) but, of course, all these provisions extend to women as well. The Sex Discrimination Act and the Equal Pay Act mean that women have in all respects to be treated on an equal footing with men. You cannot advertise a job in such a way as to prevent or even discourage applicants from persons of either sex and you have to pay men and women doing similar jobs the same rate for it.

There are some additional hazards to employing women of childbearing age. Provided she works until 11 weeks before her confinement a woman who has been continuously in your employ for two years or more is entitled to take 29 weeks off if she becomes pregnant and, in the case of firms with more than five employees, to return to her original job, without loss of seniority, at the end of that time. Furthermore, if a woman has been in your employ for at least 26 weeks up to the fifteenth week before the expected date of confinement, she is entitled to Statutory Maternity Benefit for a period of up to 18 weeks. The employer can reclaim the gross SMP from the Department of Employment. And if you bring in a replacement for her, or any other employee who is off for any longer period of time, be very careful. Her replacement could sue you for unlawful dismissal unless you notify him or her in writing that the appointment is a temporary one and give notice when it is coming to an end.

The damages awarded in unfair dismissal cases are not usually very large. The real cost is in the time they take up and the damage they may do to staff morale. Prevention – by getting rid of people before the two years are up if they look like becoming a problem – is better than cure. If you have to undertake the latter, advice from the franchisor's legal department should be sought.

Redundancy

Redundancy is a ripe area for misunderstanding. Redundancy occurs when a job disappears, for example, because a firm ceases trading or has to cut down on staff. It does not have the same restrictions as dismissal, but nevertheless does involve some financial penalties for employers if the employee has been continuously employed by the firm concerned for two years or more. In that case he will be entitled to redundancy pay on a formula based on length of service and rate of pay. About 35 per cent of this can be recovered from the Department of Employment if you employ fewer than ten people, which you should notify if you intend to make anyone redundant. As usual, there is a good deal of form filling involved. The law also requires you to give advance warning to the relevant unions if any of their members are to be made redundant.

What happens if you take over an existing franchise, together with the staff? You may, as we have pointed out, find that you do not like some of the people the previous owner took on, or that you want to change or drop some of the things he was doing, with the result that staff will be made redundant. Irrespective of the fact that you did not hire the people concerned, you are still stuck with your responsibility towards them as their current employer, so that being the proverbial new broom can be a very costly exercise. Before buying a business, therefore, it is very important to look at the staff and at the extent of any redundancy payments or dismissal situations you could get involved in. A very simple guideline is the fact that redundancy pay is linked to age, length of service and the employee's rate of pay. The maximum award for someone with 20 years' service would be £4740.

Health and safety

In the same context, another Act of Parliament you should keep an eye open for when buying a business is the Health and Safety at Work Act which lays down standards to which working premises have to conform. Before putting down your money you should check with the inspectors of the Health and Safety Executive that any premises you are buying or leasing as part of the deal meet those standards. With the Fire Officer the same action needs to be taken in respect of the Fire Precautions Act. In many cases the franchisor will undertake these checks for you, but it is still up to you actually to ensure that he has done so.

Recruitment

The cost of discharging staff, whether because of redundancy or dismissal, makes it imperative that you should make the right decisions in picking people to work for you in the first place. Personnel selection can be described as a gamble but there are ways in which you can cut down on the odds against you.

The most obvious question to ask yourself is whether you really do need to take someone on permanently at all. The principle that is often put forward for the purchase of equipment – never buy anything outright unless you are sure you have a continuing use for it and that it will pay for itself over a reasonable interval of time – also applies to personnel. The legal constraints that cover part-time or full-time employees do not extend to personnel from agencies or outside work done on contract, and this could well be the best way of tackling a particular problem, such as an upward bump in demand, until you are sure that it is going to last. It is worth remembering, too, that when you take on staff you take on a good many payroll and administrative overheads in addition to their salary. These can add quite significantly to your costs.

Sooner or later, though, if you want your business to grow (and growth of some kind seems to be an inevitable concomitant of success) you are going to need people. But even then you should ask yourself what exactly you need them for and how much you can afford to pay. Clarifying these two issues is not only important for itself, but it will also give you the basis of a job description which you can use in your press advertising or approach to a recruitment agency, at the interview and, finally, in the contract of employment. Around it you should also build a series of questions to ask the interviewee that should give you some indication of his competence to do the job. Such questions should call for a detailed response rather than a 'yes' or 'no' type of answer. For example, if you are interviewing a waitress, asking her whether she has worked in that capacity before will tell you something, but not nearly as much as asking where she has worked and for how long she was employed in each earlier job.

Competence is part of the story. Equally important is the interviewee's track record: how many previous employers he has had and whether his progress has been up, down or steady. Too many job changes at frequent intervals can be a bad sign and it is fair to ask searching questions about this if it is part of the employment pattern. It is also wise to be cautious about people who are willing to take a large drop in salary. In these days when good jobs are hard to come by there can be a perfectly good reason for this, but you ought to tactfully find out what it is.

Health is another important point to check on because, as stated in the previous section, dismissing people on medical grounds is very difficult, though there is no obligation to take them on in the first instance. For this reason some employers ask all job candidates to fill in an application form on which, among other questions, that of health is raised. Clearly if the applicant had misled you on the state of his health, that would materially weaken his case at a tribunal. What can be done to establish whether he has any commitments in the way of public or trade union duties which might affect his ability to work the hours required is a much more difficult issue. Putting anything to them in writing would, no doubt, produce an outcry, so perhaps such questions should only be raised verbally, if at all.

Possibly the references will give you a clue and you should always ask for and check references. They are not always reliable – most employers are reasonable people and they will not speak ill of an ex-employee if they can help it (though they should be aware that it is illegal to misrepresent the abilities or overstate the capability of an employee or ex-employee to another employer) – but they will generally alert you to real disaster areas. Telephone reference checks are widely reckoned to be more reliable than written ones because referees are nearly always more forthcoming in conversation than in a letter, since the law of libel and industrial relations law looms large in any written deposition.

Pensions for the self-employed

Amid all the excitement of setting up as a franchisee, thinking about what happens when you retire will very likely rank rather low on your list of priorities.* Apart from anything else, you probably feel that you have enough paperwork on your plate without getting involved in sorting out the complexities of your various pension options. Unfortunately, too, pension proposals are mostly written in a jargon of their own, which makes the whole subject seem much more difficult to grasp than it really is.

However, there are compelling reasons why you need to take self-employed pensions seriously, even at this early stage in your career as a self-employed person. Retirement may seem a long way off now, but by the time your thoughts begin to turn to it, it is often too late to build up anything useful in the way of a pension at all. In the meantime you may have missed some literally golden opportunities to mitigate your tax burden and provide for your future simultaneously. We therefore urge you to read this section (which in the main reproduces the information about pensions contained in Godfrey Golzen's *Daily Telegraph* guide, *Working for Yourself*), in the belief that it successfully explains, in simple language, a topic which generally sends newspaper readers straight to the less demanding pastures of page 3; or depending on taste, age and the paper you read, to the sports pages.

State schemes

Everyone in the UK now has a pension provision of some kind, by law. You either belong and contribute to the state scheme (even if you are self-employed – through your NI contributions) or to a

---

*A 1986 survey reported that less than one in two self-employed people had made pension provisions.

scheme set up by your employer which has to provide benefits at least equal to those offered by the state. The state scheme provides a small basic pension topped up by an earnings related amount and it has a number of serious disadvantages. One is that the earnings related element is calculated on a formula based on your earnings over 20 years from the start of the scheme and without going into the details of this, the effect is that you cannot get the full benefit of it if you retire before 1998. A second disadvantage is that there is no lump sum provision on retirement or death, as is the case with most private schemes. A third drawback is the top limit on earnings, on which the earnings related benefit is limited to £265 a week. Thus, the more highly paid you are on retirement, the worse your benefit is in comparison.

However, from the point of view of the self-employed, the biggest drawback is that you are not eligible for earnings related benefit at all, on the grounds that the fluctuating nature of self-employed earnings makes it difficult to set up such a scheme. All you are entitled to is the basic pension, which is generally admitted to be quite inadequate on its own.

Tax benefits

This is in itself a reason why you should make additional arrangements as soon as you possibly can, but for the self-employed there is another compelling incentive. Investing in a pension scheme is probably the most tax beneficial saving and investment vehicle available to you at this time. Here are some of its key features:

1. Tax relief is given on your contributions at your top rate of tax on earned income. This means that if you are paying tax at the top rate of 60 per cent, you can get £1000-worth of contributions to your pension for an outlay of only £400.
2. Pension funds are in themselves tax exempt – unlike any company in whose shares you might invest. Thus your capital builds up considerably more quickly than it would do in stocks and shares.
3. When you finally come to take your benefits – and you can take part of them as a lump sum and part as a regular pension payment (of which more later) the lump sum will not be liable to capital gains tax and the pension will be treated as earned income from a tax point of view, as distinct from investment income which is regarded as 'unearned' and taxed much more severely.
4. Lump sum benefits arising in the event of your death are paid out to your dependants free of capital transfer tax. This may enable you to build up pension funds to the extent where liability to CTT is reduced quite drastically on other

assets from which income has been siphoned to provide a pension.

The advantages of all this over various DIY efforts to build up a portfolio of stocks and shares – even if you are more knowledgeable about the stock market than most – should be obvious; you are contributing in that case out of taxed income, the resultant investment income is taxed at unearned rates and capital gains tax is payable on the profits you make from selling your holdings.

The convinced adherent of the DIY road may at this point say: ah, but under my own provisions I can contribute as, when and how much I can afford and I am not obliged to make regular payments to a pension plan when it might be highly inconvenient for me to do so. Pensions, however, are not like life insurance. You need not contribute a regular amount at all. You can pay a lump sum or a regular amount. In fact you need not make a payment every year. There are even a number of plans now available under which you are entitled to borrow from your pension plan.

The only restriction that is put on you is imposed by the government and relates to tax benefits. In order for self-employed pensions not to become a vehicle for tax avoidance, the amount you can contribute to them is limited to 17.5 per cent of your income. You are however allowed to 'average out' your contributions over any six-year period to arrive at an overall percentage per year of 17.5.

There was a further concession in the 1982 Finance Act for older people making their own pension plans. If you were born between 1916 and 1933 you can contribute 20 per cent of your relevant earnings. The concessions are even higher for people older than that (up to 24 per cent for those born back in 1912) but in that case your interest in pension plans might be somewhat academic.

Since an increasing number of self-employed people – and their financial advisers – have come to recognise the merits of these schemes, a great many companies have moved into the market for self-employed pensions. Under a fair amount of jargon and an often confusing lineage of fine print, the plans they offer boil down to the following options.

Pension policy with profits. In essence this is a method of investing in a life assurance company, which then uses your money to invest in stocks, shares, government securities or whatever. The advantage from your point of view is that pension funds are tax exempt, so the profits from their investments build up more quickly. These profits are used to build up, in turn, the pension fund you stand to get at the end of the period over which you can contribute. There is no time limit on this period, though obviously the more you do contribute the greater your benefits will be and vice versa; and you can elect to retire any time between 60 and 75.

At retirement you can choose to have part of your pension paid as a lump sum and use it to buy an annuity. This could in some circumstances have a tax advantage over an ordinary pension, but the situation is quite complicated and you should seek professional advice in making your decision. With an annuity, you can use it to buy an additional pension, the provider of which takes the risk that if you live to a ripe old age he might be out of pocket. Equally you might die within six months, in which case the reverse would be true. The statistical probabilities of either of these extremes have been calculated by actuaries and the annuities on offer are based on their conclusions.

One important point about a conventional with-profits pension that often confuses people is that it is not really a form of life insurance. If you die before pensionable age, your dependants and your estate will not usually get back more than the value of the premiums you have paid, plus interest. The best way of insuring your life is through term assurance, of which more later.

Unit linked pensions. Unit linked policies are a variant of unit trust investment, where you make a regular monthly payment (or one outright purchase) to buy stocks and shares across a variety of investments through a fund, the managers of which are supposed to have a special skill in investing in the stock market.

Combining investment with a pension plan sounds terribly attractive and much more exciting than a conventional with-profits policy and it is true that in some instances unit linked policies have shown a better return than their more staid rivals. However, units can go down as well as up and if you get into one of the less successful unit trust funds – and there are quite wide variances in their performance – you may do less well than with a conventional policy.

There are also, of course, fluctuations in the stock market itself which affect the value of your holdings. Over a period of time these fluctuations should even themselves out – you can get more units for your money when the market is down, and fewer when share prices are high. The only problem is that if your policy terminates at a time when share prices are low you will do worse than if you cash in on a boom. However, there is nothing to compel you to sell your holdings when they mature. Unless you desperately need the money you can keep them invested until times are better. Remember, though, since this policy is for your pension, you may not be able to delay using the funds for too long.

Most unit trust companies run a number of funds, invested in different types of shares and in different markets; for instance there are funds that are invested in the US, Australia or Japan, or in specialist sectors, like mining or energy. If you find that the trust you are in is not performing as well as you had hoped (prices are quoted daily in the press) most trusts will allow you to switch from one fund to another at quite a modest administration charge.

Term assurance. While this is not a form of pension at all, it may be attractive to add term assurance to your pension policy for tax purposes. Term assurance is a way of insuring your life for a given period by paying an annual premium. The more you pay, the more you (or rather your dependants) get. If you do not die before the end of the fixed term (eg 20 years) nothing is paid out. As with any other form of insurance, your premiums are simply, if you like, a bet against some untoward event occurring. There is no tax concession on life assurance premiums; it was 15 per cent until 1984.

The one thing that all types of pension schemes have in common is that their salesmen are all eagerly competing for the self-employed person's notional dollar. Your best plan in making your selection is to work through a broker and to let him make the recommendation, but that does not mean that you can abdicate responsibility altogether. For one thing, in order for a broker to make the right selection of pension plans appropriate to your circumstances, you have to describe what your needs and constraints are:

1. Can you afford to make regular payments?
2. Does the irregular nature of your earnings mean that the occasional lump sum payment would be better?
3. Do you have any existing pension arrangements – eg from previous employment?
4. When do you want to retire?
5. What provision do you want to make for dependants?

Very likely he or she will come up with a mix of solutions – for instance, a small regular payment to a pension scheme, topped up by single premium payments. The suggestion may also be made that you should split your arrangements between a conventional with-profits policy and some sort of unit linked scheme; certainly you will be recommended to review your arrangements periodically to take care of inflation and possible changes in your circumstances.

Brokers have to be registered nowadays, so it is unlikely that you will be unlucky enough to land up with someone dishonest. Check that the person you are dealing with really is a *registered* broker – not a consultant, because anyone can call themselves that. Some very big household names among brokers are not, in fact, registered but the majority are. Whoever you deal with though, there are, as in other things in life, differences in the quality of what you get, which in this case is advice. It is as well to have a few checks at your elbow which will enable you to assess the value of the advice you are being given. For instance, national quality newspapers like the *Telegraph, Guardian* and the *Financial Times,* as well as some specialist publications such as the *Economist* and *Investor's Chronicle* publish occasional surveys of the pension business which include performance charts of the various unit trust funds, showing those at the top and bottom of the league table over one, five and ten year periods. There are also tables of benefits offered by the various life companies showing what happens in each case if, for instance, you invest £500 a year over 10 years. There are quite considerable differences between what you get for your money from the most to the least generous firms. If your broker is advising you to put your money in a scheme that appears to give you less than the best deal going, you should not commit yourself to it without talking to your accountant; but with brokers, as with many other professional advisers, the best recommendation is word of mouth from someone you can trust and who can vouch for the ability of the person in question.

Professional advice

You will need the services of an accountant or lawyer, preferably someone you have chosen yourself because otherwise you can never be quite sure that his advice will be impartial. For a small business such as franchising, it is better to go to the more modest High Street type of professional who knows local circumstances and byelaws (as well as possibly having some inside information on people you will be dealing with), rather than to a big, centrally-located firm.

You will also need to make sure that *insurance* is fully taken care of. Normally, the franchisor will see to it that this is done, but since the business is effectively yours, the responsibility for it rests on you. The main kinds of cover you will need are:

1. Insurance of your premises.
2. Insurance of the contents of your premises.
3. Insurance of your stock.
4. Employer's liability if you employ staff on the premises, even on a part-time basis.
5. Public liability in case you cause injury to a member of the public or his premises in the course of business. You will also need third-party public liability if you employ staff or work with partners.
6. Legal insurance policies cover you against prosecution under Acts of Parliament which relate to your business (eg those covering unfair dismissal and fair trading).
7. Insurance against losing your driving licence, important if your business depends on your being able to drive.

The National Federation of Self-Employed and Small Businesses now includes automatic legal insurance in its membership subscription. This covers professional and legal fees of up to £10,000 for appeals to VAT tribunals, defence of Health and Safety at Work prosecutions, 90 per cent of the cost of an Industrial Tribunal Award and defence of private and business motoring prosecutions. The NFSE also runs a voluntary top-up scheme to supplement this basic legal cover.

Chapter 8

Current Franchise Opportunities – a Guide

Finding out about the franchise opportunities on offer is a costly and time-consuming business. This guide pulls together facts from various sources, including both government- and company-provided information, and presents them in an easy-to-read form.

Any attempt to provide a complete guide to current franchise opportunities in the UK, or perhaps anywhere, would be difficult. The present state of the UK franchise market, with new franchisors being 'born' every few months, makes such a guide a near impossibility.

This guide, while not complete, is comprehensive. Almost every current business category of franchise is included. Whether you are looking for a particular market, product, size of franchise organisation, cost of entry, product or service, industrial or consumer market based franchise, you will find it here. The guide provides a useful framework within which you can evaluate new franchisors as they bring their business concepts to the market place.

Why look at franchisor companies anyway?

Much of the detail of the guide looks at the franchisor's organisation rather than simply at the franchise opportunity on offer. We think that in evaluating a business proposal both the proposer and the proposal are equally important subjects for analysis. Indeed, unless you know something of the former, it is very difficult to estimate the substance and credibility of the latter.

Your view of the merits of any advice would be influenced by the qualifications and experience of the adviser. A twice bankrupted and down-at-heel stranger would not command quite the same respect for his business proposal as, for example, a millionaire industrialist.

What has to be remembered is that successful 'business format' franchising requires much more than just a good, or even a unique idea or product. What a franchisee is buying is the franchisor's capability of 'reproducing' success with a good (or unique) product or service. So prospective franchisees need to be able to see something of the substance (or otherwise) of the franchisor's company because it is that organisation that holds the key to whether or not the franchise chain can be securely developed for mutual profit.

What should you look at?

Most of the content of this book is intended to give you a clearer understanding of franchising and the specific questions to ask a franchisor.

In the opportunities guide we have tried to summarise the key information that you need to help you make decisions, not decisions about whether or not to invest in a particular franchise, but decisions on which ones to pursue further. It is extremely important to take appropriate professional advice before committing yourself and your funds to any franchise agreement.

The information in this guide is given in sections.

1. Company and business profile of each franchise

A summary sheet is given for each franchisor setting out facts in the following way:

The name of the franchise organisation is given first, together with a 'thumbnail' sketch of the franchise concept and name and position of the person to contact for details of the franchise. This is followed by four sections giving: company information, the costs of taking up a franchise and where available, the franchisor's market growth and the financial data on the franchisor's performance over the past few years.

Information on the company is given under five headings:

The names of the directors. You should ask which of these are working directors and what, if any, other directorships they hold or have held. It is in the business expertise of these people that you are investing, as well as in your own energy and enthusiasm.

The date of the incorporation is provided so you can see how long the organisation has been around in one form or another.

The issued share capital gives some idea of the liability the owners are prepared to accept. For example, two £1 shares is the minimum. This is little more than a token gesture, whereas a £10,000 paid-up share capital company shows considerably more faith in the venture by the owners.

Knowing *the ultimate holding company* can fundamentally affect your view of the whole franchise proposal. For example, knowing that Baskin-Robbins is a subsidiary company of Allied Breweries indicates a level of financial and managerial strength beyond a simple look at their balance sheet or trading statistics. So this information is also provided.

We have also told you whether or not the franchisor is a *member of the British Franchise Association* whose members are listed on pages 315-19. The BFA is the UK's self-regulating body for business format franchising. It has rules for membership which in themselves tell you something about the franchisor. However, it must be pointed out that many very reputable companies are not members of the BFA, just as the same is true, for example, of the Confederation of British Industries.

For obvious reasons the costs associated with each franchise can only be an approximate figure. Within each franchise there can be several different types or size of franchise on offer, and the costs are subject to alteration over time. Certainly the relationship of the initial fees to royalties is an important consideration. You should be suspicious of anyone offering a very 'front loaded' contract; that is, asking for a very high fee and a very low or non-existent royalty. There may be a sound reason. For example, the franchisor may supply the 'goods' and take a margin on these. Although a possible source of irritation later on, the royalty fees are one sure way of maintaining the franchisor's commitment to developing the business, and providing good advice and support in the future.

The section on market growth shows when the organisation started franchising and how successful the franchisors have been at opening new outlets. It also tells you if they own and operate any outlets themselves. If they don't, then perhaps they won't be able to see and react to changes in the market-place. Or being less charitable, you might question their ability to tell franchisees how to run a business in which they are not themselves involved.

Established companies such as Holland & Barrett have substantial retail operations which come under the heading of company owned, and have only recently started franchising off existing outlets and developing new areas. Others maintain only a few owner-run outlets to serve as a training school for new franchisees and to keep the franchisors' management in tune with a changing environment. Some have a deliberate policy of developing a strong chain of owned outlets.

Each of these strategies can be successful from the potential franchisee's point of view, but it is important to get the franchisor's policy clear at the outset.

Finally, financial data on the franchisor's trading over the past few years are provided where available. Quite a number of franchisors are too new to have their results filed at Companies House and some have neglected to file returns. (Those founded after 1985 are unlikely to have filed trading results.) At least one franchisor operates as a partnership, which eliminates the need for making financial returns. Nevertheless, as a potential investor, you do have a legitimate right to ask a franchisor questions about his financial strength.

Where UK sales are shown you need to understand the nature of the franchisor's business relationship with his franchisees to make good use of these figures. If, for example, the franchisor is supplying the franchisees with a large proportion of their end product (say, fast food), the figures will be quite different from one where only advice is provided and royalties collected.

The net profit figures show you how good the franchisor is at running his own business. You may feel that if he can't make much of a profit himself he's unlikely to be able to help you.

The net worth gives you some idea of how substantial the franchisor's organisation is. Look back to the table on page 91 to see how you calculated your own net worth.

The current ratio (where available) shows you how well the franchisor is in control of the day-to-day cash position. The ratio is calculated by relating current assets (cash debtors and stock etc) to current liabilities (overdraft, creditors, tax due etc). If the ratio is not at least 1:1 then in theory the company is illiquid and cannot meet its current financial obligations. In other words it has cash flow problems. These are bound to reflect adversely on its trading relations with its franchise network.

2. Index of franchises by business category

This table shows you at a glance all the franchisors in each industry sector, for example, Food, Printing, Motor Vehicles etc. In this way you can compare one proposal with another in your chosen business field.

3. Ranking of franchises by minimum investment levels

In this section the franchise opportunities are listed in investment level bands. £0-£5000, £5001-£15,000, £15,001-£30,000, £30,001-£75,000, and £75,001 plus.

This will help you to identify and examine all the franchise proposals within your financial reach. Don't forget that in many cases the franchisors will be able to help you raise a proportion of the investment required, so the governing factor is likely to be how much you would be prepared to risk, rather than how much cash you have available.

4. Company ranking by number of UK franchise outlets
(company owned and franchised)

You may feel that the franchisor with the best developed network and greatest number of franchises has 'proved' his business concept beyond reasonable doubt. Conversely you may feel that you would like to get in at the start of a new but sound venture.

1. Company and business profile of each franchise

Note: Telephone dialling codes given may not apply to local calls. The franchisors listed in this directory are not all currently offering franchises, as their programmes may be full for the time being. Their listing here is not an endorsement by us or the *Daily Telegraph*.

A1 Damproofing
New Side Mill
Charnley Fold Lane
Bamber Bridge
Preston PR5 6AA
Tel: 0772 35228
Contact: J B Pickup

Business description
Specialists in the treatment of woodworm, woodrot and rising
damp.

Company information
Directors: G Ainley, JB Pickup (Managing Director)
Date of incorporation: 30 August 1985
Company name: A1 Damproofing (UK) Ltd
Issued share capital: £10,000
Associate company: Industrial Chemical Co (Preston) Ltd
BFA member: No

Costs
Start-up capital (minimum): £10,000
Initial fee: £4000
Royalties: 10 per cent
Proportion of start-up capital that can be arranged: 100 per cent
  (with security)

Market growth	1984	1985	1986
UK franchise outlets:	—	4	10
UK company owned outlets:	1	1	1
Date of first UK franchise: October 1985			

Financial data	1984	1985	1986
Turnover:	N/A	N/A	£207,000
Net profit:	N/A	N/A	£46,500

N/A: Information exists but is not available.

The Accounting Centre
Elscot House
Arcadia Avenue
London N3 2JE
Tel: 01-349 3191
Contact: Ivor Davies

Business description
A monthly accounting service to small-medium sized businesses developing nationally with support from banks and firms of accountants. A proven route to independence for qualified-accountant franchisees who concentrate on supervising the bookkeeping, interpreting accounts, providing general business advice etc – leaving the franchisor to carry out all the 'number crunching' on mainframe computers with established software.

Company information
Company name: The Accounting Centre
Issued share capital: N/A
Parent company: Inspectorate UCC Ltd
BFA member: Yes

Costs
Start-up capital (minimum): £15,000 including initial licence fee
Initial fee: £7500
Royalties: 10 per cent
Proportion of start-up capital that can be arranged: 66 per cent

			(30 June)
Market growth	1984	1985	1986
UK franchise outlets:	16	25	25
UK company owned outlets:	1	1	1
Date of first UK franchise: 1983			

Financial data	1983	1984	1985
Turnover:	£575,000	£682,000	£864,000
Net profit:			£15,156
*Net worth:			£107,556
Current ratio:			1.03:1

*Fixed assets = Current assets minus liabilities. Shares in subsidiaries and loans to associated companies are excluded.

N/A: Information exists but is not available.

Anicare Group Services (Veterinary) Ltd
23 Buckingham Road
Shoreham-by-Sea
West Sussex BN4 5UA
Tel: 0273 463022
Contact: J P Sheridan

Business description
Anicare comprises a number of animal veterinary practices linked
to central resources for diagnostic, surgical and in-patient
facilities. Franchisees have to be fully qualified and members of
the Royal College of Veterinary Surgeons. Practice
accommodation is to a set pattern and help is given with site
selection.

A range of business management systems is provided, covered by
written instructions. Office stationery, forms and promotional
material are included in the franchise package.

There is regular exchange of information between practices and
arrangements for locum cover.

Company information
Directors: JP Sheridan, MD Sheridan
Date of incorporation: 1977
Company name: Anicare Group Services (Veterinary) Ltd
Authorised share capital: £1000
Parent company: N/A
BFA member: Yes

Costs
Start-up capital (minimum): £15,000
Initial fee: £3750
Royalties: 8 per cent
Proportion of start-up capital that can be arranged: 60-70 per cent

			(30 June)
Market growth	1984	1985	1986
UK franchise outlets:	7	7	8
UK company owned outlets:	1	1	1
Date of first UK franchise: 1972			

Financial data	1983	1984	1985
Turnover:	£56,806	£57,423	N/A
Net profit:	£5,020	£4,302	—
*Net worth:	£75,820	£79,066	—
Current ratio:	0.55:1	0.48:1	—

*Fixed assets = Current assets minus liabilities. Shares in subsidiaries and loans to
associated companies are excluded.

152

Apollo Window Blinds Ltd
Johnstone Avenue
North Cardonald Industrial Estate
Glasgow G52 4YM
Tel: 041-810 3021
Contact: Mrs Nan Stevenson, Franchise Executive

Business description
Apollo is a leading company in a market worth £150 million
annually. Opportunities are available in many parts of England,
Wales and Eire. The franchisees assemble and retail from high
street locations an exclusive range of window blinds to domestic,
commercial and trade customers. Full training and set-up
assistance are provided, together with a high degree of ongoing
support. Apollo also provides franchisees with strong corporate
assistance on TV, in Yellow Pages and women's magazines.

Company information
Directors: J McNeil, R McNeil, JW Watson
Date of incorporation: 1973
Company name: Apollo Window Blinds Ltd
Issued share capital: N/A
Parent company: Yes
BFA member: Yes

Costs
Start-up capital (minimum): £20,000
Initial fee: £4000
Royalties: Nil
Proportion of start-up capital that can be arranged: 70 per cent

Market growth	1984	1985	(30 June) 1986
UK franchise outlets:	65	80	98
UK company owned outlets:	1	—	—
Date of first UK franchise: 1975			

Financial data	1983	1984	1985
Group turnover:	£9m	£12m	£12m

N/A: Information exists but is not available.

153

Badgeman Ltd
544 Chiswick High Road
London W4 5RG
Tel: 01-994 0826
Contact: David Mackie

Business description
Badgeman is the industry leader in the manufacture of high
quality personalised lapel badges. Badgeman also supplies desk
plates and door plates incorporating company logotype.

Company information
Directors: AJ Coles, DH Hargreaves, DG Mackie
Date of incorporation: 1979
Company name: Badgeman Ltd
Issued share capital: £100
Ultimate holding company: Sketchley Services Division
BFA member: Yes

Costs
Start-up capital (minimum): £15,000 plus VAT plus working capital
Initial fee: £15,000 plus VAT
Royalties: 10 per cent of gross turnover
Proportion of start-up capital that can be arranged: 50 per cent

			(30 June)
Market growth	1984	1985	1986
UK franchise outlets:	10	11	11
UK company owned outlets:	1	1	1
Date of first UK franchise: 1980			

Financial data	1983	1984	1985
Turnover:	—	£176,146	£197,960
Net profit:	—	£20,899	£44,244
*Net worth:	—	£17,431	£48,955
Current ratio:	—	1.05:1	1.69:1

*Fixed assets = Current assets minus liabilities. Shares in subsidiaries and loans to
associate companies are excluded.

Balloon
26 High Street
Merstham
Surrey RH1 3EA
Tel: 07374 4211

No franchises are currently being offered.

The Bath Doctor
Denbigh House
Denbigh Road
Milton Keynes
Buckinghamshire MK1 1YP
Tel: 0908 270007
Contact: Mike Robertson

Business description
A low-cost, high-profit business that is worked from home,
serving the consumer direct and the commercial world of
hospitals, schools etc. The renovation of bathroom suites is new,
cost-effective, and the Bath Doctor is market leader.

Company information
Directors: M Robertson, J Barnes
Date of incorporation: 1 February 1986
Company name: Rosendale Properties Ltd
Issued share capital: £1000
Parent company: —
BFA member: Registered

Costs
Start-up capital (minimum): £2500
Royalties: £25-£100 per month
Proportion of start-up capital that can be arranged: 75 per cent

			(30 June)
Market growth	1984	1985	1986
UK franchise outlets:	30	40	50
UK company owned outlets:	—	—	—
Date of first UK franchise: 1982			

Financial data: New company. No accounts filed.

Beardsley Theobalds Businesses
Leygore Manor
Northleach
Cheltenham GL54 3NY
Tel: 0451 60667
Contact: John Hine

Business description
Computer-linked business transfer agents and finance brokers.
Beardsley Theobalds Businesses has been serving the East
Midlands business community as a business transfer agent for the
past six years and decided to expand nationally only two years ago
through owned or franchised agencies. The network which is
connected by Prestel to a central computer in London now has
over 1000 varied businesses for sale and more than 9000
prospective buyers looking for businesses throughout the United
Kingdom.

Company information
Directors: J Beardsley, J Hine, K Curran
Date of incorporation: December 1984
Company name: B T Businesses Ltd
Issued share capital: £210,000
Parent company: London & Manchester Group owns 40 per cent of the
    ordinary shares and all the preference shares
BFA member: No

Costs
Start-up capital (minimum): £30,000
Initial fee: £11,000
Royalties: 10 per cent of relevant fees after twelve months' trading
Proportion of start-up capital that can be arranged: 50 per cent

			(30 June)
Market growth	1984	1985	1986
UK franchise outlets:	—	5	11
Associate owned outlets:	5	5	5
Date of first UK franchise: 22 April 1985			

Financial data	1985
Turnover:	£70,000
Net profit:	£1,000
*Net worth:	£210,000

*Fixed assets = Current assets minus liabilities. Shares in subsidiaries and loans to
associated companies are excluded.

Bodyreform
Reform Cosmetics
Natural Beauty Products Ltd
Unit 5 Kingsway Buildings
Bridgend Industrial Estate
Bridgend
Mid-Glamorgan CF31 3SD
Tel: 0656 57101/645400
Contact: A R Lees

Business description
Bodyreform shops are the franchised retail outlets for Reform
cosmetics, natural, not animal-tested cosmetics, manufactured by
Natural Beauty Products Ltd. Items include skin/hair/body care
decorative cosmetics, perfumes, colognes, toiletries and
aromatherapy.

Company information
Directors: AR Lees, MR Oliver, KG Ueber, MF Ueber
Date of incorporation: 1984
Company name: Natural Beauty Products Ltd
Issued share capital: £112,500
BFA member: No

Costs
Start-up capital (minimum): £25,000
Initial fee: £3750
Royalties: None
Proportion of start-up capital that can be arranged: 66 per cent

			(30 June)
Market growth	1985	1986	1987
UK franchise outlets:	1	18	37
UK company owned outlets:	1	2	5
Date of first UK franchise:			
December 1985			

Financial data: No separate accounts are filed.

The Bread Roll Company
Unit 6
224 London Road
St Albans
Hertfordshire
Tel: 0727 35291
Contact: Mark Dixon

Business description
Specialist supplier of rolls and allied products to trade and retail customers. High profile distribution and sales service.

Company information
Directors: M Dixon, GR Ives
Date of incorporation: 1983
Company name: The Bread Roll Company (St Albans) Ltd
Issued share capital: £100
Parent company: —
BFA member: No

Costs
Start-up capital: £16,000
Initial fee: None
Royalties: None
Proportion of start-up capital that can be arranged: 60 per cent

			(June 30)
Market growth	1984	1985	1986
UK franchise outlets:	1	3	10
UK company owned outlets:	1	1	0
Date of first UK franchise: 1984			

Financial data	1983	1984	1985
Turnover:	£90K	£150K	£297K
Net profit:	£16.2K	£30K	£65.34K
*Net worth:	£ − 10K	£20K	£85.34K

*Fixed assets = Current assets minus liabilities. Shares in subsidiaries and loans to associated companies are excluded.

159

Brewer and Turnbull
Your Friendly Mr Mover
Waverley Freight Terminal
Miller Road
Preston PR1 5QS
Tel: 0772 797896
Contact: Max C Godfrey

Business description
Home and overseas removals and storage. Local and long distance
moving part loads. Branches throughout the UK.

Company information
Directors: MA Whittle, DR Wiggin, DN Whittle
Date of incorporation: 1932
Company name: Brewer and Turnbull Ltd
Issued share capital: —
Parent company: —
BFA member: No

Costs
Start-up capital: £15,000
Initial fee: £1000-£5000
Royalties: 5 per cent
Proportion of start-up capital that can be arranged: Nil

			(June 30)
Market growth	1984	1985	1986
UK franchise outlets:	16	20	24
UK company owned outlets:	—	—	1
Date of first UK franchise: 1984			

Financial data: The company was a partnership until September 1986, and
accounts are confidential. (No accounts are filed.)

British Damp Proofing
The Old School
Fleetwood Road
Esprick
Preston PR4 3HJ
Tel: 039 136 441
Contact: B Wainwright

Business description
Specialists in the treatment of rising damp and timber decay;

160

three-week comprehensive residential training course including technical, marketing and sales programmes.

Company information
Directors: B Wainwright (Chairman), AF Haslam (Managing Director), JC Lavelle
Date of incorporation: 1984
Company name: BDP Ltd
Issued share capital: £3000
BFA member: Yes

Costs
Start-up capital (minimum): £10,500
Initial fee: £3500
Royalties: Fixed fee or 10 per cent
Proportion of start-up capital that can be arranged: 50 per cent

			(30 June)
Market growth	1984	1985	1986
UK franchise outlets:	19	32	45
UK company owned outlets:	2	2	2

Date of first UK franchise: 1984

Financial data	1985
Turnover:	£483,140
Net profit:	£56,041
*Net worth:	£46,543
Current ratio:	0.95:1

*Fixed assets = Current assets minus liabilities. Shares in subsidiaries and loans to associated companies are excluded.

Bruce & Company
43 Bridge Street
Leatherhead
Surrey KT28 8BN
Tel: 0372 375161
Contact: I W Lynch

Business description
The company acts as agents in the business transfer market, selling a wide range of different types of business in the retail and service sectors. The 14 offices cover most of England and Wales.

Company information
Partners: IW Lynch
Date of incorporation: 1973
Company name: Bruce & Company
BFA member: No

161

Costs
Start-up capital (minimum): £15,000
Initial fee: £5000
Royalties: 5 per cent
Proportion of start-up capital that can be arranged: Nil

			(30 June)
Market growth	1984	1985	1986
UK franchise outlets:	9	11	13
UK company owned outlets:	1	1	1

Date of first UK franchise: 1981

Financial data: The company is a partnership. No accounts are filed.

Budget Rent A Car International Inc
International House
85 Great North Road
Hatfield
Hertfordshire AL9 5EF
Tel: 07072 68266
Contacts: Keith Harman or Bernard Glover

Business description
Budget Rent A Car operates a car and van hire business.
Franchisees have a defined locality, with franchise costs based on
market potential.

Vehicles are obtained by the company through links with
manufacturers. Office signs, fittings and stationery are issued
corporately. There is a business system, with regular returns to the
company, and checks on trading efficiency.

Training includes vehicle operation, sales and management
techniques.

District meetings are held and marketing and management
literature is circulated. All personnel are uniformed and vehicles
carry company livery.

Company staff help through the initial stages and there is
continuing support on business effectiveness and training.

Company information
Directors: PL Crouch, M McHardy, D Tett, M McRae, K Harman,
   N Summerville, T Alexander
Date of incorporation: 1958
Company name: Budget Rent A Car International Inc
Issued share capital: N/A
Parent company: Gibbons, Green, van Amerongen
BFA member: Yes

Costs
Start-up capital (minimum): £75,000
Initial fee: £15,000 plus depending on area
Royalties: 10 per cent
Proportion of start-up capital that can be arranged: Not encouraged

			(30 June)
Market growth	1984	1985	1986
UK franchise outlets:	102	108	115
UK company owned outlets:	2	2	2

Date of first UK franchise: 1966

Financial data: No separate accounts are filed.

N/A: Information exists but is not available.

Burger King UK Ltd
20 Kew Road
Richmond
Surrey TW9 2NA
Tel: 01-940 6046
Contact: Mrs Farrah Rose

Business description
Fast food hamburger restaurants.

Company information: N/A
Parent company: Pillsbury Company (USA)
BFA member: Yes

Costs
Initial fee: US $25,000
Royalties: 4 per cent per month
Proportion of start-up capital that can be arranged: Nil

			(30 June)
Market growth	1985	1986	1987
UK franchise outlets:	—	—	12
UK company owned outlets:	—	—	—

Date of first UK franchise:
  5 January 1987

Financial data: No separate accounts are filed.

N/A: Information exists but is not available.

Business Transfer Consultants (Franchise) Ltd
712 Green Lane
Goodmayes
Essex RM8 1YX
Tel: 01-597 2302
Contact: Rhonda Brooke-Taylor

Business description
Business transfer agents, selling a wide range of businesses from corner grocery stores to the largest hotels, empty premises, factories and all other commercial propositions. In addition to selling businesses, the company offers in-house services including finance and insurance.

Company information
Directors: Rhonda Brooke-Taylor, Maureen McCadden
Date of incorporation: 28 October 1983
Company name: Business Transfer Consultants (Franchise) Ltd
Issued share capital: £100
Parent company: —
BFA member: No

Costs
Start-up capital (minimum): £30,000
Initial fee: £15,000
Royalties: 10 per cent
Proportion of start-up capital that can be arranged: 50 per cent

			(30 June)
Market growth	1984	1985	1986
UK franchise outlets:	—	5	9
UK company owned outlets:	1	1	1
Date of first UK franchise: September 1983			

Financial data	1983	1984	1985
Turnover:	N/A	£80,000	£180,000
Net profit:	N/A	£7,000	£20,000

N/A: Information exists but is not available.

Business Transfer Consultants (Franchise) Ltd.

Development of our planned expansion
programme now offers further opportunities
in a number of areas for suitable persons to
join our fast growing Franchise network selling
businesses and commercial properties
nationwide.

The Franchise package includes a full training
programme — own limited company —
corporate image advantage and full
development back-up.

Capital requirement £30,000 to include
Franchise fee, initial set-up costs and the initial
budget requirement.

If you have business acumen and the ability to
exercise your own initiative we would like to
hear from you.

KEY HOUSE
712 GREEN LANE, GOODMAYES, ESSEX, RM8 1YX
TELEPHONE: 01-597 2302
FAX NO: 01-590 4470

Carpet Master Ltd
Shop Unit 36
Bradford Road
Off Buckingham Avenue
Trading Estate
Slough
Berkshire SL1 4PG
Tel: 0753 691584
Contact: Hugh Jones

Business description
Carpet Master Ltd is a young and energetic company which is quickly reshaping the retail carpet market. Carpet Master offers all its franchisees total support and back-up, every mobile carpet showroom being equipped with the very best carpets and curtains from all of the leading manufacturers.

Company information
Directors: G Luttrell, H Jones
Date of incorporation: 16 January 1987 (trading as Carpet Master for the past ten years)
Company name: Carpet Master Ltd
Issued share capital: £200
Parent company: —
BFA member: No

Costs
Start-up capital (minimum): £3721.66 plus VAT
Initial fee: As above
Royalties: None
Proportion of start-up capital that can be arranged: 100 per cent

Market growth	1984	1985	(20 February) 1986
UK franchise outlets:			3

Cartons Boulangeries
Unit 2
Telegraph Hill Estate
Laundry Road
Minster
Ramsgate
Kent CT12 4HJ
Tel: 0843 821940
Contact: Bob Peel

Business description
High class French bakery, patisserie, for consumption on or off the premises.

Company information
Directors: AR King, TW Chatfield, Mrs CW Macleod
Date of incorporation: 14 July 1986
Company name: Cartons Boulangeries Ltd
Issued share capital: N/A
Parent company: —
BFA member: No

167

Costs
Start-up capital (minimum): £20,000
Initial fee: £5000
Royalties: Starting at 7½ per cent, reducing as turnover increases
Proportion of start-up capital that can be arranged: 50 per cent

	(30 June)
Market growth	1986
UK franchise outlets:	5
UK company owned outlets:	1
Date of first UK franchise:	

N/A: Information exists but is not available.

Chapter and Verse Bookshops
41 Park Street
Bristol BS1 5NL
Tel: 0272 214670
Contact: T A G Foss

Business description
General and academic bookselling. This is a new franchising
venture and no franchises have been offered so far. Sites are being
sought.

Company information
Director: TAG Foss
Date of incorporation: 1971
Company name: Chapter and Verse Bookshop Ltd
Issued share capital: £10,000
BFA member: No

Costs
Start-up capital (minimum): £75,000
Initial fee: £4500
Royalties: 2½ per cent gross sales
Proportion of start-up capital that can be arranged: 50 per cent

Financial data: No trading accounts as yet.

Cico Chimney Linings
Westleton
Saxmundham
Suffolk IP17 3BS
Tel: 072 873 608
Contact: J Wilkin

Business description
Lining and restoration of domestic and non-domestic chimneys.

Company information
Director: RT Hadfield
Date of incorporation: 28 February 1982
Company name: Cico Chimney Linings Ltd
Issued share capital: £1000
Parent company: —
BFA member: Yes

Costs
Start-up capital (minimum): £11,000
Initial fee: £6500
Royalties: 10 per cent
Proportion of start-up capital that can be arranged: 66 per cent

			(30 June)
Market growth	1984	1985	1986
UK franchise outlets:	13	16	20
UK company owned outlets:	1	1	1
Date of first UK franchise:			
June 1982			

169

Circle 'C' Stores Ltd
24 Fitzalan Road
Roffey
Horsham
Sussex RH13 6AA
Tel: Horsham 61698
Contact: J A Wormull

Business description
Convenience stores situated in neighbourhood locations offering a range of products sold by grocers, bakers, greengrocers, chemists, newsagents, confectioners, stationers, off licences and video hire shops, all in one shop. Trading hours are 7.30 am to 9 pm, seven days a week.

Company information
Directors: JA Wormull, SP Wormull, Mrs KA Wormull
Date of incorporation: 1975
Company name: Circle 'C' Stores Ltd
Issued share capital: £100,000
Parent company: J'N'K Markets Ltd
BFA member: Registered

Costs
Start-up capital (minimum): £25,000
Initial fee: £5000
Royalties: 3 per cent
Proportion of start-up capital that can be arranged: 60 per cent

Market growth	1984	1985	(30 June) 1986
UK franchise outlets:	1	2	7
UK company owned outlets:	6	12	15
Date of first UK franchise: N/A			

Financial data	1983	1984	1985
Turnover: (Group)	£3m	£4m	£8m
Net profit: (Group)	£117,000	£150,000	£222,000
*Net worth:	£130,000	£204,000	£372,000
Current ratio:	0.8:1	0.9:1	0.8:1

Group = All company stores operating under Circle C.

*Fixed assets = Current assets minus liabilities. Shares in subsidiaries and loans to associated companies are excluded.

N/A: Information exists but is not available.

Clarks Shoes
Box 106
40 High Street
Street
Somerset BA16 0YA
Tel: 0458 43131 ext. 2399
Contact: Paul D Monaghan, Franchise Manager

Business description
Clarks Shoes franchising developed out of franchise-type businesses previously set up by the company's retail consultancy, Torlink Ltd. Franchises usually sell the Clarks brand exclusively, and are not based on territories, but limited by the brand market share in a particular town. A complete package is offered: property acquisition, highly competitive loan-finance, a unique design scheme, marketing and continuing support from a field force of consultants. Footwear experience is not essential as full classroom and practical training is provided.

Company information
Directors: JE Dixon, WB Johnston, BB Rees
Date of incorporation: 1965
Company name: Torlink Ltd

Issued share capital: N/A
Parent company: C & J Clark Ltd
BFA member: Yes

Costs
Start-up capital (minimum): £80,000
Initial fee: £5000 as contribution to obtaining site plus head lease,
   business plan, pre-opening consultancy and full training
Royalties: None
Proportion of start-up capital that can be arranged: 66 per cent

Market growth	1984	1985	1986
UK franchise outlets:	8	15	27
UK company owned outlets:	5	15	70
Date of first UK franchise: 1984			

Financial data
Company is wholly owned by C & J Clark Ltd.

N/A: Information exists but is not available.

Coffeeman
73 Woolsbridge Industrial Park
Wimborne
Dorset BH21 6SU
Tel: 0202 823501
Contacts: S Bayless, R Troon

Business description
Supplying caterers, offices, factories, all possible outlets with
fresh ground coffees and teas, and sundry items ie sugar, creamer
etc.

Company information
Director: S Bayless
Date of incorporation: 1 October 1984
Company name: Coffeeman Management Ltd
Issued share capital: £120
BFA member: No

Costs
Start-up capital (minimum): Between £9000 and £15,000
Initial fee: Franchise fee £4500 included in above
Royalties: None
Proportion of start-up capital that can be arranged: 60 per cent

Market growth	1984	1985	(30 June) 1986
UK franchise outlets:	18	25	33
UK company owned outlets:			1

Date of first UK franchise: 1979

Financial data: N/A

N/A: Information exists but is not available.

Colour Counsellors
187 New King's Road
London SW6 4NZ
Tel: 01-736 8326
Contact: Virginia Stourton

Business description
Interior decoration and supplies.

Company information
Director: V Stourton
Date of incorporation: 1977
Company name: Colour Counsellors Ltd
Issued share capital: £100
BFA member: Yes

Costs
Start-up capital (minimum): £4500
Initial fee: £3500
Royalties: Fixed fee system £1750 pa
Proportion of start-up capital that can be arranged: 50 per cent

Market growth	1984	1985	(30 June) 1986
UK franchise outlets:	50	60	65
UK company owned outlets:	1	1	1

Date of first UK franchise: 1974

Financial data	1983	1984	1985
Turnover:	£504,502	£608,139	N/A
Net profit:	£6,321	(1,824)	
*Net worth:	£2,892	£1,068	
Current ratio:	0.95:1	0.93:1	

*Fixed assets = Current assets minus liabilities. Shares in subsidiaries and loans to associated companies are excluded.

N/A: Information exists but is not available.

Command Performance
High End
Troutstream Way
Loudwater
Hertfordshire WD3 4LQ
Tel: 0923 777 636
Contact: Iain Macaulay

Business description
A business suitable for single men, women or couples. A modern hairstyling salon, sometimes with beauty department, nail centre, gymnasium/health centre. Usually high street locations, appealing to the 18-40 year-old man or woman, just below the top 5 per cent of the market.

Company information
Directors: JG Macaulay, V Macaulay, JA Macaulay, CM Youngman,
    L Charm, E Kohn
Date of incorporation: N/A
Company name: Command Performance International Ltd
Issued share capital: £50,000
BFA member: Yes

Costs
Start-up capital (minimum): £50,000
Initial fee: £5000
Royalties: 5 per cent
Proportion of start-up capital that can be arranged: 70 per cent

Market growth	1984	1985	1986
UK franchise outlets:	2	5	10
UK company owned outlets:	5	5	3
Date of first UK franchise: September 1984			

Financial data	1983	1984	1985
Turnover:	£200,000	£275,000	£500,000
Net profit:	—	—	—
*Net worth:	(£24,585)	£26,010	£34,330
Current ratio:	0.28:1	0.97:1	0.88:1

*Fixed assets = Current assets minus liabilities. Shares in subsidiaries and loans to associated companies are excluded.

N/A: Information exists but is not available.

HAIR CARE SALONS
A BUSINESS WITH STYLE

- ● FULL TRAINING
- ● PROVEN SYSTEMS
- ● FULL ADMIN. PACKAGE
- ● ASSISTANCE WITH SITE SELECTION
- ● SALON DESIGN AND SHOP FITTING PACKAGE
- ● TOP PROFESSIONALS IN MANAGEMENT MARKETING

Command Performance is one of the largest chains of franchised salons in the world with 350 salons in the USA. We are now in the UK with 16 salons opened and 10 in the 'pipeline'. No hairdressing experience necessary, good social working hours. Total capital minimum £50,000 (£15,000 own cash recommended).

OUR FRANCHISES HAVE IN COMMON:—

- ● A desire for independence.
- ● A prestigious name in business.
- ● Good return on capital.
- ● Feel 'comfortable' about investment.
- ● Support from leaders in their industry.

Command Performance®
STYLING SALONS

We've got the style for you.

£1.3 billion market likely to be around for another '2000 years'.

Write for details to:—
COMMAND PERFORMANCE INTERNATIONAL LTD
High End, Trout Stream Way, Loudwater, Herts WD3 4LQ Tel (0923) 777636

175

Compleat Cookshop
Buckingham Road
Aylesbury
Buckinghamshire HP19 3QQ
Tel: 0296 431296
Contact: J C Frankling, Franchise Recruitment
   Manager

Business description
Fashion housewares retailing.

Company information
Directors: RW Faulkner, AN Barnard
Date of incorporation: 1980
Company name: Compleat Cookshop Ltd
Issued share capital: N/A
BFA member: No

Costs
Start-up capital (minimum): £20,000
Initial fee: £2500
Royalties: Nil
Proportion of start-up capital that can be arranged: up to 70 per cent

			(30 June)
Market growth	1984	1985	1986
UK franchise outlets:	7	12	15
UK company owned outlets:	7	7	7
Date of first UK franchise:			

Financial data	1983	1984	1985
Turnover:	—	—	—
Net profit:	£13,645	£122,211	—
*Net worth:	£80,485	£156,988	—
Current ratio:	1.02:1	1.04:1	—

*Fixed assets = Current assets minus liabilities. Shares in subsidiaries and loans to associated companies are excluded.

N/A: Information exists but is not available.

176

Complete Weed Control Ltd
Industrial Estate
Bourton-on-the-Water
Gloucestershire GL54 2EN
Tel: 0451 20985
Contact: Mr R W Turner

Business description
Weed control service to local authorities, government
departments, industry, amenity and commercial areas – wherever
weed growth presents a problem in non-agricultural areas.

Company information
Directors: RW Turner (Managing Director), A Muirhead, D Pryse,
   P Stott, NJ Nattrass
Date of incorporation: 1972
Company name: Complete Weed Control Ltd
Issued share capital: £100
BFA member: Registered

Costs
Start-up capital (minimum): £20,000 plus VAT
Initial fee: £8000 plus VAT
Royalties: 10 per cent on sales turnover
Proportion of start-up capital that can be arranged: 66 per cent

			(30 June)
Market growth	1984	1985	1986
UK franchise outlets:	8	10	13
UK company owned outlets:	1	1	1
Date of first UK franchise: N/A			

Financial data	1983	1984	1985
Turnover:	£450,000	£600,000	£670,000

N/A: Information exists but is not available.

ComputerLand
UK Regional Office
518 Elder House
Elder Gate
Central Milton Keynes
Buckinghamshire MK9 1LR
Tel: 0908 664244
Contact: Clive Booth, UK Area Director

Business description
ComputerLand is an international network of microcomputer
business centres. Full training for new franchises is given at
European head office in Luxembourg. Assistance is given for the
whole opening phase (usually six months to commence trading).
Ongoing involvement includes central purchasing, technical
advice, and advertising.

Company information
Director: Paul Helminger (Managing Director)
Date of incorporation: June 1977 in the USA
Company name: ComputerLand Europe SA
Issued share capital: N/A
Ultimate holding company: ComputerLand Corporation (in California)
BFA member: Yes

Costs
Start-up capital (minimum): £200,000-£260,000 depending on location
Initial fee: £13,000-£20,000 depending on location
Royalties: 3.5 per cent plus 1 per cent for advertising

Market growth	1984	1985	1986
UK franchise outlets:	10	14	15
UK company owned outlets:	0	0	0
Date of first UK franchise: September 1982			

Financial data: No trading accounts filed for UK operation.

N/A: Information exists but is not available.

Concorde One Hour Photo Labs
46 Church Street
Enfield
Middlesex EN2 6AZ
Tel: 01-367 4762 (day), 01-360 9645 (evening)
Contact: John Fairley

Business description
One-hour high street photographic developing and retailing of
photographic accessories. The partnership emphasises business
financing and management, based on an intimate knowledge of
mini-lab operations over seven years' direct involvement. The
founder is a qualified accountant with twelve years' experience as
a business management consultant.

Company information
The business operates as a partnership.
BFA member: No

Costs
Start-up capital (minimum): £20,000
Initial fee: £5000
Royalties: 5 per cent
Proportion of start-up capital that can be arranged: 75 per cent

	(30 June) 1986
Market growth	
UK franchise outlets:	1
UK company owned outlets:	2
Date of first UK franchise:	
March 1985	

Financial data: The company is a partnership. No accounts are filed.

	(31 Dec) 1986
*Net worth:	£163,000

*Fixed assets = Current assets minus liabilities. Shares in subsidiaries and loans to
associated companies are excluded.

179

Conder Clentech
Abbotts Barton House
Worthy Road
Winchester
Hampshire SO23 7SJ
Tel: 0962 63577

No franchises are currently being offered.

Countrywide Garden Maintenance Services
164-200 Stockport Road
Cheadle
Cheshire SK8 2DP
Tel: 061-428 4444
Contact: Martin Stott

Business description
The concept of the franchise is to provide to both the private and industrial sectors a first class garden maintenance service on a regular weekly basis all the year round. The enormous attraction of this service franchise is that the clients contract to use the service every week of the year. Consequently, the franchisee will see his business expand quickly in a controlled and planned fashion.

Company information
Directors: M Stott, Y Stott
Date of incorporation: 31 January 1986
Company name: Garden Maintenance Ltd
Issued share capital: £100
BFA member: No

Costs
Start-up capital (minimum): £14,000 including working capital
Initial fee: £2600
Royalties: 8 per cent of turnover
Proportion of start-up capital that can be arranged: 70 per cent

Market growth	1984	1985	(30 June) 1986
UK franchise outlets:	0	0	3
UK company owned outlets:	1	1	1

Date of first UK franchise: Pilot scheme January 1986

Countrywide Garden Maintenance Services

The concept of our Franchise is to supply to the Private, Industrial and Public Sectors a first class Garden Maintenance Service on a fixed price contract every week, 52 weeks a year. Plus Interior Plant Rental and Maintenance for offices and hotels etc.

The market of this service is enormous and the key attraction of the Franchise is that once acquired the customer contracts to employ your company all year around, consequently the Franchisee will see his business expanding quickly in a controlled and planned fashion. But there is no upper limit to the size the business can grow to.

BRITAINS NO.1 PRIVATE AND INDUSTRIAL GARDEN MAINTENANCE CONTRACTORS

THE HEALTHY OUTDOOR FRANCHISE

Countrywide Garden Maintenance Services, 164-200 Stockport Road, Cheadle, Cheshire SK8 2DP.
Tel: 061-428 4444

Coversure Insurance Services
4 Longstaff Way
Wartford
Huntingdon
Cambridgeshire PE18 7XT
Tel: 0480 413858
Contact: P Theakston

Business description
Motor, commercial and life assurance consultants.

Company information
Director: Peter David Theakston
Date of incorporation: 1985
Company name: Insurance Management Services
BFA member: No

Costs
Start-up capital (minimum): £10,000
Initial fee: £1500

181

Royalties: 1½ to 2 per cent of premium income
Proportion of start-up capital that can be arranged: up to 50 per cent
subject to status.

	(30 June)
Market growth	1986
UK franchise outlets:	1
UK company owned outlets:	3
Date of first UK franchise: 1986	

Financial data: N/A

N/A: Information exists but is not available.

Crimecure 30 Ltd
Darley House
Cow Lane
Garston
Watford
Hertfordshire WD2 6PH
Tel: 0923 663322
Contact: Ann Stunt, Franchise Manageress

Business description
Installations of burglar alarms, door and window locks and
security systems to residential, commercial and industrial
buildings. Franchisees are given full in-house training in technical,
installation, administration and sales in company training school.

Company information
Directors: J M Darley, Carole E Darley
Date of incorporation: 1986 (Part of the Dampcure-Woodcure/30 Ltd
Stable)
Company name: Crimecure/30 Ltd
Issued share capital: N/A
Parent company: None
BFA member: No

Costs
Start-up capital (minimum): £7500
Initial fee: £7500
Royalties: 15 per cent
Proportion of start-up capital that can be arranged: up to 100 per cent

	(30 June) 1986
Market growth	
UK franchise outlets:	20
UK company owned outlets:	1
Date of first UK franchise:	
July 1986	

N/A: Information exists but is not available.

Dampco
21 Lythalls Lane
Coventry
West Midlands CV6 6FN
Tel: 0203 687683
Contact: Ron Ferrans

Business description
The treatment of woodworm and dry rot. The insertion of
chemical damp proof courses by injection.

Company information
Directors: JE Middleton, AE Middleton, WEJ Middleton, BA Middleton
Date of incorporation: October 1968
Company name: Dampco (UK) Ltd
Issued share capital: £20,000
BFA member: No

Costs
Start-up capital (minimum): £10,500 plus VAT
Initial fee: £1050 plus VAT
Royalties: 10 per cent
Proportion of start-up capital that can be arranged: 66 per cent

			(30 June)
Market growth	1984	1985	1986
UK franchise outlets:	—	—	—
UK company owned outlets:	—	—	—
Date of first UK franchise: March 1987			

Financial data	1983	1984	1985
Turnover:	£726,543	£736,710	£732,439
Net profit:	£56,846	61,450	£62,510
*Net worth:	35%	43.5%	38.07%
Current ratio:	—	—	—

*Fixed assets = Current assets minus liabilities. Shares in subsidiaries and loans to
associated companies are excluded.

Dampcure Woodcure/30 Ltd
Darley House
Cow Lane
Garston
Watford
Hertfordshire WD2 6PH
Tel: 0923 663322/41514/23842
Contact: Ann Stunt, Franchise Manageress

Business description
Specialists in the treatment of timber and dampness in buildings. The company has been carrying out this work for 28 years and are members of the country's leading trade organisations. All franchisees are trained at the company's own training school for three to four weeks. Training includes technology and work in the field office, administration and sales.

Company information
Directors: JM Darley, Carole E Darley
Date of incorporation: commenced trading 1959

Company name: Dampcure Woodcure/30 Ltd
Issued share capital: N/A
Parent company: —
BFA member: Yes

Costs
Start-up capital (minimum): £9000
Initial fee: £9000
Royalties: 15 per cent
Proportion of start-up capital that can be arranged: up to 100 per cent

			(30 June)
Market growth	1984	1985	1986
UK franchise outlets:	8	21	31
UK company owned outlets:	1	1	1

Date of first UK franchise: 1982

Financial data	1984	1985
Turnover:	£152,594	£412,286
Net profit:	(£180)	(£10,227)
*Net worth:	(£1,987)	£43,097
Current ratio:	0.68:1	0.31:1

*Fixed assets = Current assets minus liabilities. Shares in subsidiaries and loans to associated companies are excluded.

N/A: Information exists but is not available.

Dial A Char
77 London Road
East Grinstead
Sussex
Tel: 0342 28391/315764
Contact: Marcella van Veen

Business description
Domestic services, ie, cleaning, ironing, gardening, baby/granny sitting, convalescent help, catering, silver service/party help, car valeting, property management. FTA member.

Company information
Directors: M van Veen, RE van Veen
Company name: Dial A Char Ltd
Issued share capital: £100
BFA member: No

Costs
Start-up capital (minimum): £12,500
Initial fee: £7500
Royalties: 3 per cent advertising; 5 per cent royalties
Proportion of start-up capital that can be arranged: 60 per cent

			(30 June)
Market growth	1984	1985	1986
UK franchise outlets:	2	6	13
UK company owned outlets:	1	2	3

Date of first UK franchise: 1 May 1983

Financial data	1983	1984	1985
Turnover:	£42,000	£87,000	£146,000
Net profit:	£7,560	£13,920	£32,120
*Net worth:	£65,000	£115,000	£185,000

*Fixed assets = Current assets minus liabilities. Shares in subsidiaries and loans to associated companies are excluded.

Dyno-Electrics
143 Maple Road
Surbiton
Surrey KT6 4BJ
Tel: 01-549 9711
Contacts: T Fellowes, P Woodward

Business description
Dyno-Electrics provide an emergency repair and installation service to the domestic, commercial and industrial markets on a 24-hour basis.

With the franchising experience of Dyno-Rod behind them, Dyno-Electrics is rapidly expanding to become the UK's first service of its type with national recognition.

Work details are passed to the operators in the company's comprehensive communications network who operate a 24 hours a day 365 days a year manned answering service.

The company aims to further strengthen its position in the electrical market by providing aggressive marketing and advertising support to capitalise upon the awareness of the Dyno name.

Company information
Directors: JF Zockoll, MA Cowler
Date of incorporation: —
Company name: Dyno-Rod Developments
Issued share capital: —
Parent company: Dyno-Rod plc
BFA member: Yes

Costs
Start-up capital (minimum): £1250 licensed operator
Initial fee: —
Royalties: 22½ per cent

			(30 June)
Market growth	1984	1985	1986
UK franchise outlets:	4	8	16
UK company owned outlets:	0	0	1

Date of first UK franchise: 1984

Financial data: No separate accounts are filed.

Dyno-Rod
143 Maple Road
Surbiton
Surrey KT6 4BJ
Tel: 01-549 9711
Contacts: D Tonchin, C R Smith

Business description
Dyno-Rod provides pipework maintenance services nationally to industry, commerce, local authorities and the home on a 24-hour emergency or planned maintenance basis.

A wide range of techniques is used, designed to clear and diagnose blockages, and solve restricted bore or structural problems in all types of pipe systems: drains, municipal sewers, boiler tubes, heat exchangers, chemical plant, food processing plant and water mains.

The company has achieved a leading market position through adherence to disciplined training and operational standards and by providing aggressive marketing and advertising support which, for example, includes television, press, radio, direct mail and Yellow Pages.

Company information
Directors: JF Zockoll, MA Cowler, AW Cook, SM Zockoll
Date of incorporation: 1963
Company name: Dyno-Rod plc
Issued share capital: N/A
Parent company: N/A
BFA member: Yes

Costs
Start-up capital (minimum): £12,000 owner/operator, £50,000 territorial
Initial fee: £5000 owner/operator, £12,000 territorial
Royalties: 45 per cent owner/operator, 23 per cent territorial
Proportion of start-up capital that can be arranged: 70 per cent

			(30 June)
Market growth	1984	1985	1986
UK franchise outlets:	62	75	86
UK company owned outlets:	3	4	5
Date of first UK franchise: 1965			

Financial data	1983	1984	1985
Turnover:	£2,713,524	£3,313,291	N/A
Net profit:	£417,601	£622,752	
*Net worth:	£881,141	£1,010,325	
Current ratio:	1.88:1	1.28:1	

*Fixed assets = Current assets minus liabilities. Shares in subsidiaries and loans to associated companies are excluded.

N/A: Information exists but is not available.

Everett Masson & Furby Ltd
18 Walsworth Road
Hitchin
Hertfordshire SG5 9SP
Tel: 0462 32377
Contact: Ian Littlewood

Business description
Business and commercial property agents.

Company information
Directors: I Littlewood, A Madden
Date of incorporation: 1963
Company name: Everett Masson & Furby Ltd
Issued share capital: N/A
BFA member: Yes

Costs
Initial fee: £20,000
Royalties: 10 per cent
Proportion of start-up capital that can be arranged: depends on applicant

			(30 June)
Market growth	1984	1985	1986
UK franchise outlets:	16	17	19
UK company owned outlets:	2	2	2
Date of first UK franchise: September 1971			

Financial data	1983	1984	1985
Turnover:	—	£349,230	—
Net profit:	£30,691	£28,522	—
*Net worth:	£85,400	£105,272	—
Current ratio:	1.24:1	1.38:1	—

*Fixed assets = Current assets minus liabilities. Shares in subsidiaries and loans to associated companies are excluded.

N/A: Information exists but is not available.

Exchange Travel
Exchange House
Parker Road
Hastings
East Sussex TN34 3UB
Tel: 0424 423571
Contact: Dennis Beechinor, Franchise Development
   Manager

Business description
Exchange Travel, a large family-owned travel and leisure group employing a staff of over 300, is one of the UK's foremost retail travel multiples concentrating primarily on holiday and leisure sales.

Company information
Directors: GL McNally (Chairman), RG McNally (Managing Director),
   GP McNally, AJ McNally, HL Wilcox, RK Palmer, S Gray, K Riddle
Date of incorporation: 31 December 1969
Company name: Exchange Travel Agency Ltd
Issued share capital: £10,000
Parent company: Exchange Travel (Holdings) Ltd
BFA member: Yes

Costs
Start-up capital (minimum): £25,000-£30,000 plus working capital funding £35,000-£65,000 depending on location
Initial fee: £6000
Royalties: 10½ per cent of gross profit

Market growth	1984	1985	1986
UK franchise outlets:	4	21	40
UK company owned outlets:	56	17	22
Date of first UK franchise: July 1984			

	March	March	October
Financial data	1983	1984	1985
Turnover:	£3,987,300	£4,016,700	£4,404,300
Net profit:	(£209,600)	£558, 200	£53,600
*Net worth:	£122,000	£684,500	1,369,200
Current ratio:	0.9:1	1:1	1.2:1

*Fixed assets = Current assets minus liabilities. Shares in subsidiaries and loans to associated companies are excluded.

Fastframe Instant Picture Framing
28 Blandford Street
Sunderland
Tyne and Wear SR1 3JH
Tel: 091-565 2233
Contact: Margaret Hewison

Business description
High street picture framing of oil paintings, watercolours, photographs, prints, tapestries, three-dimensional items and other works of art. Ready-framed prints and pictures are also offered for sale.

Company information
Directors: HI Johnson, JL Scott, M Hewison, R Blake, JJ McCreal
Date of incorporation: 1983
Company name: Fastframe Franchises Ltd
Issued share capital: £100
Parent company: —
BFA member: Yes

Costs
Start-up capital (minimum): £35,000
Initial fee: £15,000
Royalties: 12½ per cent (6¼ per cent marketing, 6¼ per cent royalty)
Proportion of start-up capital that can be arranged: 66 per cent

191

Market growth	1984	1985	1986
UK franchise outlets:	20	32	44
UK company owned outlets:	3	3	3
Date of first UK franchise: July 1984			

Financial data	1983	1984	1985
Turnover	N/A	—	—
Net profit:		—	—
*Net worth:		(£27,783)	—
Current ratio:		0.54:1	—

*Fixed assets = Current assets minus liabilities. Shares in subsidiaries and loans to associated companies are excluded.

N/A: Information exists but is not available.

Fatso's Pasta Joint
3 Palace Gate Parade
Hampton Court
East Molesey
Surrey KT8 9BN
Tel: 01-783 1664
Contact: Ron Patmore

Business description
Fatso's Pasta Joint has been developed by Theme Holdings plc. The first Fatso's Pasta Joint opened in Old Compton Street, London W1 in 1979. Franchising began in June 1986. Customers are offered as much pasta as they can eat with sauces for £2.60. A cocktail bar is incorporated in the design. Food costs are low.

Company information
Directors: R Myers, A Lubin, KED Jones, PD Langan (non executive), N Kerman (non executive)
Date of incorporation: 25 May 1984 as Fortalice plc. Name changed to Theme Holdings plc 13 February 1985
Company name: Theme Holdings plc (Fatsos Pasta Joint)
Issued share capital: 5500,000 shares at 40p
Parent company: Theme Holdings plc
BFA member: No

Costs
Start-up capital (minimum): £70,000
Initial fee: £5000
Royalties: 5 per cent and 3 per cent advertising
Proportion of start-up capital that can be arranged: 66 per cent

Market growth	1984	1985	(30 June) 1986
UK franchise outlets:	0	0	0
UK company owned outlets:	1	1	2
Date of first UK franchise: February 1987			

Financial data	1985
Turnover	£3,063,000
Net profit:	£323,000
*Net worth:	£2,279,000
Current ratio:	—

*Fixed assets = Current assets minus liabilities. Shares in subsidiaries and loans to associated companies are excluded.

Fersina International
Cestrum House
Industry Road
Carlton
Barnsley
South Yorkshire S70 3NH
Tel: 0226 728310
Contact: Ian Woodward, National Franchise Manager

Business description
Sale, manufacture and installation of upvc doors windows and conservatories.

Company information
Directors: G Sykes, J Sykes
Date of incorporation: 1981
Company name: Cestrum Ltd
Issued share capital: N/A
BFA member: No

Costs
Start-up capital (minimum): £30,000 (including franchise fee)

Initial fee: up to £10,000
Royalties: 2½ per cent of retail sales
Proportion of start-up capital that can be arranged: 70 per cent

Market growth	1984	1985	(30 June) 1986
UK franchise outlets:	25	35	50
UK company owned outlets:	1	1	1

Date of first UK franchise: 1981

Financial data	1983	1984	1985
Turnover	—	£3,191,000	£3,899,000
Net profit:	—	£168,000	£211,000
*Net worth:	—	£148,000	£209,000
Current ratio:	—	1.1:1	0.99:1

*Fixed assets = Current assets minus liabilities. Shares in subsidiaries and loans to associated companies are excluded.

N/A: Information exists but is not available.

Fidelity Franchising Ltd
Le Brun House
3A Chislehurst Road
Orpington
Kent BR6 0DE
Tel: 0689 38498
Contact: Geoffrey Birch

Business description
Electrical spares and repairs, but not television and radio.

Company information
Directors: G Birch, AW Barton
Date of incorporation: January 1986
Company name: Fidelty Franchising Ltd
Issued share capital: £100
Parent company: Help Electrical (Orpington) Ltd
BFA member: No

Costs
Start-up capital (minimum): £12,000
Initial fee: £3000
Royalties: Yes
Proportion of start-up capital that can be arranged: Negotiable

Market growth
Pilot scheme in operation.

Fires and Things
Heat House
4 Brighton Road
Horsham
West Sussex RH13 5BA
Tel: 0403 56227
Contact: B D Simpson

Business description
Retails everything from fireplaces and stoves to pokers through high quality prestige shops. Offers a service which includes complete packages for new or refurbished homes.

Company information
Director: BD Simpson
Date of incorporation: May 1985
Company name: Fires & Things Ltd
Issued share capital: £100
Parent company: Apex Associated Group Holdings plc
BFA member: No

Costs
Start-up capital (minimum): £25,000
Initial fee: £4000
Royalties: 1 per cent of turnover
Proportion of start-up capital that can be arranged: 66 per cent

		(30 June)
Market growth	1985	1986
UK franchise outlets:	2	4
UK company owned outlets:	2	3
Date of first UK franchise: September 1985		

Financial data: First year's audited account to August 1986 not yet available.

Fixit Mobile Fastening Centre
98 Braemar Avenue
South Croydon
Surrey CR2 0QB
Tel: 01-668 4567
Contact: Mr F A Gear

Business description
Supplying a fast-moving expendable range of products from a

196

mobile vehicle specially fitted out, to the construction industry, local authorities, engineering industries and many other outlets. The product range includes fixings, fastenings, hand tools and power tools.

Company information
Directors: FA Gear (Managing Director), PH Jackman, DF Gear
Date of incorporation: January 1973
Company name: Fixit Tools Ltd
Issued share capital: £1000
BFA member: No

Costs
Start-up capital (minimum): £3500
Initial fee: £6500, stock £5500
Royalties: Nil
Proportion of start-up capital that can be arranged: 70 per cent

Market growth	1984	1985	(30 June) 1986
UK franchise outlets:	—	—	2
UK company owned outlets:	—	1	—
Date of first UK franchise: October 1986			

Financial data	1983	1984	1985
Turnover:	£294,878	£252,375	£252,319
Net profit:	(£9,432)	(£13,978)	£2,994
*Net worth:	£11,910	(£2,068)	£926
Current ratio:	1.1:1	0.91:1	0.94:1

*Fixed assets = Current assets minus liabilities. Shares in subsidiaries and loans to associated companies are excluded.

Foto Inn
19A Acton Park Estate
The Vale
London W3 7QE
Tel: 01-743 2131
Contact: Sally Levy

Business description
Foto Inn offers a fast 60-minute service for high quality developing and printing using the latest in photo processing technology. The shops have high street locations and a corporate image designed to reflect professionalism and the specialist nature of the business. The company's own engineers provide the vital technical support and quality control.

Company information
Managing Director: A Khorshid
Date of incorporation: 1981
Company name: Foto Inn plc
Issued share capital: N/A
BFA member: No

Costs
Start-up capital (minimum): £85,000
Initial fee: £5000
Royalties: 7 per cent plus 2 per cent advertising
Proportion of start-up capital that can be arranged: 70 per cent

			(30 June)
Market growth	1984	1985	1986
UK franchise outlets:	—	—	1
UK company owned outlets:	6	5	6
Date of first UK franchise: N/A			

Financial data	1983	1984	1985
Turnover:	£272.7	£430.4	£809.4
Net profit:	(£3.1)	£81.5	£77.5
*Net worth:	£38.1	£89.6	£162.5
Current ratio:	0.43:1	1.03:1	N/A

*Fixed assets = Current assets minus liabilities. Shares in subsidiaries and loans to associated companies are excluded.

N/A: Information exists but is not available.

The Frame Factory
67 Vivian Avenue
London NW4 3XE
Tel: 01-202 2499
Contact: Stephen Godfrey

Business description
Picture framing, posters and art supplies. Sale of decorative mirrors and aesthetic wall claddings.

Company information
Directors: Erik Drummond, Jef Goodchild, Stephen Godfrey,
   David Henderson
Date of incorporation: 1986
Company name: The Frame Factory Franchise Ltd
Issued share capital: £5000
BFA member: No

Costs
Start-up capital (minimum): £30,000
Initial fee: £7500
Royalties: 8 per cent
Proportion of start-up capital that can be arranged: 75 per cent

Market growth	1984	1985	(30 June) 1986
UK franchise outlets:	3	5	6
UK company owned outlets:	1	2	2

Financial data	1983	1984	1985
Turnover:	£53,000	£85,000	£132,000
Net profit:	£13,500	£19,000	£36,000
*Net worth:	£7,000	£13,000	£33,000
Current ratio:	1:1	2:1	1.3:1.0

*Fixed assets = Current assets minus liabilities. Shares in subsidiaries and loans to associated companies are excluded.

Freezavan Ltd
Fleet Estate Office
Fleet
Nr Spalding
Lincolnshire PE12 8LR
Tel: 0406 22727
Contact: Roy Lowe

Business description
Freezavan is the leading frozen food home delivery service offering a comprehensive range of branded frozen foods to the door on a regular monthly basis.

Company information
Directors: AJL Worth, DWR Evans, GR Donaldson, GR Fieldsend,
   RK Lowe, PM Merrikin, PR Hurley
Date of incorporation: 17 February 1984
Company name: Freezavan Ltd
Issued share capital: £151,099
Parent company: Frozen Quality Ltd
BFA member: No

Costs
Start-up capital (minimum): £7000
Initial fee: £4500
Royalties: 7½ per cent
Proportion of start-up capital that can be arranged: 60 per cent

Market growth	1984	1985	(30 June) 1986
UK franchise outlets:	—	—	16
UK company owned outlets:	5	16	11
Date of first UK franchise: March 1986			

Financial data	1985
Turnover:	£350,000
Net profit:	—
*Net worth:	—
Current ratio:	—

*Fixed assets = Current assets minus liabilities. Shares in subsidiaries and loans to associated companies are excluded.

Garden Building Centres Ltd
Coppice Gate
Lye Head
Bewdley
Worcestershire DY12 2UX
Tel: 0299 266361
Contact: Ian A Jackson, Sales Director

Business description
The sale of garden buildings, such as conservatories, greenhouses and sheds, from garden centres. Training is provided for franchisees.

Company information
Directors: DW Pound (Chairman), Mrs J Pound, IA Jackson, MF French FCA (Secretary), JF Anson, Mrs B Boxley
Date of incorporation: 4 March 1986
Company name: Garden Buildings
Issued share capital: £100
Parent company: DW Pound Garden Buildings Ltd
BFA member: No

Costs
Start-up capital (minimum): £10,000 cash plus £15,000 facility
Initial fee: £5000
Royalties: 6 per cent of turnover
Proportion of start-up capital that can be arranged: 60 per cent

Market growth	1985	(30 June) 1986
UK franchise outlets:	—	3
UK company owned outlets:	3	3
Date of first UK franchise: February 1986		

Financial data of Parent Company	1983/4	1984/5	1985/6**
Turnover:	£2,642,875	£3,032,913	£3,473,499
Net profit:	£143,817	£48,322	£32,063
*Net worth:	£197,322	£235,000	£256,000

*Fixed assets = Current assets minus liabilities. Shares in subsidiaries and loans to associated companies are excluded.

**Nine month year – end of year moved from March to December.

203

The Gold Vault Ltd
26 Skelty Park Road
Skelty
Swansea SA2 9AS
Tel: 0792 207194
Contact: S A Ramsey-Williams

Business description
Purchasers of used precious metals, suppliers of dental products (consumables).

Company information
Directors: SA Ramsey-Williams (Managing Director), SG Williams,
   E Ramsey, J Ramsey-Williams, EI Ramsey
Date of incorporation: 1980
Company name: The Gold Vault Ltd
Issued share capital: N/A
BFA member: No

Costs
Start-up capital (minimum): £2000
Initial fee: £2000
Royalties: approx 10 per cent
Proportion of start-up capital that can be arranged: 50 per cent

	(30 June)
Market growth	1986
UK franchise outlets:	N/A
UK company owned outlets:	N/A
Date of first UK franchise: 1985	

Financial data: No accounts filed.

N/A: Information exists but is not available.

Herbal World Natural Body Care
North Eastern Chambers
Station Square
Harrogate
North Yorkshire HG1 1SY
Tel: 0423 525865
Contact: T R Cottier

Business description
Retailer of natural body care products and ancillary items.
All products are naturally based and not tested on animals.

Company information
Directors: TR Cottier FCA (Chairman), JW Maud, R Padwick,
    L Wilkinson
Date of incorporation: August 1986
Company name: Herbal World Group Ltd
Issued share capital: £80,000
BFA member: No

Costs
Start-up capital (minimum): £35,000
Initial fee: Franchise licence fee £7500
Royalties: 5 per cent of turnover as management fee
Proportion of start-up capital that can be arranged: 50 per cent

Market growth
Date of first UK franchise: January 1987

Highway Windscreens
Unity House
Southend Road
Woodford Green
Essex IG8 8HD
Tel: 01-551 0214
Contact: J C Frankling, Franchise Recruitment
   Manager

Business description
Mobile windscreen replacement.

Company information
Directors: R Fitzjohn, P Diegler, B Cassidy
Date of incorporation: 1973
Company name: Highway Windscreens UK Ltd
Issued share capital: N/A
BFA member: No

Costs
Start-up capital (minimum): £6000
Initial fee: £2500
Royalties: 12½ per cent
Proportion of start-up capital that can be arranged: up to 70 per cent

Market growth	1984	1985	(30 June) 1986
UK franchise outlets:	7	8	11
UK company owned outlets:	3	5	7
Date of first UK franchise: 1979			

Financial data	1983	1984	1985
Turnover:	—	—	—
Net profit:	£17,392	£4,489	—
*Net worth:	£19,070	£22,759	£24,277
Current ratio:	1.15:1	1.04:1	1.15:1

207

*Fixed assets = Current assets minus liabilities. Shares in subsidiaries and loans to associated companies are excluded.

N/A: Information exists but is not available.

House of Something Different
12-16 Church Hill
Loughton
Essex
Tel: 0584 811515
Contact: R Padwick

Business description
Fireplaces and auxiliary goods, gas, electric and coal fires, grates and fretts, reproduction beams and mouldings for DIY home improvement.

Company information
Directors: M Moore, S Moore, P Moore, RPA Padwick
Date of incorporation: 1974
Company name: House of Something Different Ltd
Issued share capital: N/A
BFA member: No

Costs
Start-up capital (minimum): £30,000
Initial fee: £6000
Royalties: 2½ per cent
Proportion of start-up capital that can be arranged: 70 per cent

Market growth	1984	1985	1986
UK franchise outlets:	1	2	4
UK company owned outlets:	5	5	4
Date of first UK franchise: —			

Financial data	1983	1984	1985
Turnover:	£233,000	£542,000	£703,000
Net profit:	—	—	—
*Net worth:	—	—	—
Current ratio:	—	—	—

*Fixed assets = Current assets minus liabilities. Shares in subsidiaries and loans to associated companies are excluded.

N/A: Information exists but is not available.

Hyde-Barker Travel
Market Street
Mansfield
Nottinghamshire NG18 1SR
Tel: 0623 31121
Contact: M A Hyde-Barker

Business description
Retail travel agency, selling all packaged holidays in the UK, Europe and worldwide; British Rail and IATA appointed; all forms of travel and independent holidays.

Company information
Directors: MA Hyde-Barker, Mrs C Hyde-Barker
Date of incorporation: 1948
Company name: D N Hyde-Barker (Agents) Ltd
Issued share capital: £15,000
BFA member: No

Costs
Start-up capital (minimum): £35,000 +
Initial fee: £2000 +
Royalties: 1 per cent of turnover
Proportion of start-up capital that can be arranged: subject to discussion

Market growth	1984	1985	(30 June) 1986
UK franchise outlets:	0	1	1
UK company owned outlets:	5	6	7
Date of first UK franchise: December 1985			

Financial data	1983	1984	1985
Turnover:	£3,675,509	£3,172,832	£3,073,147
Net profit:	£4,026	£3,004	£9,548
*Net worth:	£53,582	£55,668	£60,469

*Fixed assets = Current assets minus liabilities. Shares in subsidiaries and loans to associated companies are excluded.

Infopoint
4-5 Hanborough Business Park
Long Hanborough
Oxfordshire OX7 2LH
Tel: 0993 881991
Contact: Philip Flook or Anthony Brooks

Business description
Infopoint has developed a system to provide sightseers and travellers with attractive information cards about places they are visiting. The A5 cards, which are vended from rugged, outdoor non-electrical units, are made in waterproof plastic material. This ensures they do not deteriorate on site but retain their high quality and vend reliably.

Company information
Directors: G Flook, Anthony W Brooks
Date of incorporation: 1 August 1985
Company name: Infopoint Ltd
Issued share capital: £10,000
BFA member: No

Costs
Start-up capital (minimum): £5450
Initial fee: £3000
Royalties: None
Proportion of start-up capital that can be arranged: 70 per cent

Market growth	(April) 1987
UK franchise outlets:	—
UK company owned outlets:	4

Financial data: No accounts filed.

210

infopoint
INFORMATION
SYSTEMS

Where do I go?
What can I see?

Infopoint has developed a system to provide sightseers and tourists with attractive information cards about the places they are visiting. The A5-sized cards, which are vended from rugged, outdoor, non-electrical units, are in weatherproof PVC. This ensures that they retain their high quality and vend reliably when on site.

We are now inviting ambitious people with the ability to recognise its vast potential to operate the business exclusively within major tourist towns/cities throughout the country (and indeed other countries). The easy-to-operate system could be started on a part-time basis and expanded as and when the profits grow. It is designed to be as flexible as possible to cater for all levels of commitment.

UK investment is £3000 upwards, dependant upon numbers of sites operated.

For further information return the coupon to Philip Flook or Tony Brooks at Infopoint, Hanborough Business Park, Long Hanborough, Oxon. OX7 2LH. Tel: (0993) 881991

Please send me further information about Infopoint.

Name

Address

211

Intacab Ltd
Service House
West Mayne
Basildon
Essex SS15 6RW
Tel: 0268 415891
Contact: Mel Lilley

Business description
Operating taxis and private hire cars with provision of courier
services to private and commercial clients.

Company information
Directors: Michael J Toomey, Peter A Dance, Barry Hawkins,
   Jeremy P Griffiths, Albert E Gale
Date of incorporation: 1974
Company name: Intacab
Issued share capital: N/A
Parent company: Laindon Holdings Ltd
BFA member: No

Costs
Start-up capital (minimum): £80,000
Initial fee: £5000
Royalties: 7½ per cent of net turnover

Market growth: N/A

Financial data: N/A

N/A: Information exists but is not available.

START A JOURNEY ON THE ROAD TO SUCCESS...

...by completing the coupon below and sending it to **INTACAB LTD.,** Service House, West Mayne, Basildon, Essex, SS15 6RW — or telephone **MEL LILLEY on BASILDON (0268) 415891.**

Please send me the **INTACAB FRANCHISE PROSPECTUS,** without obligation, which will show me how to become an **INTACAB FRANCHISEE.**

Name: _____

Address: _____

_____

'A better way to get you there'

In-toto Ltd
Wakefield Road
Gildersome
Leeds LS27 0QW
Tel: 0532 524131
Contact: Malcolm Eccleston, Franchise Operations
Manager

Business description
In-toto Ltd offers a franchise in the marketing of quality fitted
kitchens from quality showrooms in key locations. The kitchens
are manufactured by Wellmann and electrical appliances are
supplied by Philips. Each store offers a complete service,
including design and installation, tiles, accessories and dining
furniture, as well as the furniture and appliances.

In-toto Ltd provides franchisees with full marketing and
advertising support and comprehensive training on an ongoing
basis. The showrooms are also supported by advertising
campaigns and local promotions jointly founded by the
franchisees.

Company information
Directors: FB Davies, JR Kinder, SE Strecker, MD Wellmann
Date of incorporation: 1980
Company name: In-toto
Issued share capital: N/A
Parent company: Wellmann Ltd
BFA member: Yes

Costs
Start-up capital (minimum): £25,000-£40,000
Initial fee: £5000
Royalties: Nil
Proportion of start-up capital that can be arranged: 60 per cent

Market growth	1984	1985	(30 June) 1986
UK franchise outlets:	24	26	31
UK company owned outlets:	—	1	1
Date of first UK franchise: 1980			

Financial data	1983	1984	1985
Turnover	£299,537	—	—
Net profit:	£1,074	—	—
*Net worth	(£140,780)	(£158,868)	—
Current ratio:	0.36:1	0.26:1	—

*Fixed assets = Current assets minus liabilities. Shares in subsidiaries and loans to associated companies are excluded.

N/A: Information exists but is not available.

Isodan (UK) Ltd
55b Colebrook Road
Royal Tunbridge Wells
Kent TN4 9DP
Tel: 0892 44822
Contact: S John Holt, Managing Director

Business description
Isodan is a system for filling external cavity walls with insulation material. The method is dry with no mixing of ingredients, and the filler, Isofill, is exclusive to Isodan and their franchisees.

A defined area of operations is agreed and insulation operators trained to an approved standard. The operating machine is included in the franchise but a vehicle and tools are found by the franchisee.

At start-up, all stationery and forms are provided. There is publicity and on-site supervision from company staff.

Promotion is in the national press, trade and technical journals.

Company information
Directors: S John Holt, SP Hayklan
Date of incorporation: 1973
Company name: Isodan (UK) Ltd
Issued share capital: £28,500
BFA member: No

Costs
Start-up capital (minimum): £7500 which includes the initial fee of
£3500 below
Initial fee: £3500
Royalties: Nil
Proportion of start-up capital that can be arranged: 100 per cent, subject
to status and bank

Market growth	1984	1985	(30 June) 1986
UK franchise outlets:	55	61	61
UK company owned outlets:	—	—	—
Date of first UK franchise: 1975			

Financial data	1983	1984	1985
Turnover:	£369,279	£381,036	£171,914
Net profit:	(£9,545)	£30,478	(£3,246)
*Net worth:	(£8,126)	£36,710	£38,724
Current ratio:	0.84:1	1.71:1	2.69:1

*Fixed assets = Current assets minus liabilities. Shares in subsidiaries and loans to
associated companies are excluded.

Kall-Kwik Printing
Kall-Kwik House
Pembroke Road
Ruislip
Middlesex HA4 8NW
Tel: 0895 632700
Contact: Mrs Anne Wright, Franchise Sales Manager

Business description
Kall-Kwik Printing is a complete printing, copying and design
service with the emphasis on speed and quality. The sole licensee
for the UK of the US Kwik-Kopy system, the system has over
1000 centres in four continents. Kall-Kwik Printing began
operating in the UK in 1978 and has over 130 high street shops.

Kall-Kwik provides a financial start-up package (with Barclays,
Lloyds, Midland, National Westminster and the Royal Bank of
Scotland), and guidance on site selection, layout, planning and
four weeks' formal training, plus extensive on-the-job experience.
This is backed by considerable opening and post-opening support,
operating manuals and ongoing technical, management and
marketing assistance. The preferred cash outlay is £25,000-
£30,000 with the balance being financed over six to seven years.

Company information
Director: M Gerstenhaber (Managing Director)
Date of incorporation: 1978
Company name: Kall-Kwik Printing (UK) Ltd
Issued share capital: £10,000
BFA member: Yes

Costs
Start-up capital (minimum): £79,000, including working capital and VAT
Initial fee: £12,000, including training
On-going franchise fee: 6 per cent plus 4 per cent for promotion and
   marketing fund
Proportion of start-up capital that can be arranged: 66 per cent

			(30 June)
Market growth	1984	1985	1986
UK franchise outlets:	86	96	111
UK company owned outlets:	1	1	—
Date of first UK franchise: 1979			

Financial data	1984	1985	1986
Turnover:	£1,512.0K	£1,241.0K	£1,382.0K
Net profit:	£75.0K	£36.0K	£82.0K
*Net worth:	£56.9K	£64.7K	£106.2K

217

Knightguard UK Ltd
14-16 Tonbridge Road
Maidstone
Kent ME16 8RP
Tel: 0622 686362
Contact: G Phelps

Business description
Manpower security.

Company information
Directors: G Phelps, A Coates, W Latter, Mrs A Self
Date of incorporation: November 1986
Company name: Knightguard UK Ltd
Issued share capital: N/A
BFA member: No

Costs
Start-up capital (minimum): £10,000
Initial fee: £9750
Royalties: 10 per cent on first £250,000 pa, 5 per cent to £500,000
Proportion of start-up capital that can be arranged: Negotiable

	(30 June)
Market growth	1987
UK franchise outlets:	9
UK company owned outlets:	—
Date of first UK franchise: December 1986	

N/A: Information exists but is not available.

Knobs & Knockers Franchising Ltd
36-40 York Way
London N1 9AB
Tel: 01-278 8925
Contact: John R Staddon, Operations Director

Business description
Knobs & Knockers are leading retailers of speciality brassware and home design merchandise within the UK. Established in 1969, they operate 55 retail branches with a unique shop-presentation and a range of 1200 quality products – including many exclusive designs – which are offered in an elegant and distinctive fashion.

Designers, architects and developers present a growing opportunity to generate business supported by the company's specialist 'Contract & Trade' division.

The package includes site selection advice, shop-fitting design, full training and ongoing support.

Company information
Directors: Michael C Warshaw, Leonard C Warshaw, Arthur W Monk,
    John R Staddon
Date of incorporation: 12 February 1986
Company name: Knobs & Knockers Franchising Ltd
Issued share capital: £100,000 (£50,000 paid up)
Parent company: Jennings Monk Ltd
BFA member: Associate

Costs
Start-up capital (minimum): £55,000
Initial fee: £7000
Royalties: 7½ per cent
Proportion of start-up capital that can be arranged: 70 per cent

			(30 June)
Market growth	1984	1985	1986
UK franchise outlets:	—	—	—
UK company owned outlets:	40	47	53
Date of first UK franchise:			
August 1986			

Kwik Strip
Units 1-2
The 306 Estate
242 Broomhill Road
Brislington
Bristol BS4 5RA
Tel: 0272 772470
Contact: I M Chivers

Business description
Kwik Strip specialises in serving the growing stripping/restoration market with a well-proven process which is designed specifically for the UK. The process will efficiently strip paint, varnish and polyurethanes from all types of wood and metal. Its company-owned pilot operation at Bristol shows audited net profits for the past four years.

Kwik Strip offers within its package assistance in finding the right location, all equipment plus starter pack, one week's training at Bristol headquarters covering all aspects of business including bookkeeping, product knowledge, after-sales service, followed by continuous back-up from HQ.

Company information
Directors: IM Chivers, Mrs SA Coatsworth
Date of incorporation: March 1982
Company name: Kwik Strip (UK) Ltd
Issued share capital: N/A
BFA member: No

Costs
Start-up capital (minimum): £8500 plus VAT
Initial fee: £4250 plus VAT
Royalties: 5 per cent
Proportion of start-up capital that can be arranged: 40 per cent

			(30 June)
Market growth	1984	1985	1986
UK franchise outlets:	11	14	17
UK company owned outlets:	1	1	1
Date of first UK franchise: January 1983			

Financial data	1983	1984	1985
Turnover	£136,533	£137,132	£173,929
Net profit	(£9,660)	£5,485	£18,968
*Net worth:	(£7,004)	(£9,560)	N/A
Current ratio:	0.9:1	0.76:1	N/A

*Fixed assets = Current assets minus liabilities. Shares in subsidiaries and loans to associated companies are excluded.

N/A: Information exists but is not available.

The Late Late Supershop (UK) Ltd
CWS Ltd
P O Box 53
New Century House
Manchester M60 4ES
Tel: 061-834 1212 ext 5416
Contact: Mrs Kathryn R Sharp

Business description
Convenience retailer of a wide range of goods including groceries,
fresh foods, wines and spirits, books and magazines etc.
Franchisor is a wholly owned subsidiary of the Cooperative
Wholesale Society, whose other subsidiaries include the Co-op
Bank and CIS.

Company information
Directors: DB Campion, Mrs JM Campbell
Date of incorporation: 1984
Company name: The Late Late Supershop (UK) Ltd
Issued share capital: £2
Parent company: Cooperative Wholesale Society Ltd
BFA member: Yes

Costs
Start-up capital (minimum): £75,000 plus stock
Initial fee: £8000
Royalties: 2 per cent of sales
Proportion of start-up capital that can be arranged: 70 per cent

			(30 June)
Market growth	1984	1985	1986
UK franchise outlets:	—	4	2
UK company owned outlets:	—	2	1
Date of first UK franchise:			
February 1985			

Financial data: N/A

N/A: Information exists but is not available.

MAPS Marketing Ltd
160 Molesworth Road
Stoke
Plymouth
Devon
Tel: 0752 556688/660030
Contact: JW Macleod, V Macleod or P Edrich

Business description
Simple advertising and promotion at low cost. The only
equipment necessary is an office and a telephone; the service can
be operated from home. Each franchisee has a specific area which
is reflected in the purchase price according to population.

Company information
Directors: JW Macleod, S Gourlay, E Macleod-Johnstone
Date of incorporation: 1986
Company name: MAPS Marketing Ltd
Issued share capital: £1000
BFA member: No

Costs
Start-up capital (minimum): £3000
Initial fee: £1000
Royalties: 7 per cent
Proportion of start-up capital that can be arranged: 50 per cent

	(30 June)
Market growth	1986
UK franchise outlets:	2
UK company owned outlets:	4
Date of first UK franchise: July 1986	

Micrex Microfilm Express Ltd
Microfilm House
Thrupp Lane
Radley
Oxfordshire OX14 3NG
Tel: 0235 22275
Contact: Bryan Baillie

Business description
Microfilm service centre: 48 hours collection, processing and
delivery microfilming service, both 16mm and 35mm work
undertaken. Equipment and special materials supplier.

Company information
Directors: B Baillie, Jennifer Toh
Date of incorporation: July 1974
Company name: Micrex Microfilm Express Ltd
Issued share capital: £4900
BFA member: No

Costs
Start-up capital (minimum): £40,000
Initial fee: £5000
Royalties: 10 per cent
Proportion of start-up capital that can be arranged: 50 per cent

Market growth	1984	1985	(30 June) 1986
UK franchise outlets:	0	0	0
UK company owned outlets:	1	1	1
Date of first UK franchise: March 1987			

Financial data	1984	1985	1986
Turnover:	£78,000	£124,000	£140,000
*Net profit:	£18,500	£34,900	£77,000
**Net worth:	£72,500	£158,500	£163,200

*Trading profits before special provisions.

**Fixed assets = Current assets minus liabilities. Shares in subsidiaries and loans to associated companies are excluded.

Midas (Great Britain) Ltd
107 Mortlake High Street
London SW14 8HH
Tel: 01-878 7803
Contact: Ken I Phillips

Business description
Automotive aftermarket retailer of brakes and exhaust services, steering, tyres and MOT. Services available in many locations.

Company information
Directors: Robert C Foster (Managing Director), Ken I Phillips
Date of incorporation: 1967
Company name: Midas (Great Britain) Ltd
Issued share capital: N/A
Parent company: I C Industries
BFA member: Yes

RUN YOUR OWN BUSINESS

(WITH A LITTLE HELP FROM THE WORLD'S LARGEST EXHAUST AND BRAKE SPECIALISTS).

Midas are the world's largest specialists in brakes, exhausts and under-car servicing. A large part of this business is conducted through a highly successful franchising operation.

Midas's U.K. business is growing fast, and they're now looking for franchisees both to take over existing Midas centres and to start, own and run new centres from scratch.

You could buy into an already profitable centre; we currently have opportunities at **Leicester, Burton, Blackpool, Walsall, Longbridge, Cheltenham, Gloucester, Barnstaple, Weston-super-Mare, Exeter, Hendon** and **New Cross.**

Alternatively, you might already own a garage, whose potential you could expand. Or you might own a suitable site or property which could be developed into a centre.

While you'll need finance, we're not looking for financiers. We're looking for people who are prepared to take an active day-to-day part in the running of their business. Our success is based on the quality of our service, and we'll expect you to implement this. In return, we'll give you all the training, back-up and advice you need.

The challenge is considerable, but so too can be the rewards: you'll be taking part in an established and profitable success story.

If you're up to the Midas challenge, write to:

Mr K Phillips, Marketing Manager, Midas (Great Britain) Limited, 107 Mortlake High Street, London SW14 8HH.

EXHAUSTS · BRAKES · TYRES · SHOCK ABSORBERS

Costs
Start-up capital (minimum): £100,000-£150,000
Initial fee: £10,000
Royalties: 6 per cent royalty; 6 per cent advertising of gross sales
    (after VAT)
Proportion of start-up capital that can be arranged: 70 per cent

			(30 June)
Market growth	1984	1985	1986
UK franchise outlets:	9	9	9
UK company owned outlets:	30	32	34
Date of first UK franchise: 1967			

Financial data	1983	1984	1985
Turnover:	£4,969K	£4,245K	£5,591K
Net profit:	(£252K)	(£1,214K)	(£283K)
*Net worth:	£1,788K	£598K	£869K
Current ratio:	1.1:1	0.6:1	0.64:1

*Fixed assets = Current assets minus liabilities. Shares in subsidiaries and loans to associated companies are excluded.

N/A: Information exists but is not available.

Midland Waterlife
154-156 High Street
Bromsgrove
Worcestershire
Tel: 0527 70676
Contact: Richard Edge or Roy Miles

Business description
Franchised retail aquatic centres sited within selected garden centres.

Company information
Directors: R Edge, R Miles, P Webb, M Martin
Date of incorporation: 4 March 1986
Company name: Midland Waterlife Franchising Ltd
Issued share capital: 96 £1 shares
BFA member: No

Costs
Start-up capital (minimum): £25,000
Initial fee: Franchise fee £3000
Royalties: None (Advertising 2 per cent net turnover)
Proportion of start-up capital that can be arranged: 60 per cent
    with security

	(30 June)
Market growth	1986
UK franchise outlets:	1
UK company owned outlets:	1

Date of first UK franchise: May 1986

Mixamate Concrete
Bourne Way
Hayes
Kent BR2 7EY
Tel: 01-462 8011
Contact: Peter Slinn

Business description
Mixamate is a unique specialised service to builders and home improvers for the provision of mixed concrete.

The system is based on a patented purpose built vehicle designed to carry aggregate, cement and water. A concrete mixer is an integral part of the vehicle which also carries wheelbarrows and shovels in fact all the materials and equipment the driver requires to mix concrete at site, ready for the customer to lay.

With Mixamate the customer neither has to mix the concrete himself nor take a bulk delivery of ready mixed concrete.

When the Mixamate vehicle arrives on site, the driver starts to mix the concrete ready for the customer to lay. So the customer gets only the amount of freshly made concrete that he needs for the job – no more, no less – unlike traditional ready-mixed concrete where the customer either under orders because of poor estimating, or over orders because he wants to make sure he is not left short.

Company information
Directors: Peter Bates, Peter Slinn
Date of incorporation: 26 September 1978
Company name: Mixamate Holdings Ltd
Issued share capital: £1000
Parent company: Mixamate Ltd
BFA member: Yes

Costs
Start-up capital (minimum): £15,000
Initial fee: £3000
Royalties: 6 per cent
Proportion of start-up capital that can be arranged: 70 per cent

Market growth: N/A

Financial data	1983	1984	1985
Turnover:	£546,329	£876,818	N/A
Net profit:	£13,151	£34,700	
*Net worth:	£79,486	£114,186	
Current ratio:	0.86:1	0.85:1	

*Fixed assets = Current assets minus liabilities. Shares in subsidiaries and loans to associated companies are excluded.

N/A: Information exists but is not available.

Mr Lift
The Lifthouse
Gloucester Road
Almondsbury
Bristol BS12 4HY
Tel: 0454 618181
Contact: Rupert Crook

Business description
Mr Lift hires, sells and services fork-lift trucks. Mr Lift's speciality is the sale of quality rebuilt fork-lift trucks imported directly from Japan. This full business format franchise offers thorough training and support.

Company information
Directors: AC Day, M Day
Date of incorporation: 1976
Company name: Mr Lift Ltd
Issued share capital: £100,000
Parent company: Tony Day Handling plc
BFA member: Registered

Costs
Start-up capital (minimum): £82,500
Initial fee: £7500
Royalties: 5 per cent management services fee, 2½ per cent advertising fund contribution
Proportion of start-up capital that can be arranged: £55,000

			(30 June)
Market growth	1984	1985	1986
UK franchise outlets:	—	—	3
UK company owned outlets:	3	3	3

Date of first UK franchise: 1985

231

Financial data	1983	1984	1985
Turnover:	£3,602	£43,905	—
Net profit:	£1,117	£2,016	—
*Net worth:	£893	£1,967	(£74,706)
Current ratio:	1.33:1	0.86:1	0.20:1

*Fixed assets = Current assets minus liabilities. Shares in subsidiaries and loans to associated companies are excluded.

Mr Slade Dry Cleaning
Mr Slade Franchises Ltd
Maritime Chambers
1 Howard Street
North Shields
Tyne and Wear NE30 1AR
Tel: 0632 596421
Contact: Eunice Hesslegrave

Business description
Mr Slade Dry Cleaning uses the best of the industry's products and equipment. The old concept of a dry cleaning shop has been transformed into a bright, superbly presented business.

Company information
Directors: RP Slade, TW Nicholson, GW Robinson
Date of incorporation: 1982
Company name: Mr Slade Dry Cleaning
Issued share capital: N/A
Parent company: Aglossin Ltd
BFA member: No

Costs
Start-up capital (minimum): £15,000
Initial fee: £5500
Royalties: 10 per cent
Proportion of start-up capital that can be arranged: 60 per cent

			(30 June)
Market growth	1984	1985	1986
UK franchise outlets:	11	11	11
UK company owned outlets:	17	17	15
Date of first UK franchise: 1983			

Financial data	1983	1984	1985
Turnover:	£26,585	£73,535	N/A
Net profit:	(£46,867)	£12,123	
*Net worth:	(£83,148)	(71,000)	
Current ratio:	0.07:1	0.08:1	

*Fixed assets = Current assets minus liabilities. Shares in subsidiaries and loans to associated companies are excluded.

N/A: Information exists but is not available.

National Vacuum Cleaner Services
Hampton House
5 Hampton Pier Avenue
Herne Bay
Kent CT6 8EW
Tel: 0227 374656
Contact: Dennis Wall

Business description
Specialists in the servicing and repairs to all makes of floor cleaning machines (electrical, commercial and industrial). Coverage is throughout the UK; there are local and national contacts with major establishments and reputable national companies.

Company information
Partners: D Wall, Barbara Wall
Date of commencement: 1 September 1983
Company name: National Vacuum Cleaner Services
BFA member: No

Costs
Start-up capital: £4473.50
Initial fee: £3890 plus VAT (= £4473.50)
Royalties: Nil
Proportion of start-up capital that can be arranged: Nil

			(30 June)
Market growth	1984	1985	1986
UK franchise outlets:	9	21	42
UK company owned outlets:	0	0	0
Date of first UK franchise:			
5 September 1983			

Financial data	1984	1985
Turnover:	£26,000	£55,000
Net profit:	£13,000	£27,500
*Net worth:	—	—
Current ratio:	—	—

*Fixed assets = Current assets minus liabilities. Shares in subsidiaries and loans to associated companies are excluded.

Natural Life Health Foods Ltd
15 Queen Street
Salisbury
Wiltshire SP1 1EY
Tel: 0584 811518
Contact: Ron Padwick

Business description
Health food retailers and coffee/restaurant operators.

Company information
Directors: RPA Padwick, Richard Mistlin (Managing Director)
Date of incorporation: 1985
Company name: Natural Life Health Foods Ltd
Issued share capital: £500
BFA member: No

Costs
Start-up capital (minimum): £70,000
Initial fee: £7500
Royalties: 4.5 per cent
Proportion of start-up capital that can be arranged: 70 per cent

	(30 June) 1986
Market growth:	
UK franchise outlets:	4
UK company owned outlets:	1
Date of first UK franchise: 1986	

Financial data: N/A

N/A: Information exists but is not available.

New Moves
15 South Street
Exeter EX1 1DZ
Tel: 0392 219922
Contact: Mike Biswell

Business description
Property shop offering a full range of estate agency services. We are able to provide the homeowner with the opportunity to sell his property at vastly reduced cost. Insurance and mortgage brokerage is included in our service. A full training package is provided.

Company information
Directors: M Biswell, Josephine Biswell
Date of incorporation: N/A. New company.
Company name: New Moves Property Shops Ltd
Issued share capital: £20,000
BFA member: No

Costs
Start-up capital (minimum): £15,000
Initial fee: £5000
Royalties: 10 per cent
Proportion of start-up capital that can be arranged: By individual
  arrangement.

N/A: Information exists but is not available.

Oasis Trading
7-8 Cave Street
Oxford OX4 1BA
Tel: 0865 723561
Contact: Andrew Thomas

Business description
Oasis Trading is a wholesaler and retailer of an exclusive range of
imported merchandise, chiefly ladies fashions, jewellery, giftware,
basketware, fashion accessories, rugs and other items for the
home. Nearly all products are designed by Oasis Trading's in-
house designers in the light of the company's experience as a
retailer and knowledge of the requirements of the market.

Company information
Directors: G Brown, Edwina Brown, P Evans, A Thomas
Date of incorporation: April 1976
Company name: Pinecord Ltd
Issued share capital: £3000
BFA member: No

Costs
Start-up capital (minimum): £30,000-£80,000
Initial fee: £10,000
Royalties: Nil
Proportion of start-up capital that can be arranged: 66 per cent

			(30 June)
Market growth	1984	1985	1986
UK franchise outlets:	8	9	12
UK company owned outlets:	6	9	8
Date of first UK franchise: 1980			

Financial data	1983	1984	1985
Turnover:	£1,909,421	£1,997,937	£2,575,066
Net profit:	£65,362	£151,983	£66,905
*Net worth:	£186,823	£338,806	£402,911

*Fixed assets = Current assets minus liabilities. Shares in subsidiaries and loans to
associated companies are excluded.

Olivers Hot Bread and Coffee Shops
Eagle Court
Harpur Street
Bedford MK40 1JZ
Tel: 0234 328181

No franchises are currently being offered.

The Original Art Shop
28 Hemmells
Laindon
Essex SS15 6ED
Tel: 0268 415822
Contact: Mike Francis

Business description
Retail shop operation offering a product range of a wide selection
of original pictures including oils, watercolours, prints, posters,
graphics etc. A first class picture framing service is incorporated
on the premises.

Company information
Directors: MD Francis, CT Platt
Date of incorporation: January 1981
Company name: Original Art Shops Ltd
Issued share capital: N/A
BFA member: Registered

Costs
Start-up capital (minimum): £35,000
Initial fee: £2500
Royalties: 10 per cent of turnover
Proportion of start-up capital that can be arranged: 66 per cent

			(30 June)
Market growth	1984	1985	1986
UK franchise outlets:	4	4	4
UK company owned outlets:	25	20	21
Date of first UK franchise: November 1982			

Financial data	1983	1984	1985
Turnover:	£405,853	N/A	N/A
Net profit:	£27,262		
*Net worth:	£22,912		
Current ratio:	0.92:1		

*Fixed assets = Current assets minus liabilities. Shares in subsidiaries and loans to
associated companies are excluded.

N/A: Information exists but is not available.

An artistic licence for a bright future...

Original Art Shops are bringing the widest range of pictures right into Britain's shopping centres. Realistically-priced originals and prints, oils, watercolours, drawings, posters, maps and imaginative graphic ideas.

This unbeatable selection is complemented by a fast, efficient, on-the-spot framing service.

An Original Art Shop will give you an absorbing and versatile business in an attractive environment.

Full training and support are provided, but you must have the dedication and commitment to build yourself an independent and prosperous future.

**TOTAL CAPITAL INVESTMENT
£35,000**

**MINIMUM CAPITAL REQUIRED
£12,000**

Finance available from Barclays & Nat West Banks

Contact Mike Francis at:—

The ORIGINAL Art Shop

The Original Art and Framing Franchise

**12 Southchurch Road
Southend-on-Sea, Essex
Tel: Southend-on-Sea (0702) 460391**

239

Perfect Pizza
65 Staines Road
Hounslow
Middlesex TW3 3HW
Tel: 01-577 1711
Contact: Mr R Mendoza

Business description
Perfect Pizza is the UK's leading pizza takeaway and delivery
franchise.

Company information
Directors: J Barry, M Clayton
Date of incorporation: Wholly owned subsidiary
Parent company: United Biscuits (UK) Ltd
BFA member: Yes

Costs
Start-up capital (minimum): approx £56,000
Initial fee: £4000
Royalties: 5 per cent royalty, 3 per cent advertising
Proportion of start-up capital that can be arranged: 66 per cent

Market growth	1986
UK franchise outlets:	57
UK company owned outlets:	3
Date of first UK franchise: 1982	

Financial data: No separate accounts are filed.

PIP Instant Printers
Black Arrow House
2 Chandos Road
London NW10 6NF
Tel: 01-965 0700
Contact: Dermot Waters

Business description
PIP Instant Printing produces fast professional printing and
copying. FranPrint, the UK master licence holder, headed by
leading franchise expert Dick Crook, draws not only on its own
experience, but on the success of over 1100 shops under the
publicly quoted American parent.

Suitable candidates, who need have no previous printing
experience, benefit from expert site selection and in-depth training

in printing processes and management. Advertising, marketing and field support are strong features of the franchise.

Company information
Directors: R Crook, D Waters
Date of incorporation: 1985
Company name: FranPrint Ltd
Issued share capital: £200,000
Parent company: Franchise Investors Ltd
BFA member: Yes

Costs
Start-up capital (minimum): £65,000 total
Initial fee: £8000
Royalties: 7½ per cent plus 2½ advertising fund contribution
Proportion of start-up capital that can be arranged: 66 per cent

			(30 June)
Market growth	1984	1985	1986
UK franchise outlets:	40	53	65
UK company owned outlets:	0	0	3
Date of first UK franchise: 1982			

Financial data	1983	1984	1985
Turnover:	£138,833	£336,153	N/A
Net profit:	(£211,425)	(£160,004)	
*Net worth:	(£239,258)	(£399,262)	
Current ratio:	0.35:1	0.25:1	

*Fixed assets = Current assets minus liabilities. Shares in subsidiaries and loans to associated companies are excluded.

N/A: Information exists but is not available.

Pizza Express
29 Wardour Street
London W1V 3HB
Tel: 01-437 7215
Contact: Jonathan Dell

Business description
Pizza Express are table service, licensed restaurants with a menu based on a variety of pizzas, with desserts, Italian wines and beer. Premises have standard design with individual distinctions.

The company liaises at all stages of the selection and preparation of the premises and there is a staff training programme prior to commencement of trading and continuing later to a regular pattern. Business management and technical advice are available during the start-up phase and throughout the life of the franchise.

Company information
Directors: PJ Boizot, R Simson, IS Neill, R Fowler
Date of incorporation: 1965
Company name: Pizza Express Ltd
Issued share capital: £50,000
BFA member: Yes

Costs
Start-up capital (minimum): £150,000
Initial fee: £12,500
Royalties: 4 per cent
Proportion of start-up capital that can be arranged: 50-60 per cent

			(30 June)
Market growth	1984	1985	1986
UK franchise outlets:	19	25	28
UK company owned outlets:	9	13	14
Date of first UK franchise: 1972			

Financial data	1983	1984	1985
Turnover:	£2,691,317	£3,502,365	N/A
Net profit:	£96,271	£151,425	
*Net worth:	£325,114	£429,350	
Current ratio:	1.2:1	1.29:1	

*Fixed assets = Current assets minus liabilities. Shares in subsidiaries and loans to associated companies are excluded.

N/A: Information exists but is not available.

Pizza Hut
Venture House
Hartley Avenue
London NW7 2HX
Tel: 01-959 3677

No franchises are currently being offered.

Poppies (UK) Ltd
31 Houndgate
Darlington DL1 5RH
Tel: 0325 488699
Contact: Beverley Clayton

Business description
High quality domestic service franchising specialising in regular domestic help and commercial cleaning.

Company information
Directors: Mrs S Rørstad, Mrs L Hislop, G Iszatt
Date of incorporation: 1983
Company name: Poppies (UK) Ltd
Issued share capital: N/A
Parent company: N/A
BFA member: Yes

Costs
Start-up capital (minimum): £10,000 plus VAT
Initial fee: £4000
Royalties: £2000 fixed levy
Proportion of start-up capital that can be arranged: 70 per cent

			(30 June)
Market growth	1984	1985	1986
UK franchise outlets:	1	24	45
UK company owned outlets:	1	1	0

Date of first UK franchise: 1983

Financial data	1983	1984	1985
Turnover:		£25,000	£150,000
Net profit:		(£25,000)	£21,000
Net worth: fixed assets		£8,500	£12,000
Current ratio:		—	—

Fixed assets = Current assets minus liabilities. Shares in subsidiaries and loans to associated companies are excluded.

N/A: Information exists but is not available.

Potholes
Prospect Road
Alresford
Hampshire SO24 9QF
Tel: 0962 73 3025
Contact: C T Bayles

Business description
A range of all-British, top-quality products enables franchisees to offer a year-round maintenance, repair, refurbishing and coating service to industry, public utilities, government departments, health authorities, farms and commerce, on concrete and asphalt, indoors and outdoors.

Company information
Directors: CT Bayles, P Lambert, A Stott, G Stott
Date of incorporation: 1981
Company name: Potholes International Ltd
Issued share capital: £31,000
BFA member: No

Costs
Start-up capital (minimum): approx £20,000, including working capital
and vehicle
Initial fee: £7500 plus VAT
Royalties: 6 per cent including advertising contributions
Proportion of start-up capital that can be arranged: varies according to
circumstances

			(30 June)
Market growth	1984	1985	1986
UK franchise outlets:	1	1	5
UK company owned outlets:	1	1	1
Date of first UK franchise: December 1983			

Financial data	1983	1984	1985
Turnover:	—	—	N/A
Net profit:	£1,634	(£16,980)	
*Net worth:	£1,734	£154	
Current ratio:	0.67:1	0.62:1	

*Fixed assets = Current assets minus liabilities. Shares in subsidiaries and loans to
associated companies are excluded.

N/A: Information exists but is not available.

PRB Self Drive Hire
Unit 8
Cape Road Industrial Estate
Warwick CV34 4JW
Tel: 0926 499867
Contact: Mrs H R Burnett

Business description
Nationwide vehicle hire depots using vehicles up to 12 months old,
at a most competitive rate.

Company information
Directors: Mrs HR Burnett, PR Birtwistle
Date of incorporation: 8 November 1984
Company name: PRB Vehicle Hire (Contract & Franchising) Ltd
Issued share capital: £50,000
BFA member: No

Costs
Start-up capital (minimum): £12,000
Initial fee: £7500
Royalties: 7 per cent
Proportion of start-up capital that can be arranged: 50 per cent

Market growth	1984	1985	(30 June) 1986
UK franchise outlets:	3	12	15
UK company owned outlets:	2	3	3
Date of first UK franchise: 10 June 1984			

Financial data	1983	1984	1985
Turnover:	£38,000	£150,000	£230,000
Net profit:	nil	£14,000	£25,000
*Net worth:	—	—	£250,000

*Fixed assets = Current assets minus liabilities. Shares in subsidiaries and loans to associated companies are excluded.

Professional Appearance Services
1 Queen Square
Bath BA1 2HE
Tel: 0225 312756
Contact: Malcolm Shaw

Business description
National autovaleting of new and used cars and commercial vehicles for dealerships, auction centres, fleet users etc, plus the sale and application of vehicle paint and fabric sealants and anti-theft devices. Commercial contract cleaning to shops, hotels and offices, plus carpet and upholstery cleaning and treatments.

Company information
Directors: DJ Crook, J Crook, RL Sewell, MG Shaw, T Jackson
Date of incorporation: 8 February 1980
Company name: Professional Appearance Services Ltd
Issued share capital: £93 (in £1 shares)
BFA member: Registered

Costs
Start-up capital (minimum): £11,940 plus VAT
Initial fee: included in start-up figure
Royalties: 8 per cent of turnover
Proportion of start-up capital that can be arranged: 70 per cent

Market growth	1984	1985	(30 June) 1986
UK franchise outlets:	5	8	10
UK company owned outlets:	—	—	—
Date of first UK franchise: September 1983			

Financial data	1983	1984	1985
Turnover:	£53,824	£29,083	32,012
Net profit:	£3,048	(£3,035)	(£2,332)
*Net worth:	(£15,104)	(£17,893)	(£20,725)
Current ratio:	0.24:1	0.26:1	0.30:1

*Fixed assets = Current assets minus liabilities. Shares in subsidiaries and loans to associated companies are excluded.

Prontaprint
Coniscliffe House
Coniscliffe Road
Darlington DL3 7EX
Tel: 0325 483333
Contact: David Pooley

Business description
Prontaprint offers fast process printing, copying, typesetting, graphic design and artwork services with the boast that if it involves paper and ink 'We can do it'.

The company assesses business potential in the area, selects premises and develops them to a standard formula. Training, theoretical and practical, includes staffing, accounting, customer relations, sales and the principles of offset printing.

There is a launch publicity campaign and company activity to promote and develop the franchise. Prontaprint insist that it is very much a people business, and only those who truly enjoy dealing with the public are likely to succeed.

Company information
Directors: KH Rostron, MA Spence, KG Craney, J Cooper
 (non-executive), B Donnelly, D Pooley, J Easterby
Date of incorporation: 1971
Company name: Prontaprint plc
Issued share capital: £74,200
Parent company: Prontaprint Holdings Ltd
BFA member: Yes

Costs
Start-up capital (minimum): £55,000
Initial fee: £12,500
Royalties: 10 per cent
Proportion of start-up capital that can be arranged: 70 per cent

Market growth	1984	1985	(30 June) 1986
UK franchise outlets:	251	287	291
UK company owned outlets:	1	1	1
Date of first UK franchise: 1971			

Financial data	1983/4	1984/5	1985/6
Turnover:	£2.59m	£2.94m	£3.30m
Net profit:	£364,647	£528,370	£563,467
Net worth:	£349,083	£625,495	£889,458
Current ratio:	1.109:1	1.345:1	1.572:1

Fixed assets = Current assets minus liabilities. Shares in subsidiaries and loans to associated companies are excluded.

Pronuptia de Paris Bridalwear
70-78 York Way
Kings Cross
London N1 9AG
Tel: 01-278 0343
Contact: Alex Henning, Retail Controller

Business description
Pronuptia de Paris is the leading retail bridalwear specialist in the UK, associated with the main Pronuptia operation in Paris who control over 300 locations worldwide. There is an inter-company connection with Young's Formal Wear for Men and commonly, both departments operate together in the same location.

Franchisees need no previous experience in the trade as the company gives training on management, display and dealing with the public.

Premises can be sited off the main shopping areas and company advice is available on suitable locations and shopfitting.

National advertising is in women's magazines, with fashion shows, point of sale aids and co-ordinated local publicity.

Company information
Directors: C Spencer (Chairman), LA Fielding (Managing Director), CJ Hounsell (Finance Director), VR Young
Date of incorporation: 25 November 1985
Company name: Youngs Franchise Ltd
Issued share capital: £1000
BFA member: Yes

Costs
Start-up capital (minimum): 40,000
Initial fee: £10,000 (£15,000 for a combined Pronuptia and Young's location)
Royalties: 10 per cent, including 3 per cent spent on advertising and promotion
Proportion of start-up capital that can be arranged: 66 per cent

Market growth	1984	1985	1986
UK franchise outlets:	60	60	57
UK company owned outlets:	17	16	14

Date of first UK franchise: 1978

Ryman Ltd
Ryman House
59 Markham Street
London SW3 3NR
Tel: 01-351 5671
Contact: John Wynne Williams

Business description
Retailers of office stationery, equipment and furniture.

Company information
Directors: Jennifer d'Abo, J Wynne-Williams, S Billyeald, K Bull,
   C Lumley-Ellis, R d'Abo, D Dunn, R Hambro
Date of incorporation: 1985
Company name: Ryman Group plc
Issued share capital: N/A
BFA member: No

Costs
Start-up capital (minimum): £90,000
Initial fee: £6500
Royalties: 10 per cent
Proportion of start-up capital that can be arranged: 60-70 per cent

Market growth		1985	(30 June) 1986
UK franchise outlets:		1	2
UK company owned outlets:		44	52

Financial data	1984	1985	1986
Turnover:	£12,751	£14,332	£17,177
Net profit:	(£508)	£116	£554
*Net worth:	—	—	—
Current ratio:	0.76:1	0.67:1	—

*Fixed assets = Current assets minus liabilities. Shares in subsidiaries and loans to associated companies are excluded.

N/A: Information exists but is not available.

Safeclean
Delmae House
Home Farm
Ardington
Wantage
Oxon OX12 8PN
Tel: 0235 833022
Contact: Brian Duckett

Business description
Safeclean operators provide a complete furnishing care service to the top of the domestic market. All fabrics can be cleaned on-site, or protected against soiling, stains, fire and static electricity. Using the company's unique equipment and chemicals, the operator guarantees to cause no shrinkage or colour-run.

Safeclean operators are often one-man businesses, but many employ service people. There is full initial and continuing training and support from the company. Overheads are low as the operator works from home, using the family car (signwritten) for his business.

Company information
Directors: DG Cook, ER Cook, BJ Duckett
Date of incorporation: 1969
Company name: D G Cook Ltd
Issued share capital: £5000
Parent company: —
BFA member: Yes

Costs
Start-up capital (minimum): £9750
Initial fee: —
Royalties: Approx 7 per cent of turnover
Proportion of start-up capital that can be arranged: 65 per cent

			(30 June)
Market growth	1984	1985	1986
UK franchise outlets:	50	62	68
UK company owned outlets:	—	—	—
Date of first UK franchise: January 1972			

Financial data	1983	1984	1985
Turnover:	—	£148,754	£230,453
Net profit:	—	£2,913	£11,791
*Net worth:	—	£16,339	£22,230
Current ratio:	—	0.69:1	0.55:1

*Fixed assets = Current assets minus liabilities. Shares in subsidiaries and loans to associated companies are excluded.

Seekers Estate Agency
200B Haverstock Hill
London NW3
Tel: 01-794 7194

Business description
Estate agency.

Company information
Director: M Nyman
Date of incorporation: 1979
Company name: Thorn Ganby Ltd
Issued share capital: £100
Parent company: —
BFA member: No

Costs
Start-up capital (minimum): £25,000
Initial fee: £10,000
Royalties: 10 per cent
Proportion of start-up capital that can be arranged: 50 per cent

			(30 June)
Market growth	1984	1985	1986
UK franchise outlets:	—	—	45
UK company owned outlets:	—	—	—
Date of first UK franchise: May 1981			

251

Financial data	1983	1984	1985
Turnover:	£644,348	—	—
Net profit:	£88,412	(£39,161)	—
*Net worth:	£110,644	—	(£20,904)
Current ratio:	1.14:1	0.4:1	0.2:1

*Fixed assets = Current assets minus liabilities. Shares in subsidiaries and loans to associated companies are excluded.

Serviceman Service Centres
2nd Floor
Northgate House
High Pavement
Basildon
Essex SS14 1EA
Tel: 0268 293355
Contact: Michael P Timmins, Franchise Director

Business description
Car servicing, repairs, tuning, MOT testing.

Company information
Directors: MJ Hallybone (Chairman), RJ Clare (Managing Director),
DG Gilbey, MP Timmins
Date of incorporation: 19 April 1985
Company name: Serviceman Franchise plc
Issued share capital: £1,115,000
BFA member: No

Costs
Start-up capital (minimum): £42,000
Initial fee: £11,500
Royalties: 6.5 per cent management service plus 3 per cent ground rent
Proportion of start-up capital that can be arranged: 70 per cent, subject
    to status

		(30 June)
Market growth:	1986	1987
UK franchise outlets:	6	9
UK company owned outlets:	—	3

Financial data: N/A

N/A: Information exists but is not available.

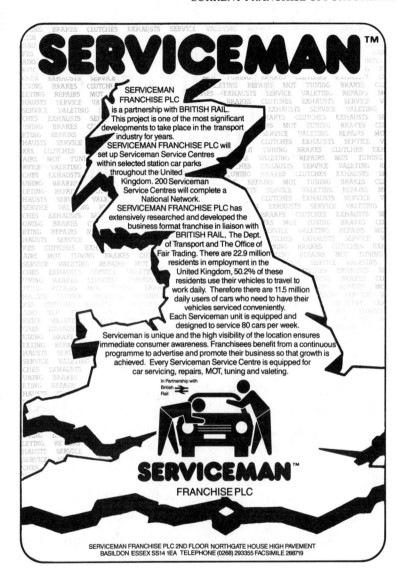

If you're interested in franchising this is where you start.

Name

Company

Address

Please send me by return a copy of the Franchisee Guide.
I enclose a cheque for £5.95 (to include postage and packing).

Return to: Franchise Desk, Scottish Development Agency,
21-25 Bothwell Street, Glasgow G2 6NR.

There are very significant franchising opportunities in Scotland. But before you commit yourself in any way you should ask a number of questions.

Are you a suitable person to become a franchisee? Does the franchisor have a good track record? Has the business format been properly tested?

Scottish Development Agency,

The SDA has prepared a "Franchisee Guide" to help you answer all these questions. The guide costs £5.95 (including postage and packing) and will be sent to you by return when you complete this coupon. It is also available through our Franchise Desk on 041-248 3315.

21-25 Bothwell Street, Glasgow G2 6NR.

ServiceMaster
50 Commercial Square
Freemans Common
Leicester LE2 7SR
Tel: 0533 548620
Contacts: Philip Tait, Brenda Bruton

Business description
ServiceMaster is the world's leading cleaning organisation, with
more than 3000 licensees worldwide.

Two franchises are offered in the UK: one providing daily
cleaning services to commercial premises and the other based on
in situ carpet and upholstery cleaning in domestic and commercial
situations. In both cases full preparation training is provided,
covering every aspect of the business, and regular courses and
workshops are held in an ongoing training programme. Back-up
support is provided for marketing, sales, finance and
administration.

Company information
Directors: BA Smith, DV Horsfall, RA Armstrong
Date of incorporation: 1976
Company name: ServiceMaster Ltd
Issued share capital: N/A
Parent company: ServiceMaster Industries Inc
BFA member: Yes

Costs
Start-up capital (minimum): £9000
Initial fee: £4000
Equipment: £5000
Royalties: contract cleaning: 7-4 per cent scale. On location: 10 per cent
Proportion of start-up capital that can be arranged: 66 per cent

			(30 June)
Market growth	1984	1985	1986
UK franchise outlets:	175	173	187
UK company owned outlets:	—	—	—
Date of first UK franchise: 1959			

Financial data	1983	1984	1985
Turnover:	£644,348	N/A	N/A
Net profit:	£88,412		
*Net worth:	£110,644		
Current ratio:	1.14:1		

*Fixed assets = Current assets minus liabilities. Shares in subsidiaries and loans to
associated companies are excluded.

N/A: Information exists but is not available.

Signtalk Ltd
266 Church Street
Blackpool
Lancashire FY1 3PZ
Tel: 0253 293774
Contact: Mr K L Harber

Business description
Suppliers of a tremendous range of business promotional and incentive products including licence holders, rear window stickers, roof boards, pens, coasters, banners, bunting, shop window display material, general printed stationery, badges, magnetic panels etc. Preparatory training is given at headquarters and a bookkeeping system is provided. Suitable for salesmen or women with ambition, and areas are generous.

Company information
Directors: KL Harber, L Holland
Date of incorporation: January 1986
Company name: Signtalk Ltd
Issued share capital: N/A
BFA member: No

Costs
Start-up capital (minimum): £5000
Initial fee: £1200
Royalties: None; 1 per cent of purchases as advertising contribution
Proportion of start-up capital that can be arranged: —

	(30 June) 1986
Market growth	
UK franchise outlets:	4
UK company owned outlets:	1
Date of first UK franchise: March 1986	

N/A: Information exists but is not available.

Silver Shield Windscreens
Wheler Road
Seven Stars Estate
Coventry CV3 3LA
Tel: 0203 307755
Contact: John A Oliver

Business description
24-hour windscreen replacement service.

Company information
Directors: JA Oliver (Managing Director), W Evans (Financial Director)
Date of incorporation: 1978
Company name: Silver Shield Screens Ltd
Issued share capital: £500
BFA member: Yes

Costs
Start-up capital (minimum): £18,000
Initial fee: £6950
Royalties: 10 per cent
Proportion of start-up capital that can be arranged: 50 per cent

			(30 June)
Market growth	1984	1985	1986
UK franchise outlets:	58	60	62
UK company owned outlets:	—	—	—
Date of first UK franchise: 1978			

Financial data	1983	1984	1985
Turnover:	£5.5m	£8m	£11m
Net profit:	N/A	N/A	N/A
*Net worth:	£120,348	£116,454	N/A
Current ratio:	1.22:1	1.1:1	N/A

*Fixed assets = Current assets minus liabilities. Shares in subsidiaries and loans to associated companies are excluded.

N/A: Information exists but is not available.

Sketchley Franchises Ltd
P O Box 7
Rugby Road
Hinckley
Leicestershire LE10 2NE
Tel: 0455 38133
Contact: Keith J Twyman, Franchise Manager

Business description
Dry cleaning and shoe repair shops offering a comprehensive
service of personal garment and household item cleaning, while-
you-wait shoe repairs, garment repairs, dyeing and specialist
services including suedes, sheepskins, leathers, curtains, duvets,
eiderdowns and pillows.

Company information
Directors: SFR Bee, RF Adams, R Gudger, FH Lambert, WG Evans
Date of incorporation: Sketchley plc 1916; Sketchley Cleaners 1932
Company name: Sketchley Cleaners Ltd
Issued share capital: £5,771,667 (Sketchley plc)
Parent company: Sketchley plc
BFA member: Yes

Costs
Start-up capital (minimum): £77,000
Initial fee: £5000
Royalties: 6 per cent management fee, 4 per cent advertising fund
Proportion of start-up capital that can be arranged: 70 per cent

			(30 June)
Market growth	1984	1985	1986
UK franchise outlets:	—	—	4
UK company owned outlets:	486	479	479
Date of first UK franchise: September 1985			

Financial data	1983	1984	1985
Turnover:	£83,730,000	£101,225,000	£159,170,000
Net profit:	£9,319,000	£10,830,000	£10,154,000
*Net worth:	£44,223,000	£67,341,000	£71,317,000

*Fixed assets = Current assets minus liabilities. Shares in subsidiaries and loans to
associated companies are excluded.

Clean-up with Sketchley franchise wise.

If you're thinking of going into business, a Sketchley dry cleaning and shoe repair franchise is the wise one you can really clean-up with.

As Britain's largest and best known name in cleaning, we're now offering exceptional opportunities to franchise bright new shops in many locations.

Using our name, knowledge and experience gained from operating 500 outlets, you'll run your own shop with the security and reputation of the Sketchley name behind you. And the prospect of real potential growth and development ahead of you.

In addition, we'll train you and your personnel with all the technical and business knowledge you need to run a successful shop.

You'll also have the powerful support of our marketing which smaller businesses cannot enjoy!

Phone 0455 38133 or write for more information on joining the team that knows the meaning of cleaning-up franchise wise.

Sketchley

WE KNOW THE MEANING OF CLEANING.

Keith Twyman, Franchise Manager, Sketchley Franchises Ltd., Rugby Road, Hinckley, Leics. LE10 2NE.

Slim Gym Ltd
Bingswood Industrial Estate
Whaley Bridge
Stockport SK12 7LY
Tel: 06633 4545
Contact: Mr N McKechnie

Business description
Health and leisure consultants. Design of fitness orientated clubs including necessary management and control systems. Smallest project 1000 sq ft; largest 4000.

Company information
Directors: LS Bloom, AC Thompson, N McKechnie, R Kelly
Date of incorporation: 1983
Company name: Slim Gym Ltd
Issued share capital: £40,000
BFA member: No

Costs
Start-up capital (minimum): £50,000
Initial fee: N/A
Royalties: N/A

Market growth	1983	1984	(30 June) 1985
UK franchise outlets:	2	5	9
UK company owned outlets:	—	—	—
Date of first UK franchise: September 1983			

Financial data	1984	1985
Turnover:	—	—
Net profit:	—	—
*Net worth:	£14,138	£69,083
Current ratio:	1.46:1	1.36:

*Fixed assets = Current assets minus liabilities. Shares in subsidiaries and loans to associated companies are excluded.

N/A: Information exists but is not available.

Snap-On-Tools
Palmer House
150-154 Cross Street
Sale
Cheshire M33 1FU
Tel: 061-969 0126
Contact: Mrs Jackie Coulding

Business description
Snap-On-Tools retail tools for the motor vehicle garage trade, the role of the franchisee being to visit appropriate outlets and sell a range of company supplied products. Someone with previous sales experience is envisaged as a franchisee.

Preparatory training in the technical and sales aspects is given and there is a business management system.

Company information
Directors: RR Gadsby, M Lancaster, N Cooper, MF Gregory,
   LA Ameche, LL Larson, JR Olson
Date of incorporation: 1965
Company name: Snap-On-Tools Ltd
Issued share capital: N/A
BFA member: Yes

Costs
Start-up capital (minimum): £6000
Initial fee: Nil
Royalties: Nil
Proportion of start-up capital that can be arranged: Nil

			(30 June)
Market growth	1984	1985	1986
UK franchise outlets:	306	308	314
UK company owned outlets:	N/A	N/A	N/A
Date of first UK franchise: 1965			

Financial data	1983	1984	1985
Turnover:	£20,222K	—	—
Net profit:	£1,580K	—	—
*Net worth:	£5,075K	—	—
Current ratio:	1.7:1	—	—

*Fixed assets = Current assets minus liabilities. Shares in subsidiaries and loans to associated companies are excluded.

N/A: Information exists but is not available.

Spud-U-Like
34-38 Standard Road
London NW10 6EU
Tel: 01-965 0181
Contact: Michael Porritt

Business description

Spud-U-Like is a fast food retailing business specialising in potatoes baked with a variety of fillings. The company will select premises, or if suitable, accept the franchisee's, giving assistance with planning permission, external and internal design.

Preparation for trading includes business advice and staff training.

Specialist equipment and catering products can be bought through company facilities.

There is an opening advertising campaign and ongoing publicity.

Company information

Directors: T Schlesinger (Chairman), M Porritt (Managing Director), DA Jacobs, JN Malin
Date of incorporation: 1974

265

Company name: Spud-U-Like Ltd
Issued share capital: £10,000
Parent company: British School of Motoring
BFA member: Yes

Costs
Start-up capital (minimum): £50,000 (including VAT)
Initial fee: £5000 plus VAT
Royalties: 5 per cent, plus 3 per cent advertising
Proportion of start-up capital that can be arranged: up to 70 per cent

			(30 June)
Market growth	1984	1985	1986
UK franchise outlets:	55	50	40
UK company owned outlets:	6	5	5
Date of first UK franchise: June 1981			

Financial data: There are no separate accounts.

Stained Glass Overlay
PO Box 65
Norwich
Norfolk NR6 6EJ
Tel: 0603 485454
Contacts: D Hubbard or S Lawrence

Business description
Selling, marketing and production of designs on glass using coloured films and lead strips. The process can create freeform designs on glass as well as simulations of traditional stained glass and lead light windows.

Company information
Directors: GG Williams, DG Whayman, A Keizer, WC Hancock, JB Hart, AJ Bowkett, WD Madel
Date of incorporation: N/A
Company name: Anglian Windows Ltd
Issued share capital: N/A
Parent company: BET plc
BFA member: No

Costs
Start-up capital (minimum): £35,000
Initial fee: £13,000 included in above
Royalties: 7½ per cent management services fee, 2½ per cent national advertising fund
Proportion of start-up capital that can be arranged: —

Market growth	1984	1985	(30 June) 1986
UK franchise outlets:	—	—	—
UK company owned outlets:	—	—	1
Date of first UK franchise: 29 August 1986			

Financial data: No separate accounts are filed.

N/A: Information exists but is not available.

Stockcheck
The Courtyard
Harewood Estate
Harewood
Leeds LS17 9LS
Tel: 0532 886565
Contact: J C Gilpin

Business description
Food and liquor stocktaking and stock control in the hotel and leisure industry and licensed trade. A high level of consultancy advice service is provided. Only applicants with career backgrounds in the above industries are considered.

Company information
Proprietor: JC Gilpin
Parent company: John Gilpin Ltd
BFA member: No

Costs
Start-up capital (minimum): £7500 including working capital
Initial fee: £3500
Royalties: 7½ per cent plus 2½ per cent to marketing fund

Market growth	1984	1985	(30 June) 1986
UK franchise outlets:	6	9	13
UK company owned outlets:	—	—	—
Date of first UK franchise: October 1983			

Financial data	1983	1984	1985
Turnover:	£60,000	£120,000	£205,000

Stop-a-Thief!
Unit 9
Avenue 1
Business Park
Letchworth
Hertfordshire SG6 2BB
Tel: 0462 670555
Contact: Phil Aston

Business description
The company supplies and fits a wide range of vehicle security systems for the trade, fleet and retail markets. The main feature of the service is the 'on site' service carried out by the local franchisee.

Company information
Directors: L Small (Managing Director), P Weston (Sales), P Aston (Franchises)
Date of incorporation: new incorporation 1 February 1986
Company name: Stop Thief (UK) Ltd
Issued share capital: N/A
Parent company: Gamma Electronics
BFA member: No

Costs
Start-up capital (minimum): £9500
Initial fee: £4995
Royalties: £25 per week
Proportion of start-up capital that can be arranged: 30 per cent

			(30 June)
Market growth	1984	1985	1986
UK franchise outlets:	20	20	22
UK company owned outlets:	1	2	3
Date of first UK franchise: January 1983			

N/A: Information exists but is not available.

Subway Sandwiches and Salads (UK) Ltd

PO Box 153   25 High Street
London N11 3JU   Milford CT 06460
Tel: 01-361 9546   USA
                             Tel: Freefone 0800 89 11 83

UK contact: Neil Taylor

Business description
Sells sandwiches and salads, fast food. With over 1200 stores in operation worldwide, Subway is the world's largest sandwich company.

Company information
Directors: FA de Luca, P Buck
Date of incorporation: 13 February 1986
Company name: N/A .
Issued share capital: £500,000
Parent company: N/A (in USA)
BFA member: No

Costs
Start-up capital (minimum): £40,000
Initial fee: £5000 plus VAT
Royalties: 8 per cent plus 2 per cent advertising
Proportion of start-up capital that can be arranged: 50 per cent

	(30 June) 1986
Market growth	
UK franchise outlets:	1
UK company owned outlets:	—
Date of first UK franchise: September 1986	

N/A: Information exists but is not available.

Swinton Insurance
31-33 Princess Street
Manchester M2 4EW
Tel: 061-236 8697
Contact: Peter W Lowe

Business description
Swinton are the largest privately owned insurance brokers in the
UK, having pioneered the high street shop style of operation more
than 25 years ago.

A full support package includes a property location and
shopfitting service, pre-entry training and continued press and tv
advertising and promotional back-up. The company also offers a
centralised accounts administration service, computerised
quotation facilities, and regular liaison with experienced
personnel.

A strong company corporate image is adhered to in all cases.

Experience of, or qualifications, in the insurance business is
necessary.

271

Company information
Directors: K Scowcroft, BD Blake, PW Lowe, BK Scowcroft, F Blashill,
   K Bryan, R Wilkinson
Date of incorporation: N/A
Company name: Swinton Franchising Ltd
Issued share capital: N/A
Parent company: N/A
BFA member: Yes

Costs
Start-up capital (minimum): £18,000
Initial fee: £2300
Royalties: 6 per cent to include advertising and central accounting
Proportion of start-up capital that can be arranged: up to 75 per cent

			(30 June)
Market growth	1984	1985	1986
UK franchise outlets:	20	27	70
UK company owned outlets:	100	121	150
Date of first UK franchise: 1984			

Financial data	1983	1984	1985
Premium income:	£48m	£56m	66m

N/A: Information exists but is not available.

System-Text (UK) Ltd
System-Text House
Beavor Lane
London W6 9BL
Tel: 01-741 7461
Contact: Derek R Fiddaman

Business description
System-Text was created in Sweden over 25 years ago as a self-
adhesive lettering system which has now developed into one of the
largest variable sign making and decorative systems. By using the
latest CAD/CAM production technology we are able to supply
the majority of needs to a variety of markets.

Company information
Directors: MJ Green (Managing Director), S Thollin, L Thulin
Date of incorporation: 3 December 1979
Company name: System-Text (UK) Ltd
Issued share capital: N/A
Parent company: System-Text AB, Malmö, Sweden
BFA member: No

Costs
Start-up capital (minimum): £12,750 includes three months' working
  capital
Initial fee: £3500
Royalties: Fixed fee £4000 pa
Proportion of start-up capital that can be arranged: 50 per cent

			(30 June)
Market growth	1984	1985	1986
UK franchise outlets:	—	—	—
UK company owned outlets:	1	1	1
Date of first UK franchise:			
2 February 1987			

Financial data	1983	1984	1985
Turnover:	£126,710	—	—
Net profit:	(£130,127)	—	—
*Net worth:	(£252,509)	(£475,379)	(£598,552)
Current ratio:	0.65:1	0.57:1	0.64:1

*Fixed assets = Current assets minus liabilities. Shares in subsidiaries and loans to
associated companies are excluded.

N/A: Information exists but is not available.

Team
Haverscroft Industrial Estate
New Road
Attleborough
Norfolk NR17 1YE
Tel: 0953 454544
Contact: David Fossey

Business description
Distribution of radio, TV and audio equipment and accessories to
the retailer by mobile showroom.

Company information
Directors: D Fossey (Managing Director), B Simms
Date of incorporation: 1978
Company name: Team (Audio) Ltd
Issued share capital: N/A
BFA member: Registered

Costs
Start-up capital (minimum): £24,000
Initial fee: £4000
Royalties: 4.2 per cent of trade sales
Proportion of start-up capital that can be arranged: 66 per cent

			(30 June)
Market growth	1984	1985	1986
UK franchise outlets:	2	7	13
UK company owned outlets:	2	2	3
Date of first UK franchise: April 1984			

Financial data	1983	1984	1985
Turnover:	£572,000	£904,000	£1,768,000

N/A: Information exists but is not available.

Thorntons
Derwent Street
Belper
Derbyshire DE5 1WP
Tel: 077 382 4181
Contact: R E Smith

Business description
Retailers and manufacturers of high quality confectionery.

Company information
Directors: CJ Thornton, PN Thornton, MS Thornton, JS Thornton
Date of incorporation: June 1921
Company name: J W Thornton Ltd
Issued share capital: £804,330
BFA member: Yes

Costs
Start-up capital (minimum): £15,000 for shopfitting
Initial fee: £1000
Royalties: —
Proportion of start-up capital that can be arranged: —

			(30 June)
Market growth	1984	1985	1986
UK franchise outlets:	54	68	80
UK company owned outlets:	145	150	155
Date of first UK franchise: June 1968			

Financial data	1983	1984	1985
Turnover:	£29,752K	£34,794K	£39,205K
Net profit:	£2,559K	£1,647K	£2,508K
*Net worth:	£10,940K	£12,483K	£14,572K
Current ratio:	1:1.5	1:1.4	1.5:1

Fixed assets = Current assets minus liabilities. Shares in subsidiaries and loans to associated companies are excluded.

Tie Rack Ltd
70-78 York Way
London N1 9AG
Tel: 01-837 6356
Contact: Ronald Delnevo

Business description
Retailing ties, scarves, handkerchiefs, belts and accessories in prime locations, Tie Rack select and acquire the site, set the shop up for business in every respect, train the franchisee, supply stock and provide continuous support.

Company information
Directors: RC Bishko, TD Jennings, WA Hobhouse, RJ Delnevo,
  B Roback
Date of incorporation: 1981
Company name: Tie Rack Ltd
Issued share capital: N/A
Parent company: Associated Investments Ltd
BFA member: Yes

Costs
Start-up capital (minimum): £35,000
Initial fee: £5000
Royalties: 22½ per cent (inclusive of rent, rates and service charges)
Proportion of start-up capital that can be arranged: 60 per cent

			(30 June)
Market growth	1984	1985	1986
UK franchise outlets:	18	43	80
UK company owned outlets:	6	10	20
Date of first UK franchise: 1983			

Financial data	1983	1984	1985
Turnover:	—	—	—
Net profit:	—	(£26,401)	£142,232
*Net worth:	£127,212	£84,827	£175,792
Current ratio:	0.79:1	0.77:1	0.94:1

*Fixed assets = Current assets minus liabilities. Shares in subsidiaries and loans to associated companies are excluded.

N/A: Information exists but is not available.

TNT Parcel Office
TNT House
Long Street
Atherstone
Warwickshire CV9 1BS
Tel: 08277 5311
Contact: David Hadley

Business description
TNT Parcel Office is a reception point for parcels which are delivered on any of TNT's express parcel services within the UK, Europe and worldwide.

The franchisee can turn a small part of his existing business into a Parcel Office thereby utilising existing overheads and resources. The franchisee is expected to sell and promote the services within his immediate area, offer a personal service to customers and provide a collection facility if required. TNT is the market leader in the express parcels delivery sector and provides full back-up service for the franchisee.

Company information
Directors: PW Allsebrook, DM Dick, Sir P Abeles, JR Cribb,
    JH Hunter, LR Clifton-Bligh, AD Jones, C van Leeuwen,
    Lord Geddes, WV Hanley
Date of incorporation: —
Company name: TNT Parcel Office
Issued share capital: —
Parent company: TNT Roadfreight (UK) Ltd
BFA member: Yes

Costs
Start-up capital (minimum): Prime site: £5000; Secondary site: £3000
Initial fee: N/A
Royalties: Nil
Proportion of start-up capital that can be arranged: 60 per cent

Market growth	1984	1985	1986
UK franchise outlets:	305	358	419
UK company owned outlets:	—	—	—
Date of first UK franchise: 1981			

N/A: Information exists but is not available.

Trust Parts
Unit 7
Groundswell Industrial Estate
Crompton Road
Swindon
Wiltshire SN2 5AY
Tel: 0793 723749
Contact: Bob Wilson, Franchise Manager

Business description
Van sales operation supplying a comprehensive range of essential, fast moving consumable hardware to motor and allied trade workshops.

The van is driven by the franchisee and is specially fitted to carry and display stock which is sold and delivered to the customer on the spot.

Company information
Directors: R Bourne (Managing), PG McDonald, W Mackenzie
   (Chairman)
Date of incorporation: 1979
Company name: Trust Parts Ltd
Issued share capital: £265,243
BFA member: No

Costs
Start-up capital (minimum): £20,000
Initial fee: £14,000
Royalties: 5 per cent
Proportion of start-up capital that can be arranged: Nil

Market growth	1984	1985	(30 June) 1986
UK franchise outlets:	—	—	—
UK company owned outlets:	50	59	68
Date of first UK franchise: 18 August 1986			

Financial data	1983	1984	1985
Turnover:	£2,274,000	£2,688,000	£3,210,000
Net profit (pre-tax):	£186,000	£255,000	£294,000
*Net worth:	£550,000	£708,000	£836,000
Current ratio:	1.8:1	1.7:1	—

*Fixed assets = Current assets minus liabilities. Shares in subsidiaries and loans to associated companies are excluded.

Tumble Tots (UK) Ltd
Cannons Sports Club
Cousin Lane
London EC4R 3TE
Tel: 01-621 0904
Contact: David Thomas

Business description
Active physical play programme for pre-school children.

Company information
Director: R Clarke MBE
Date of incorporation: 1981
Company name: Tumble Tots
Issued share capital: N/A
Parent company: Jack Chia Group
BFA member: No

Costs
Start-up capital (minimum): £4000-£5000
Initial fee: £3100
Royalties: —
Proportion of start-up capital that can be arranged: —

			(30 June)
Market growth	1984	1985	1986
UK franchise outlets:	5	7	60
UK company owned outlets:	10	40	2

Date of first UK franchise: 1983

Financial data: Figures not available as company was bought out in 1984.

N/A: Information exists but is not available.

The UK School of Motoring Ltd
2 East Street
Newport
Isle of Wight PO30 1JN
Tel: 0983 527788
Contact: Adrian Brewer

Business description
Driving school. The provision of driving tuition to the general
public, companies, local authorities etc.

Company information
Directors: A Brewer, Sylvia Brewer, R Proctor, C Welfare
Date of incorporation: 21 February 1986
Company name: The UK School of Motoring Ltd
Issued share capital: N/A
BFA member: No

Costs
Start-up capital (minimum): £3500
Initial fee: £2500
Royalties: Management fee per vehicle operated
Proportion of start-up capital that can be arranged: 30 per cent

	(30 June)
Market growth	1986
UK franchise outlets:	1
UK company owned outlets:	2
Date of first UK franchise: November 1986	

N/A: Information exists but is not available.

Uticolor
Sheraton House
35-37 North Street
York YO1 1JD
Tel: 0904 37798
Contact: Eric S Bottomley

Business description
Uticolor is a vinyl bonding process used to repair vinyl and leather coverings which have been holed or otherwise damaged. The repair service is offered to hotels, clubs, schools, hospitals and offices.

Some manual dexterity is an advantage to the franchisee, who will be given training in all aspects of the franchise.

Company information
Directors: ES Bottomley, GA Denton, RA Dowdall
Date of incorporation: 1977
Company name: Uticolor (Great Britain) Ltd
Issued share capital: £100,000
Parent company: Sheraton House Ltd
BFA member: Yes

Costs
Start-up capital (minimum): £6000 (including working capital)
Initial fee: *c.* £3000
Royalties: 10 per cent administration fees
Proportion of start-up capital that can be arranged: 50 per cent

			(30 June)
Market growth	1984	1985	1986
UK franchise outlets:	33	35	36
UK company owned outlets:	2	2	2

Date of first UK franchise: 1978

Financial data	1983	1984	1985
Turnover:	—	—	—
Net profit:	£5,815	—	—
*Net worth:	£15,804	£18,190	—
Current ratio:	4.33:1	5.63:1	—

*Fixed assets = Current assets minus liabilities. Shares in subsidiaries and loans to associated companies are excluded.

Vandervells Business Transfer Centre

Vandervell House
72 London Road
Southampton SO1 2AJ
Tel: 0703 229271
Contact: Geoff Vandervell

Business description
Business transfer agents.

Company information
Directors: GL Vandervell, KI Vandervell
Date of incorporation: 1962
Company name: Vandervells BTC Ltd
Issued share capital: £100
BFA member: No

Costs
Start-up capital (minimum): £15,000
Initial fee: £4500
Royalties: 10 per cent
Proportion of start-up capital that can be arranged: —

Market growth	1984	1985	(30 June) 1986
UK franchise outlets:	3	3	5
UK company owned outlets:	—	—	—
Date of first UK franchise: —			

Financial data	1983	1984	1985
Turnover:	£80,125	—	—
Net profit:	(£12,748)	—	—
*Net worth:	(£17,602)	(£16,988)	(£53,971)
Current ratio:	0.13:1	—	0.05:1

*Fixed assets = Current assets minus liabilities. Shares in subsidiaries and loans to associated companies are excluded.

VDU Services
VDU House
Brook Road
Wormley
Surrey GU8 5BR
Tel: 042 879 3733
Contact: David Cooper

Business description
Computer and VDU cleaning.

Company information
Directors: DL Cooper, Mrs A Cooper
Date of incorporation: April 1984
Company name: N/A
Issued share capital: N/A
Parent company: VDU Services Franchising Ltd
BFA member: No

Costs
Start-up capital (minimum): £8350 plus VAT
Initial fee: £8350 plus VAT
Royalties: 10 per cent after 3 months
Proportion of start-up capital that can be arranged: Negotiable

Market growth
Pilot scheme in operation.

Financial data	1986
Turnover:	£32,000
Net profit:	£13,500
*Net worth:	N/A
Current ratio:	N/A

*Fixed assets = Current assets minus liabilities. Shares in subsidiaries and loans to associated companies are excluded.

N/A: Information exists but is not available.

Video Events Ltd
12 Harley House
Upper Harley Street
London NW1 4PR
Tel: 01-935 4430/0873 77379
Contact: D Ahern

Business description
To provide professional video filming services for the general public and industry at economic prices with consistent high quality.

Company information
Directors: D Ahern, Mrs V Kemp
Date of incorporation: 12 October 1984
Company name: Video Events Ltd
Issued share capital: £100,000
BFA member: No

Costs
Start-up capital (minimum): £7500
Initial fee: —
Royalties: 8 per cent plus 2 per cent advertising
Proportion of start-up capital that can be arranged: 100 per cent

		(30 June)
Market growth	1985	1986
UK franchise outlets:	1	4
UK company owned outlets:	2	2
Date of first UK franchise: 1985		

Financial data	1985
Turnover:	£122,000
Net profit:	£24,000
*Net worth:	£103,000
Current ratio:	—

*Fixed assets = Current assets minus liabilities. Shares in subsidiaries and loans to associated companies are excluded.

Wallspan Bedrooms Ltd
Industrial Estate
Maulden Road
Flitwick
Bedfordshire MK45 5BW
Tel: 0525 716161
Contact: —

Business description
The Wallspan Group is a privately owned organisation, still led by the man who started it all 25 years ago.

With one of the most modern equipped factories in Europe, Wallspan operate from their own purpose-built seven-acre freehold site in Bedfordshire, producing what is arguably the finest range of fitted bedroom furniture in the UK.

A new factory extension has recently been completed to meet the growing demand from its own wholly owned 34 showrooms as well as new business brought in by the additional 48 franchise outlets.

Through an aggressive product development programme, Wallspan have established themselves as innovators in the production of bedroom furniture.

Company information
Directors: TW Bailey, JV Bayley, JP Appleby (Company Secretary)
Date of incorporation: 1962
Company name: Wallspan Bedrooms Ltd
Issued share capital: N/A
BFA member: No

Costs
Start-up capital (minimum): —
Initial fee: —
Royalties: —
Proportion of start-up capital that can be arranged: —

			(30 June)
Market growth	1984	1985	1986
UK franchise outlets:	34	42	45
UK company owned outlets:	26	30	33
Date of first UK franchise: August 1975			

Financial data	1983	1984	1985
Turnover:	£3,867,691	£4,103,279	£3,876,793
Net profit:	£46,280	£171,478	(£255,408)
*Net worth:	£282,822	£348,553	£204,403
Current ratio:	1.02:1	1.02:1	0.62:1

*Fixed assets = Current assets minus liabilities. Shares in subsidiaries and loans to associated companies are excluded.

N/A: Information exists but is not available.

Wash 'n' Wax
19 Ainslie Place
Edinburgh EH3 6AU
Tel: 031-226 2823
Contact: Colin McCraith

Business description
Mobile vehicle valet service. Wash 'n' Wax specialise in offering a complete valeting service to the business car owner, on a contract basis, enabling the franchisee to establish a long-term customer base within his protected territory.

Company information
Directors: MH McPherson, CM Beggs, A Macdonald, PD McCraith
Date of incorporation: 1985
Company name: Wash 'n' Wax Ltd
Issued share capital: £22,000
BFA member: No

Costs
Start-up capital (minimum): £6000
Initial fee: £1500
Royalties: 10 per cent
Proportion of start-up capital that can be arranged: 80 per cent

			(30 June)
Market growth	1984	1985	1986
UK franchise outlets:	—	—	8
UK company owned outlets:	1	1	1
Date of first UK franchise: 1986			

Financial data: N/A

N/A: Information exists but is not available.

Weider Health and Fitness
Craven House
Station Road
Godalming
Surrey GU7 1JD
Tel: 04868 25544
Contact: Michael J Stearn

Business description
Distributor and retailer of health and fitness equipment, clothing, foods, food supplements and related products.

Company information
Directors: MJ Stearn, DS Riley, D Strong, K Fowler, I Sampson,
    B Weider
Date of incorporation: 1974
Company name: Weider Health and Fitness
Issued share capital: £200,000
Parent company: Craven House Marketing Ltd
BFA member: No

Costs
Start-up capital (minimum): £30,000
Initial fee: £3000
Royalties: 10 per cent (7 per cent net)
Proportion of start-up capital that can be arranged: 66 per cent

			(30 June)
Market growth	1984	1985	1986
UK franchise outlets:	1	2	4
UK company owned outlets:	3	3	3
Date of first UK franchise: December 1983			

Financial data	1983	1984	1985
Turnover:	£4000K	£5000K	£7000K
Net profit:	£180K	£190K	£200K
*Net worth:	—	—	£1.2m
Current ratio:	—	—	—

*Fixed assets = Current assets minus liabilities. Shares in subsidiaries and loans to associated companies are excluded.

Weightguard Franchise Ltd
Henlow Grange Health Farm
Henlow
Bedfordshire SG16 6DP
Tel: 0462 811111
Contact: Elizabeth Knight

Business description
Slimming clubs.

Company information
Directors: Mrs D Purdew, S Purdew
Date of incorporation: 1984
Company name: Weightguard Franchise Ltd
Issued share capital: £15,000
Parent company: Weightguard Ltd (1960)
BFA member: No

Costs
Start-up capital (minimum): £1300
Initial fee: —
Royalties: 15 per cent
Proportion of start-up capital that can be arranged: 30 per cent

			(30 June)
Market growth	1984	1985	1986
UK franchise outlets:	21	21	35
UK company owned outlets:	34	34	24
Date of first UK franchise:			
3 December 1984			

Financial data: N/A

N/A: Information exists but is not available.

Wetherby Training Services
15 Victoria Street
Wetherby
West Yorkshire LS22 4RE
Tel: 0937 63940
Contact: D G Button

Business description
Secretarial and computer training centres using a unique self-teaching system. No previous teaching experience is necessary. Full training is given and continuing marketing support.

Company information
Directors: DG Button, CJ Button, R Shuttleworth
Date of incorporation: 1976
Company name: Wetherby Training Services
Issued share capital: —
Parent company: Reach-a-Teacha Ltd
BFA member: Yes

Costs
Start-up capital (minimum): £6000
Initial fee: £1500
Royalties: Nil
Proportion of start-up capital that can be arranged: 70 per cent

			(30 June)
Market growth	1984	1985	1986
UK franchise outlets:	62	75	98
UK company owned outlets:	1	1	1
Date of first UK franchise: 1976			

Financial data: The business is not a limited company and therefore no accounts are filed.

Wimpy
10 Windmill Road
London W4 1SD
Tel: 01-994 6454
Contacts: Mike Chambers, Property and Franchise
Sales Director

Business description
Wimpy retails fast food by counter service, with a speedy throughput. Some existing outlets have table service but these are not being increased.

The company assists with site selection and viability, deals with planning permission and supervises structural and internal layout.

Business experience and sales motivation are an advantage to the franchisee who, together with his staff, will be trained in all aspects of the business. Help is available for staff selection.

There is publicity and practical support when trading starts and a continuing promotion programme.

Company information
Directors: M Woolfenden, T Abbott, N Arnold, M Chambers, J Davison,
    J Dalgleish, C Kennedy, V Nicholson, I Woodhead
Date of incorporation: 1956
Company name: Wimpy International Ltd
Issued share capital: N/A
Parent company: United Biscuits
BFA member: Yes

Costs
Start-up capital (minimum): £400,000
Initial fee: £10,000 plus VAT
Royalties: 8.5 per cent plus VAT
Proportion of start-up capital that can be arranged: 60 per cent

Market growth	1984	1985	1986
UK franchise outlets:	403	384	364
UK company owned outlets:	21	35	33

Date of first UK franchise:
    1958 Table service; 1980 Counter service

Financial data: No separate accounts are filed.

N/A: Information exists but is not available.

Young's Formal Wear for Men
70-78 York Way
Kings Cross
London N1 9AG
Tel: 01-278 0343
Contact: Alex Henning, Retail Controller

Business description
Young's is the leading formal wear hire specialist in the UK offering exclusive morning wear. There is an intercompany connection with Pronuptia bridal wear, and commonly, both bridalwear and formal wear are franchised in the same location.

Previous knowledge of the trade is not necessary as product and business training is given.

The company will guide on the selection of premises, which do not have to be in a main shopping centre. Advice and liaison with the shopfitter is also given.

The company provides publicity nationally in bride orientated magazines, with point of sale aids, and also gives advice on local franchisee advertising.

Company information
Directors: C Spencer (Chairman), LA Fielding (Managing Director), CJ Hounsell (Finance Director), VR Young
Date of incorporation: 25 November 1985
Company name: Youngs Franchise Ltd
Issued share capital: £1000
BFA member: Yes

Costs
Start-up capital (minimum): £40,000
Initial fee: £10,000 (£15,000 for a combined Young's and Pronuptia location)
Royalties: 10 per cent (includes 3 per cent spent on advertising and promotion)
Proportion of start-up capital that can be arranged: 66 per cent

Market growth	1984	1985	(30 June) 1986
UK franchise outlets:	60	60	57
UK company owned outlets:	17	16	14

Date of first UK franchise: 1978
(Young's Formal Wear for Men)

2. Index of franchises by business category

Beauty and health

Bodyreform
Command Performance
Herbal World Natural Body Care
Natural Life Health Foods Ltd
Slim Gym Ltd
Weider Health and Fitness
Weightguard Franchise Ltd

Building and maintenance

A1 Dampproofing
The Bath Doctor
British Damp Proofing
Cico Chimney Linings
Dampco
Dampcure Woodcure/30 Ltd
Dyno-Electrics
Dyno-Rod
Fersina International
Fidelity Franchising Ltd
Fires and Things
Fixit Mobile Fastening Centre
Garden Building Centres Ltd

House of Something Different
Isodan (UK) Ltd
Kwik Strip
Mixamate Concrete
Potholes
Stained Glass Overlay

Food, hotels, restaurants

The Bread Roll Company
Burger King UK Ltd
Cartons Boulangerics
Coffeeman
Fatso's Pasta Joint
Perfect Pizza
Pizza Express
Pizza Hut
Spud-U-Like
Stockcheck
Subway Sandwiches and Salads (UK) Ltd
Wimpy

Motor vehicles and associated services

Budget Rent A Car International Inc
Freezavan Ltd
Highway Windscreens
Intacab Ltd
Midas (Great Britain) Ltd
Mr Lift
PRB Self Drive Hire
Professional Appearance Services
Serviceman Service Centres
Silver Shield Windscreens
Snap-On-Tools
Stop-a-Thief!
Trust Parts
The UK School of Motoring Ltd
Wash 'n' Wax

Printing

Kall-Kwik Printing
PIP Instant Printers
Prontaprint

Retailers

Apollo Window Blinds Ltd
Balloon Ltd
Carpet Master Ltd
Chapter and Verse Bookshops
Circle 'C' Stores Ltd
Clarks Shoes
Compleat Cookshop
ComputerLand
Concorde One Hour Photo Labs
Exchange Travel
Fastframe Instant Picture Framing
Foto Inn
The Frame Factory
Hyde-Barker Travel
In-toto Ltd
Knobs and Knockers Franchising Ltd
The Late Late Supershop (UK) Ltd
Midland Waterlife
Oasis Trading
The Original Art Shop
Pronuptia de Paris Bridalwear
Ryman Ltd
Sketchley Franchises Ltd
Thorntons
Tie Rack Ltd
Wallspan Bedrooms Ltd
Young's Formal Wear for Men

Services

The Accounting Centre
Anicare Group Services (Veterinary) Ltd
Badgeman Ltd
Beardsley Theobalds Businesses
Brewer and Turnbull
Bruce and Company
Business Transfer Specialists (Franchise) Ltd
Colour Counsellors
Complete Weed Control Ltd
Countrywide Garden Maintenance Services
Coversure Insurance Services
Crimecure 30 Ltd
Dial A Char
Everett Masson & Furby Ltd
The Gold Vault Ltd

Infopoint
Knightguard (UK) Ltd
MAPS Marketing Ltd
Micrex Microfilm Express Ltd
Mr Slade Dry Cleaning
National Vacuum Cleaner Services
New Moves
Poppies
Safeclean
Seekers Estate Agency
ServiceMaster
Signtalk Ltd
Swinton Insurance
System-Text (UK) Ltd
Team
TNT Parcel Office
Uticolor
Vandervells Business Transfer Centre
VDU Services
Video Events Ltd
Wetherby Training Services

3. Ranking of franchises by investment level

£0-£5000

The Bath Doctor
Carpet Masters Ltd
Colour Counsellors
Dyno-Electrics
Fixit Mobile Fastening Centre
The Gold Vault Ltd
MAPS Marketing Ltd
National Vacuum Cleaner Services
Signtalk Ltd
TNT Parcel Office
The UK School of Motoring Ltd
Weightguard Franchise Ltd

£5001-£15,000

A1 Damproofing
The Accounting Centre
Anicare Group Services (Veterinary) Ltd
Brewer and Turnbull
British Damp Proofing
Bruce & Company

Cico Chimney Linings
Coffeeman
Countrywide Garden Maintenance Services
Coversure Insurance Services
Crimecure 30 Ltd
Dampco
Dampcure Woodcure/30 Ltd
Dial A Char
Dyno-Rod (Owner/Operator)
Fidelty Franchising Ltd
Freezavan Ltd
Highway Windscreens
Infopoint
Isodan (UK) Ltd
Knightguard (UK) Ltd
Kwik Strip
Mixamate Concrete
Mr Slade Dry Cleaning
New Moves
Poppies
PRB Self Drive Hire
Professional Appearance Services
Safeclean
ServiceMaster
Snap-On-Tools
Stockcheck
Stop-a-Thief!
System-Text (UK) Ltd
Thorntons
Uticolor
Vandervells Business Transfer Centre
VDU Services
Video Events Ltd
Wash 'n' Wax
Wetherby Training Services

£15,001-£30,000

Apollo Window Blinds Ltd
Badgeman Ltd
Beardsley Theobalds Businesses
Bodyreform
The Bread Roll Company
Burger King UK Ltd
Business Transfer Consultants (Franchise) Ltd
Circle 'C' Stores Ltd
Compleat Cookshop

Complete Weed Control Ltd
Concord One Hour Photo Labs
Everett Masson & Furby Ltd
Exchange Travel
Fersina International
Fires and Things
The Frame Factory
Garden Building Centres Ltd
House of Something Different
Midland Waterlife
Potholes
Seekers Estate Agency
Silver Shield Windscreens
Swinton Insurance
Team
Tie Rack Ltd
Trust Parts
Weider Health and Fitness

£30,001-£75,000

Budget Rent A Car International Inc
Chapter and Verse Bookshops
Command Performance
Dyno-Rod (territorial)
Fastframe Instant Print Framing
Herbal World Natural Body Care
Hyde-Barker Travel
In-toto Ltd
Knobs & Knockers Franchising Ltd
Micrex Microfilm Express Ltd
Natural Life Health Foods Ltd
Oasis Trading
The Original Art Shop
Perfect Pizza
PIP Instant Printers
Prontaprint
Pronuptia de Paris Bridalwear
Serviceman Service Centres
Slim Gym Ltd
Spud-U-Like
Stained Glass Overlay
Subway Sandwiches and Salads (UK) Ltd
Young's Formal Wear for Men

Over £75,000

Clarks Shoes
ComputerLand
Fatso's Pasta Joint
Foto Inn
Intacab Ltd
Kall-Kwik Printing
The Late Late Supershop (UK) Ltd
Midas (Great Britain) Ltd
Mr Lift
Pizza Express
Ryman Ltd
Sketchley Franchises Ltd
Wimpy

No franchises currently being offered

Balloon Ltd
Conder Clentech
Olivers Hot Bread and Coffee Shop
Pizza Hut

4. Company ranking by number of UK franchise outlets

	1985	1986
TNT Parcel Office	358	419
Wimpy	384	364
Snap-On-Tools	308	314
Prontaprint	287	291
ServiceMaster	173	187
Budget Rent A Car International Inc	108	115
Kall-Kwik Printing	96	111
Wetherby Training Services	75	98
Apollo Window Blinds Ltd	80	98
Dyno-Rod	75	86
Tie Rack Ltd	43	80
Thorntons	68	80
Swinton Insurance	27	70
Safeclean	62	68
PIP Instant Printers	53	65
Colour Counsellors	60	65
Silver Shield Windscreens	60	62
Isodan (UK) Ltd	61	61
Perfect Pizza		57
Pronuptia de Paris Bridalwear	60	57

	1985	1986
Young's Formal Wear for Men	60	57
Fersina International	35	50
The Bath Doctor	40	50
Wallspan Bedrooms Ltd	42	45
Seekers Estate Agency		45
Poppies (UK) Ltd	24	45
British Damp Proofing	32	45
Fastframe Instant Picture Framing	32	44
National Vacuum Cleaner Services	21	42
Exchange Travel	21	40
Spud-U-Like	50	40
Bodyreform	18	37
Uticolor	35	36
Weightguard Franchise Ltd	21	35
Coffeeman	25	33
In-toto Ltd	26	31
Dampcure Woodcure/30 Ltd	21	31
Pizza Express	25	28
Clarks Shoes	15	27
The Accounting Centre	25	25
Brewer & Turnbull	20	24
Stop-a-Thief!	20	22
Cico Chimney Linings	16	20
Crimecure 30 Ltd		20
Everett Masson & Furby Ltd	17	19
Kwik Strip	14	17
Dyno-Electrics	8	16
Freezavan Ltd		16
Compleat Cookshop	12	15
ComputerLand	14	15
PRB Self Drive Hire	12	15
Stockcheck	9	13
Team	7	13
Bruce & Company	11	13
Complete Weed Control Ltd	10	13
Dial A Char	6	13
Oasis Trading	9	12
Burger King UK Ltd	—	—
Highway Windscreens	8	11
Mr Slade Dry Cleaning	11	11
Badgeman Ltd	11	11
Beardsley Theobalds Businesses	5	11
Professional Appearance Services	8	10
Command Performance	5	10
A1 Damproofing	4	10

	1985	1986
The Bread Roll Company	3	10
Slim Gym Ltd	5	9
Serviceman Service Centres		6
Midas (Great Britain) Ltd	9	9
Knightguard UK Ltd	—	—
Business Transfer Specialists (Franchise) Ltd	5	9
Wash 'n' Wax	—	8
Anicare Group Services (Veterinary) Ltd	7	8
Circle 'C' Stores Ltd	2	7
The Frame Factory	5	6
Vandervells Business Transfer Centre	3	5
Potholes	1	5
Cartons Boulangeries		5
Weider Health & Fitness	2	4
Video Events Ltd	1	4
Sketchley Franchises Ltd	—	4
Signtalk Ltd		4
The Original Art Shop	4	4
Natural Life Health Foods Ltd		4
House of Something Different	2	4
Fires and Things	2	4
Mr Lift	—	3
Garden Building Centres Ltd	—	3
Countrywide Garden Maintenance	—	3
Carpet Master Ltd	—	3
Ryman Ltd	1	2
MAPS Marketing Ltd		2
The Late Late Supershop (UK) Ltd	4	2
Fixit Mobile Fastening Centre	—	2
The UK School of Motoring Ltd		1
Subway Sandwiches and Salads (UK) Ltd		1
Midland Waterlife		1
Hyde-Barker Travel	1	1
Foto Inn	—	1
Coversure Insurance Services		1
Concorde One Hour Photo Labs		1

Note. — = No information available for that year.

Chapter 9

Franchising: Growth and Opportunities

The United States

This is the world's largest business format franchise market. There is little doubt that it holds some important pointers for the future of franchising in the UK.

The US franchise business continues to outpace the growth of the economy, with 1986 sales estimated to exceed $150 billion, well up on 1985's figure of $135 billion. In 1982 sales were a 'mere' $100 billion!

Large franchisors, those with 1000 or more units each, dominate business format franchising, with 57 companies accounting for 53 per cent of sales and 55 per cent of establishments. Those figures should be viewed against a backdrop of over 2400 franchisors operating in this market, employing some 6 million people between them.

Only 70 per cent of outlets in franchise chains in North America are franchisee operated. The remainder are company owned stores using hired managers. These 'company stores' are acknowledged to be less profitable than franchised outlets.

In general, franchising is viewed as being a relatively 'safe' way into business with only a small fraction of a per cent of the country's 350,000 + franchisees failing in any one year. There is also evidence that franchisees are generally satisfied with their lot. Some 90 per cent sign up again when the term of their agreement expires.

The main growth in US business format franchising is in the service sector, encouraged in part by the low cost of entry compared with established car repair and fast food franchises, for example.

This high growth sector includes such areas as: financial counselling services, home repair, insurance, legal service centres, accounting service centres, medical services, dental clinics, business brokers, weight reduction centres, figure control centres, smoking control centres, exercise studios and safe deposit box locations.

Most of these activities are either in their infancy or non-existent in the UK franchise market. Restrictive practices permitting it seems inevitable that these types of franchise will make their presence felt in the UK in the coming decade.

Franchise growth in general in the USA is forecast to grow faster between 1985 and 1995, than in the period 1975-85, with double digit percentages the norm rather than the exception.

The United Kingdom

Franchised sales in the UK exceeded £2.2 billion in 1986, some 29 per cent higher than the 1985 figure of £1.7 billion, which was itself a record. According to the Power research survey of UK franchising, sponsored by the National Westminster Bank, about 440 business format franchise systems are now on offer in the UK. However, only a small percentage of those franchisors have got their operations together properly, and could so be viewed as a sound investment proposition for prospective franchisees.

The Power survey further revealed that the average number of franchised units per chain has risen to 45 (37 in 1985), with a total of 19,800 units in all, up some 56 per cent on the 1985 figure. Over 148,000 people were employed in franchising in the UK, a growth of 35 per cent since 1985.

The factors that have fuelled the growth of franchising in the 1980s are equally divided between changes in the economic and in the political climates. The recession of the early 1980s generated more people with large redundancy payments, who elected after losing their job to go into business for themselves instead. Franchising seemed to offer a way of combining the independence of self-employment with the security of a proven business formula.

Market factors have helped too. The growth in popularity of fast food as a result of changing lifestyles, for example, has helped to stimulate demand for franchised food outlets. The growing number of women entering work has encouraged demand for dry cleaning services, home help agencies and the emergence of US-style convenience stores which meet a need for early and late shopping in neighbourhood areas.

The government has also increasingly recognised the importance of new businesses in job creation and economic growth. This has led to a range of stimulatory measures aimed at the small business sector in general, but with an inevitable overspill that has benefited the franchise sector.

The banks, accountancy firms and legal practices have also worked in their various ways to legitimise franchising and to encourage and advise would-be franchisees.

Business format franchising in the UK is forecast to top £6.1 billion by 1991, with most sectors experiencing some growth. Ahead in the growth league will be service-type operations and those franchises with a relatively low entry cost.

City interests

Until now the City has virtually ignored the franchise market, with the exception of the clearing banks who have provided a ready source of funding for franchisees. But the financial climate for franchisors has been much improved by two funds, which will have the knock-on effect of improving the quality of franchises on offer in the UK in coming years.

Franchise Investors Ltd (FIL). This is a new fund launched by Granville & Co, the corporate finance group, to provide finance and expertise for franchisors. Its initial capital of £1.25 million is to help companies that want to expand by franchising. FIL's backers include Causeway Development Capital, Post Tel Investment Management, and Legal and General, which together own about 75 per cent of the equity. The rest is held by Granville and the founders. It plans to identify and take equity stakes in companies whose business is suitable for franchising. It also intends to buy master licences, probably from North American companies, and develop franchise networks in the UK.

The Unlisted Securities Market. On 16 April 1984, the Body Shop became the first UK franchise to make it to the USM. Launched at 95p the shares rose to £1.55 on the first day of trading, and by January 1987 stood at £8.00. While the company itself raised very little from flotation – less than £100,000 – it is now strongly placed to raise more whenever it chooses. At the same time it spread the firm's reputation and extended company ownership to both employees and franchisees.

In 1986, the Body Shop was 'promoted' from the second division and gained a full listing on the Stock Exchange – another franchising first in the UK.

Prontaprint, another franchise quoted on the USM from May 1985, was placed at 137p. After achieving a 1986 high of £1.40, the shares stood at 85p in January 1987.

Success stories

Apart from the Body Shop, a number of other franchises were conspicuously successful in 1986.

Tie Rack has expanded from a tiny shop in London's Oxford Street to become one of Britain's most exciting retail outlets, with over 100 franchises throughout the country. In the year to February 1986, its pre-tax profits more than tripled to £611,000 on revenues of £9 million. On the back of this success, Roy Bishko, Tie Rack's founder and chairman, was able to raise £1.5 million expansion capital in June 1986 from Midland Bank and its merchant banking subsidiary, Samuel Montagu.

Interlink, another franchise quoted on the Stock Exchange, was valued at £30 million when it was floated. In the three years to 1986, Interlink's turnover grew from £4.5 to £13.7 million, while pre-tax profits soared some 600 per cent from £372,000 to £2.59 million.

Interlink have recently signed a joint marketing deal with Prontoprint, involving them in promoting Interlink's despatch services in its high street outlets. For that Prontaprint get a percentage of Interlink's service charges.

Success of a different, but no less important, kind can be anticipated from GKN Dyno-Rod. In October 1986 GKN took a 60 per cent share of a joint venture with Dyno-Road, the drain cleaning company founded 23 years ago.

GKN's initial stake of £10 million is in a joint company which will develop a nationwide business in the USA where the domestic and commercial drain and pipe cleaning markets are estimated to be work a combined £1 billion per annum. This will go some way to redressing the imbalance caused by the flood of USA franchisors penetrating the UK market.

Problems

It has not been all plain sailing in the franchise world over the past couple of years.

On 15 October 1985 the eighth UK Convention of Young's Franchise Group Ltd, was held at the Grand Hotel, Brighton, and attended by a representative of Barclay's Bank, the group's major creditor. No indication was given at the Convention that the group might be in a parlous condition.

One month later, on Friday 10 November 1985, the Young's franchise group, consisting of Young's Formal Hire, Pronuptia Wedding Hire and the new La Mama fashion maternity wear chain, went into receivership without warning, with debts of £3.75 million.

Ten days later, on 25 November, Young's was sold to Cyril Spencer, former chairman of the Burton Group, who plans to continue franchise operations, for £1.5 million. After preferential creditors such as the Inland Revenue and National Insurance took their slice, what was left went to Barclays Bank, who even then were substantially out of pocket on the deal.

Many of the Young Group's franchisees suffered as a result of this débâcles, none more than the holders of La Mama franchises. All but six of the former 23 franchises have closed, many forced out of business by crippling debts, in a venture which the new management have subsequently said was inadequately researched. National Westminster Bank provided loans to 20 of the 23 initial franchises.

On 31 January 1987 Young's finally pulled out of the La Mama franchise, leaving the remaining six outlets to trade independently.

The Young Group was a senior member of the British Franchise Association.

The 333 franchisees of Homelocaters UK, a national flat finding agency, were less fortunate. In May 1986 Home locators UK was convicted as a limited company, of breaching the 1953 Accommodation Agencies Act, and ordered to pay £1550 in fines and compensation. Attempts to find the franchise founders to serve a distress warrant for the cash have so far met with no success. Homelocators were not a member of the British Franchise Association (BFA).

The Cookie Coach Company, whose franchisees sold cakes and cookies from 1920s style vans, was compulsorily wound up at the request of the Department of Trade and Industry. On 3 December 1986, Peat Marwick, the accountancy firm, was appointed receiver of the company with the task of selling the business as a going concern. The likely deficiency when the dust settles will be over half a million pounds, and the position of the 46 franchisees is uncertain to say the least. Cookie Coach Company was not a member of the BFA, but it was on the BFA Register of Qualified Non-Member Companies, developing a franchise.

Problems of a different nature are occurring at Kentucky Fried Chicken (KFC), the finger-lickin' good fast food chain. The group closed 60 franchised outlets in the six months to January 1987 and its new policy of making the KFC franchise into a restaurant-type chain looks like causing more of their 320 British outlets to close. To add to the confusion, KFC announced in December 1986 that it had formed a joint venture with Trusthouse Forte to operate the chain in the UK.

The result of the spate of KFC closures can already be seen throughout the country. Franchisees no longer having an agreement and the right to the KFC name have started using names such as Mississippi Fried Chicken, Favorite Fried Chicken and Dixie Fried Chicken. A pressure group, the Kentucky Fried Chicken Franchisee Association, claiming to represent 260 franchisees, has been formed to protect the franchisees' estimated £40 million invested in the franchise chain.

Chapter 10
Franchising Check List

After reading this book, you should work carefully through the questions in this check list, covering each franchise proposal that you are considering.

The index of franchise proposals by business category will help you to identify more than one opportunity to look at. You will find that the process of comparing one with another will sharpen up your critical faculties and provide you with plenty of bargaining ammunition.

It is important for you to recognise that entering into any franchise agreement is very much a bargaining process. The franchisor will do his best to present you with a 'take it or leave it' proposal, as any good businessman should. But this is only an opening position and one from which you should use all your negotiating skills to move him to a position of greater advantage to yourself. For example, you may see that a competitive franchisor includes full product and business training within the franchise package fee, while the one you are negotiating with does not. All other factors being equal, this opens up an opportunity for negotiating some if not all of these costs be transferred from you to the franchisor.

Not all of these questions will apply to every franchisor's proposal, but the great majority do.

1. The franchisor, his organisation and business strategy

Questions here are designed to establish how successful, substantial and honest the franchisor and his organisation are. You could make a useful start by getting the accounts from Companies House, running some fairly standard credit checks, asking the BFA what is known and contacting the franchise manager of one of the clearing banks (page 112). This will prepare you and may even save you a visit.

1.1 Is the franchisor soundly financed? Ask to see the recently audited financial statements, and look at least three years back too.
1.2 Is the franchisor a subsidiary of another company and if so whom?
1.3 Is that parent company soundly financed? Ask to see their audited accounts too.
1.4 Does the franchisor have associate companies; if so, who are they

and what exactly is their relationship?

1.5 Does either the parent company or any associates operate franchises?

1.6 If they do, would they be in competition with you?

1.7 Is their franchise operation(s) a success?

1.8 How long has the franchisor been in this type of business?

1.9 When did he start franchising?

1.10 How long has his pilot operation(s) been running?

1.11 Does he maintain an outlet as a testing ground for new ideas and product improvements?

1.12 Does the franchisor still run any outlets himself, and if so how many?

1.13 Are they buy-backs of failed franchisees or does he tend to keep prime sites for himself?

1.14 What business experience and qualifications have the franchisor's directors and managers, and what is the structure of their organisation?

1.15 How much of their own cash do the directors have in the business?

1.16 Have any of the directors or managers ever gone bankrupt?

1.17 Have they or the company recently been involved in litigation, county court judgements etc?

1.18 What is the franchisor's commercial credit rating?

1.19 How many franchise outlets does the franchisor currently have in the UK, and what has been the trend over the past three to five years?

1.20 Has he had any franchise failures or departures; if so how many, and when and why did they fail?

1.21 How many franchisee and owner-operated outlets does he plan to have in future and over what time scale? Where will they be?

1.22 Can you interview a selection of the franchisees of your own choice? Choose a mixture of experienced and new franchisees in different types of location.

1.23 Who are the franchisor's accountants, bankers, lawyers, and are there any other professional or commercial references that you can take up?

1.24 What selection criteria are used for choosing franchisees? How many are turned away?

1.25 What innovations has the franchisor introduced since he started franchising, and what plans does he have for the future (new products, services, markets etc)?

1.26 Is the franchisor a member of the BFA or any other appropriate trade body or chamber of commerce?

1.27 If it is a foreign company, how many of the answers to the above questions relate to their UK operations?

2. *The market and product (service) relationship*

The central strategy of any business lies in the 'unique' relationship between its products (or services) and its markets (or customers). Unless there is something unique about your product or your business, then there is no reason for anyone to choose to buy from you. That uniqueness may simply be that yours is the only photocopier shop in a particular business community; it may rest in an image created around a particular product, such as Kentucky Fried Chicken; or it may be built into a 'unique' service such as Drainmasters' ability to look inside drain ducting with a mobile camera eye.

In any event you must be able to satisfy yourself that the franchisor both understands and intends to preserve the essence of this strategic product/market relationship in the face of existing and likely competition. These questions will help you to probe this area.

2.1 What is the overall demand for this type of product (or service) and what is the franchisor's market share?

2.2 Is that demand seasonal? (This will affect cash flow projections and the best starting date.)

2.3 Exactly what sort of people (or business) buy their product (or service)?

2.4 What benefits do the customers get from buying the product?

2.5 Who are your competitors (not just other franchisors)?

2.6 What are their major strengths and weaknesses?

2.7 What are your franchisor's relative advantages over that competition and why do people buy from him?

2.8 How does your franchisor's quality compare?

2.9 How long has this product been on the UK market?

2.10 Is the product (or its image) protected by patents, copyright or trade marks?

2.11 What guarantees does the product carry and who is responsible for any costs or work associated with any claims or repairs?

2.12 Are there any legal or statutory controls related to the sale of this product, and if so what are they?

2.13 Are the franchisees restricted to buying stock from the franchisor?

2.14 If so, how can the franchisor guarantee competitive supplies?

2.15 Are franchisees allowed to extend or enhance the product range from sources other than the franchisor?

2.16 How is the product advertised and promoted, and who controls and pays for that (at both national and local levels)?

2.17 Are the opening hours recommended or controlled?

2.18 Does the franchisor organise national sales conferences and have a 'house' sales magazine?

2.19 Who sets the selling price of the product?

3. The territory, location or site on offer

While you may be satisfied that the general strategy of the franchisor's business is sound, you have to satisfy yourself that it will work in your area. You also need to know exactly who is responsible for all aspects of site location and development.

3.1 Is the territory exclusive and if so how is that exclusivity guaranteed?

3.2 Who chooses the location or territory, and exactly what criteria are used to establish its commercial viability?

3.3 If the franchisor makes these decisions what will he do for you if he gets it wrong and you can't make it pay?

3.4 Where are the neighbouring franchisees and company owned outlets, both current and projected?

3.5 Where are the competitors?

3.6 How well are other businesses doing in the area, and what are industrial and employment conditions like?

3.7 Does the area present any particular insurance problems?

3.8 Are any significant planning developments or road alterations expected?

3.9 Is the location to be bought or leased?

3.10 Are the equipment and fixtures specified by the franchisor?

3.11 Do these have to be obtained from him?

3.12 Is the layout of the location specified and if so can you make changes in the light of experience?

4. The franchise package and after-sales service and support

The way in which the franchisor will 'transplant' his successful business formula to the franchisee in his own area is through the franchise package. This package contains the operating details of exactly how the franchisor will help the franchisee to set up and run his business. This must include a large element of post-launch support. Any franchisor offering little or no after-sales service and support is unlikely to be offering an attractive franchise opportunity.

4.1 Does the franchisor provide an initial business and product training programme for you?

4.2 If so, how long, what exactly is the content and who pays for it?

4.3 Does the franchisor provide pre-launch advertising and promotions?

4.4 Will the franchisor provide a launch team to help you open up, and if so who pays?

4.5 Does the franchisor help select and train your staff (are there any restrictions on whom you can employ?)

4.6 Does the franchisor provide an operating manual that explains all aspects of running the business?

4.7 Who pays for the initial opening supplies?

4.8 What provision does the franchisor make for counselling and advice with operating problems? (Ask to meet the staff responsible for providing such a service.)

4.9 Does the franchisor provide regular post-opening training, if necessary?

4.10 Is there a system for inspecting franchisee's business operations?

4.11 How is quality control monitored both on franchisor supplies and franchisee operations?

4.12 What 'business systems' are provided, such as book-keeping, stock control etc?

4.13 Can the franchisor advise on appropriate professional help – accountants, surveyors, lawyers etc?

4.14 Is an initial supply of business stationery etc included in the package?

4.15 Can the franchisor prove that his support systems really work?

5. Franchise start-up costs, operating costs, projected revenues and profits

This is perhaps the most important area of all. The result of all the franchisor's plans and expectations are brought together into a set of financial statements. One element of this, the costs, can be predicted with some accuracy if you ask the right questions. The revenues, however, are simply projections, the credibility of which you must judge for yourself. The questions already asked will give you a sound base from which to evaluate the franchisor's claims.

5.1 How much does the licence fee cost and what exactly do you get for it?

5.2 Is there any initial deposit and if so, is it returnable in full?

5.3 How much long-term capital will you need to buy leases, equipment, fixtures etc?

5.4 How much working capital will you need to finance stock, debtors etc?

5.5 Do you have to buy certain minimum quantities of stock and other supplies from the franchisor and if so, what happens if your sales are too low?

5.6 How much will the franchise package cost you, and what does it consist of?

5.7 What are the royalty charges throughout the life of this agreement?

5.8 Are there any provisions for altering the royalty level when sales are poor – ie below break-even volume?

5.9 Are goods supplied by the franchisor marked up? If so, by how much?

5.10 Is there any control on increases in mark-up?

5.11 Do you have to make a regular commitment to 'central' advertising? If so, how much and how often?

5.12 How often will you have to replace equipment, machinery etc? Do you have a choice of both time and type?

5.13 How often will you have to redecorate?

5.14 What financing arrangements can the franchisor make for you? What are the terms and conditions associated with this finance, ie true interest rate, loan repayment period, capital moratoriums etc? Will you end up owning the equipment after all financing costs have been paid off?

5.15 What does the franchisor expect sales revenue to be month by month for the first 12 months and quarterly for the next two years?

5.16 What does the franchisor expect material and operating costs to be (on the same basis as above)?

5.17 So what will the projected gross and net profits be over the first three years? (Make sure your salary and interest on loans and overdrafts are deducted.)

5.18 How can the franchisor substantiate these projections? If based on other franchisees' experiences, can you see audited results? (Take a copy for your accountant to examine.)

5.19 What legal or other contractual fees are likely to be incurred in taking out this franchise?

5.20 Are there any other costs or revenues associated with running this franchise?

6. The franchise contract

This is the legal embodiment of all the terms, conditions, obligations and benefits of the franchise. You must take professional advice from your solicitor, accountant and bankers before entering into such an agreement.

6.1 Are *all* the commitments revealed in the earlier questions contained in the contract ie royalties, fees, franchisor support etc?

6.2 How long is the franchise agreement for?

6.3 What happens at the end of the contract period?

6.4 Do your leases and financing arrangements cover an appropriate time period, bearing in mind the length of the franchise agreement?

6.5 What are the conditions for renewing the contract?

6.6 Under what conditions, if any, can you assign the franchise?

6.7 How can you terminate the contract before the expiry date, for example, if you just don't like the business?

6.8 How can the franchisor terminate the contract before the expiry date?

6.9 How long do you have to correct any defaults?

6.10 Is there an arbitration process?

6.11 When terminating the contract for whatever reason, how will you be compensated for any 'goodwill' generated over the life of the contract?

6.12 What happens in the event of your illness or death?

6.13 Are there any restrictions on what other business activities you can involve yourself in (both during the franchise and after termination)?

6.14 How does the franchisor propose to maintain his good reputation and hence yours?

6.15 Have you any rights to the franchisor's innovations?

6.16 What is your position if the franchisor fails or is put into liquidation?

6.17 What happens to stock etc if the agreement is terminated?

7. Questions to ask another franchisee

You would be wise to ask to see at least two current franchisees in the franchisor's network. Most of the questions already asked could be confirmed in a discussion with them, as well as those listed below.

7.1 Were there any important costs not revealed to you by the franchisor?

7.2 Has all equipment, stock or other materials provided by the franchisor been of satisfactory quality?

7.3 Has the franchisor kept delivery promises?

7.4 How long was it before you reached break even?

7.5 Were the franchisor's projections of sales, profits, and cash flow realistic?

7.6 Was the pre-launch support programme adequate?

7.7 Has the after-sales service been adequate?

7.8 Have you had a serious disagreement with the franchisor and if so, what about?

7.9 How was that resolved?

7.10 Do you know of any problems your franchisor has had with other franchisees?

7.11 Does the franchisor make periodic visits or ask for reports?

7.12 Are you generally satisfied with the marketing and technical assistance provided by the franchisor?

7.13 If you had not taken out this franchise would you still do so now?

7.14 Would you advise anyone else to take out a franchise with this franchisor?

7.15 Have you had any territorial problems, such as a new franchisee being imposed on part of your 'territory', or franchisor-owned outlets opening or selling in prescribed areas?

Chapter 11

The British Franchise Association

It should be borne in mind that, although franchising substantially reduces the inherent risk in a new business venture, it does not automatically guarantee success.

At the same time, registration with or membership of this or any other association does not automatically protect the member company, or his franchisee, against commercial failure.

BFA Administrative Office: Franchise Chambers, 75a Bell Street, Henley-on-Thames, Oxfordshire RG9 2BD; 0491 578049

Full members

Accounting Centre (The)
Elscot House
Arcadia Avenue
London N3 2JE

Alan Paul Hairdressing plc
14 The Rake Precinct
Bromborough
Merseyside
Wirral

Alfred Marks (Franchise) Ltd
Adia House
84-86 Regent Street
London W1A 1AL

ANC Holdings Ltd
Berryhill Trading Estate
Victoria Road
Fenton
Stoke-on-Trent
Staffordshire ST4 2NS

Anicare Group Services (Veterinary) Ltd
27 Buckingham Road
Shoreham-by-Sea
West Sussex BN4 5UA

AP Autela
Autela House
PO Box 80
Tachbrook Road
Leamington Spa
Warwickshire CV31 3QR

Apollo Window Blinds Ltd
Johnstone Avenue
North Cardonald Industrial Estate
Glasgow G52 4YM

Applied Motors (Europe) Ltd
Victoria Wharf
Dragoon Road
London SE8 3NW

Avis Rent A Car Ltd
Trident House
Station Road
Hayes
Middlesex UB3 4DJ

Badgeman Ltd
544 Chiswick High Road
London W4 5RG

Bally Group (UK) Ltd
Wells House
79 Wells Street
London W1P 4JL

British Damp Proofing
The School House
Fleetwood Road
Esprick
Preston PR4 3HJ

Budget Rent A Car International Inc
International House
85 Great North Road
Hatfield
Hertfordshire AL9 5EF

Burger King (UK) Ltd
20 Kew Road
Richmond
Surrey TW9 2NA

City Link Transport Holdings Ltd
Batavia Road
Sunbury on Thames
Middlesex TW16 5LR

Clarks Shoes Ltd
40 High Street
Street
Somerset BA16 0YA

The Coca Cola Export Corporation
Pemberton House
Wright's Lane
London W8 5SN

No further franchises are available.

Colour Counsellors Ltd
187 New King's Road
London SW6 4NZ

Command Performance International
High End
Troutstream Way
Loudwater
Hertfordshire WD3 4LQ

Computerland Europe SARL
518 Elder House
Elder Gate
Central Milton Keynes
Buckinghamshire MK9 1LR

Country Rose Management (Franchise) Ltd
Country Properties
6c Brand Street
Hitchin
Hertfordshire SG5 1HX

Crown Eyeglass
Stancliffe Street
Blackburn BB2 2QR

Dampcure/Woodcure 30
Darley House
Cow Lane
Garston
Watford
Hertfordshire WD2 6PH

Don Millers Hot Bread Kitchens
166 Bute Street Mall
Arndale Centre
Luton
Bedfordshire LU1 2TL

Dyno-Services Ltd
Zockoll House
143 Maple Road
Surbiton
Surrey KT6 4BJ

Everett Masson & Furby Ltd
18 Walsworth Road
Hitchin
Hertfordshire SG5 9SP

Exchange Travel (Franchises) Ltd
Exchange House
66-70 Parker Road
Hastings
East Sussex TN34 3UB

Fastframe Franchises Ltd
28 Blandford Street
Sunderland
Tyne and Wear SR1 3JH

Fotofast (Terryford) Ltd
4th floor
Carolyn House
22-26 Dingwall Road
Croydon CR0 9XF

Global Cleaning Contracts
8-10 High Street
Sutton
Surrey SM1 1HA

Holiday Inns (UK) Ltd
Windmill House
Windmill Road
Brentford
Middlesex TW8 0QH

Holland & Barrett (Franchising) Ltd
Healthways House
Station Approach
West Byfleet
Surrey KT14 6NE

Home Tune Ltd
Home Tune House
Guildford Road
Effingham
Nr Leatherhead
Surrey KT24 5QS

Interlink Express Parcels Ltd
Portland House
22-24 Portland Square
Bristol BS2 8RZ

In-toto Ltd
Wakefield Road
Gildersome
Leeds LS27 0QW

Kall-Kwik Printing (UK) Ltd
Kall-Kwik House
Pembroke Road
South Ruislip
Middlesex HA4 8NW

Keith Hall Hairdressing
2 Oxford Street
Long Eaton
Nottingham NG10 1JR

Kentucky Fried Chicken (GB) Ltd
Wicat House
403 London Road
Camberley
Surrey GU15 3HL

The Late Late Supershop (UK) Ltd
PO Box 53
New Century House
Manchester M60 4ES

Master Thatchers Ltd
Rose Tree Farm
29 Nine Mile Ride
Finchampstead
Wokingham
Berkshire RG11 4QD

Midas (Great Britain) Ltd
107 Mortlake High Street
London SW14 8HH

Mixamate Holdings Ltd
Station Yard
Bourne Way
Hayes
Kent BR2 7EY

Mobiletuning Ltd
7a Nelson Road
London SE10 9JB

Nationwide Investigations
86 Southwark Bridge Road
London SE1 0EX

Northern Dairies Ltd
33 Hemsworth Road
Sheffield S8 8LJ

Olivers (UK) Ltd
Eagle Court
Harpur Street
Bedford MK40 1JZ

The Pancake Place Ltd
Clydesdale Bank House
30 New Road
Milnathort
Kinross KY13 7XT

Pass & Company
Passco House
635 High Road
London E11 4RD

PDC Copyprint (Franchise) Ltd
1 Church Lane
East Grinstead
West Sussex RH19 3AZ

The Perfect Pizza
65 Staines Road
Hounslow
Middlesex TW3 3HW

PIP (UK) Ltd
Black Arrow House
2 Chandos Road
London NW10 6NF

Pizza Express Ltd
29 Wardour Street
London W1V 3HB

Poppies (UK) Ltd
31 Houndgate
Darlington DL1 5RH

PPG Industries (UK) Ltd
PO Box 359
Rotton Park Street
Birmingham B16 0AD

Prontaprint Ltd
Executive Offices
Coniscliffe House
Coniscliffe Road
Darlington DL3 7EX

Pronuptia de Paris
  (Young's Franchise) Ltd
70-78 York Way
London N1 9AG

Rodier Paris
26 Curzon Street
London W1Y 7AE

Safeclean International
(D G Cook Ltd)
Delmae House
Home Farm
Ardington
Wantage
Oxfordshire OX12 8PN

ServiceMaster Ltd
50 Commercial Square
Freeman's Common
Leicester LE2 7SR

Silver Shield Screens Ltd
Wheler Road
Seven Stars Estate
Coventry
West Midlands CV3 3LA

Singer Distribution Ltd
Unit H
Grafton Way
West Ham Industrial Estate
Basingstoke RG22 6HZ

Sketchley plc
Cleaning Division
PO Box 7
Hinckley
Leicestershire LE10 2NE

Snap-On-Tools Ltd
Palmer House
150-154 Cross Street
Sale
Cheshire M33 1FU

Sperrings Ltd
13a Oakmount Road
Chandlers Ford
Southampton SO5 2LG

Spud-U-Like Ltd
34-38 Standard Road
London NW10 6EU

Swinton Insurance Brokers Ltd
31-33 Princess Street
Manchester M2 4EW

Thorntons
J W Thornton Ltd
Derwent Street
Belper
Derbyshire DE5 1WP

Tie Rack Ltd
70-78 York Way
London N1 9AG

TNT (UK) Ltd
TNT Despatch Post
TNT House
Long Street
Atherstone
Warwickshire CV9 1BS

Unigate Dairies Ltd
14-40 Victoria Road
Aldershot
Hampshire GU1 11TH

Uticolor (Great Britain) Ltd
Sheraton House
35 North Street
York YO1 1JD

Wetherby Training Services
15 Victoria Street
Wetherby
West Yorkshire LS22 4RE

Wimpy International Ltd
10 Windmill Road
London W4 1SD

Young's Formal Wear (Young's Franchise Ltd)
70-78 York Way
London N1 9AG

Yves Rocher (London) Ltd
664 Victoria Road
South Ruislip
Middlesex HA4 0NY

Ziebart International Corporation
Zeegard Car Care Ltd (UK licensee)
3 Downsbrook Trading Estate
Southdown View Way
Worthing
East Sussex BN14 8QN

Chapter 12

Useful Organisations and Publications

Note: National telephone dialling codes are given and may not apply to local calls.

Organisations

Franchise associations

The British Franchise Association
Franchise Chambers
75a Bell Street
Henley-on-Thames
Oxfordshire RG9 2BD
Tel: 0491 578049
The association was formed in 1977 to establish a clear definition of ethical franchising standards, and to help members of the public, press, potential investors and government bodies to differentiate between sound business opportunities and suspect business offers. It currently has some 70 members. Although being a member of the BFA does not guarantee the likely success of a franchise, it does show acceptance of a code of practice.

The association will provide a checklist of questions to ask a franchisor, and will answer questions on non-BFA companies if it has the information.

The International Franchise Association
1025 Connecticut Avenue NW
Suite 1005
Washington, DC 20036
USA
Founded in 1960, this is a non-profit organisation representing 350 franchising companies in the USA and around the world. It is recognised as the spokesman for responsible franchising. It could be particularly useful in providing information on the growing number of 'new' franchises arriving in the UK with claims of USA parentage.

National Franchise Association Coalition
PO Box 366
Fox Lake
Illinois 60020
USA
The coalition was formed in 1975 by franchisees in order to provide a centre for the expression of the franchisees' viewpoints, as distinct from those of the franchisors. No such organisation exists in the UK, but the American experiences provide some interesting lessons. There are areas of problems and dispute even between ethical and established franchise organisations and their franchisees.

European Franchise Federation
President: Mr Duncan Whitfield
Home Tune Ltd
Home Tune House
Guildford Road
Effingham
Nr Leatherhead
Surrey KT24 5QS
Tel: Bookham (0372) 56656

European national associations

Belgian Franchise Association
President: Mrs Betty Huby
Boulevard de l'Europe 17
Boite 8
B1420 Braine-L'Alleud
Belgium

Dutch Franchise Association
President Mr R van Dijk
1213 Vg Hilversum
The Netherlands

French Franchise Association
President: Mr B Amstutz-Mahler
9 Bd des Italiens
75002 Paris
France

German Franchise Association
President: Dr W Skaupy
Josephspital Strasse 14
8000 Munich 2
W Germany

Italian Franchise Association
President: Mr G Bonani
C so di Porta Nuova 3
20121 Milano
Italy

Norwegian Franchise Association
c/o Mr Torleif Karlesen
Astveitkogen 41
5084 Tertnes
Norway

Swedish Franchise Association
President: Mr Peter Westring
PO Box 5039
S 181 05 Lidingo
Sweden

Swiss Franchise Association
President: Mr C Seroude
c/o Gesplan
5 Rue Toepffer
Geneva
Switzerland

Non-European associations

Franchisors Association of Australia
Executive Officer: Mr B Bell
Suite 7
Ground Floor
Corporation Centre
123 Clarence Street
Sydney
New South Wales
Australia 2000

Association of Canadian Franchisors
44 Laird Drive
Toronto
Ontario
Canada M4G 3T2

Japanese Franchise Association
Elsa Building 602
3-13-12 Roppongi
Minato-Ku
Tokyo
Japan

South African Franchise Association
c/o Johannesburg Chamber of
Commerce
Private Bag 34
Auckland Park 2000
South Africa

Education

The following organisations regularly run courses on franchising:

Crown Eagle Communications Ltd
2 Bloomsbury Place
London WC1A 2QA
Tel: 01-636 0617
Contact: J K Van Wycks (Seminars Division)

Franchise Development Services Ltd
Castle House
Castle Meadow
Norwich NR2 1PJ
Tel: 0603 6677024
Contact: Bill Wood (Seminar Organiser)

Franchise World
James House
37 Nottingham Road
London SW17 7EA
Tel: 01-767 1371

Institute of Marketing & The British Franchise Association
Moor Hall
Cookham
Maidenhead
Berkshire SL6 9HQ
Tel: 06285 24922

Thames Polytechnic, School of Business Administration
Riverside House
Beresford Street
London SE18 6BH
Tel: 01-854 2030
Contact: Jackie Severn

Franchise consultants

The AFL Deeson Partnership Ltd
Ewell House
Graveney Road
Faversham
Kent ME13 8UP
Tel: 0795 535468
Contact: Tony Deeson, Sue Koster

Anglia Franchise Associates
8 Church Street
Harleston
Norfolk IP20 9BB
Tel: 0379 853833
Contact: Dennis Wisker, Norman Hulme

Business Development Corporation
150 Regent Street
London W1R 5FA
Tel: 01-734 5351
Contact: Monty Howard

Caltain Associates Ltd
Rothamsted
Broken Gate Lane
Denham
Middlesex UB9 4LB
Tel: 0895 834200

Centre for Franchise Marketing
26 High Street
Merstham
Surrey RH1 3EA
Tel: 07374 4211
Contact: John Gooderham, Michael Way

Franchise and Marketing Management Ltd
18 Lichfield Street
Walsall
West Midlands WS1 1TS
Tel: 0922 615351
Contact: Mike Matthews

Franchise Concepts
3 Castle Street
High Wycombe
Buckinghamshire HP13 6RZ
Tel: 0494 32631
Contact: Bryan Wilkes

Franchise Development Services Ltd
Castle House
Castle Meadow
Norwich NR2 1PJ
Tel: 0603 6677024
Contact: Roy Seaman

Franchise Investors Ltd
Davidson House
Green Man Lane
Hatton Cross
Feltham
Middlesex TW14 0PZ
Tel: 01-890 9896
Contact: Dick Crook

Franchise Selection and Marketing Ltd
Highpoint
Hyde Lane
Stafford ST18 9BG
Tel: 0789 3447
Contact: Peter Morrell

Frazer/Scott
28 Blandford Street
Sunderland
Tyne and Wear
Tel: 0783 625533
Contact: John Scott

GB Fast Foods Ltd
8 Pembridge Road
London W11 3HL
Tel: 01-229 6698
Contact: David Acheson, Sandra Young

Andrew James
Hilltop House
24 Cairnmuir Road
Edinburgh EH12 6LP
Tel: 031-334 8040
Contact: Andrew James

MMM
6 Mill Street
Buxton
Norfolk NR10 5JE
Tel: 060546 212
Contact: Michael Virgo

Pannell Kerr Forster
New Garden House
78 Hatton Garden
London EC1N 8JA
Tel: 01-831 7393
Contact: David Hunt

RSH Consultants Ltd
3 Jubilee Buildings
Outram Street
Sutton in Ashfield
Nottinghamshire NG17 1DE
Tel: 0623 515704
Contact: Ian Herd, Tony Roberts

Three important questions you should ask anyone offering their services in this field are:

Has the consultant been involved in successful franchising at a high level?

Has he demonstrated his ability to advise? Ask to speak to some of his past clients.

If the consultant is taking commission on the sale of the franchises his client is launching, there could well be an undesirable conflict of interest.

Lawyers listed by members

Adlers
6 Eldon Street
London EC2M 7LS
Tel: 01-481 9100
Contact: Martin Mendelsohn

Baker & McKenzie
Aldwych House
Aldwych
London WC2B 4UP
Tel: 01-242 6531
Contact: Gabriel Fisher

Drummond & Co, WS
31-32 Moray Place
Edinburgh EH3 6BZ
Tel: 031-226 5151
Contact: Michael Bell

Field Fisher & Martineau
Lincoln House
296-302 High Holborn
London WC1V 7JL
Tel: 01-242 1250
Contact: John Nelson-Jones

Ladas & Parry
52-64 High Holborn
London WC1V 6RR
Tel: 01-242 5566
Contact: Iain Baillie
(also trade mark agents)

Lorenz & Jones
Courtyard House
30 Worthing Road
Horsham
West Sussex
Tel: Horsham 69166
Contact: Ken Prichard-Jones

Macfarlanes
10 Norwich Street
London EC4A 1BD
Tel: 01-831 9222
Contact: V E Treves

Mundays
The Bellbourne
103 High Street
Esher
Surrey KT10 9QE
Tel: 0372 67272
Contact: Ray Walley

Needham & James
Windsor House
Temple Row
Birmingham B2 5LF
Tel: 021-236 9701
Contact: John Pratt

Owen White & Catlin
Gavel House
90-102 High Street
Feltham
Middlesex TW13 4ES
Tel: 01-890 2836
Contact: Anton Bates

Peters & Peters
2 Harewood Place
Hanover Square
London W1R 9HB
Tel: 01-629 7991
Contact: Raymond Cannon

Wm F Prior & Co
Temple Bar House
23-28 Fleet Street
London EC4Y 1AA
Tel: 01-353 3571
Contact: Christopher O'Grady

Paul Shrank & Co
7 Bell Yard
Temple Bar
Strand
London WC2A 2JR
Tel: 01-404 0880
Contact: Paul S Shrank

Banks and other financial institutions

Barclays Bank plc
Marketing Department
6th Floor
Juxon House
94 St Paul's Churchyard
London EC4M 8EH
Tel: 01-248 9155
Contact: F P Salaun

Black Arrow Finance Ltd
748 London Road
Hounslow
Middlesex TW3 1SE
Tel: 01-572 7474
Contact: W P Griffiths

323

Bowring UK Ltd
The Bowring Building
Tower Place
London EC3P 3BE
Tel: 01-283 3100
Contact: Robert Leather, Director
Insurance brokers with offices
throughout UK. Specialists in
arranging group schemes for
Franchisees and in personal planning
(including provision for pensions, life
insurance etc).

First National Securities Ltd
Television House
Mount Street
Manchester M2 5NB
Tel: 061-834 1107
Contact: D Owen

Lloyds Bank plc
71 Lombard Street
London EC3P 3BS
Tel: 01-626 1500
Contact: Alan Pope

Midland Bank plc
Business Sector Marketing
Head Office
Poultry
London EC2P 2BX
Tel: 01-606 9911, ext 2645
Contact: Roy Manning, Franchise
Manager

National Westminster Bank plc
Small Business Section
3rd Floor
116 Fenchurch Street
London EC3M 5AN
Tel: 01-726 1000
Contact: P Stern, Franchise Marketing
Manager

Royal Bank of Scotland
42 St Andrew's Square
Edinburgh EH2 2YE
Tel: 031-556 8555
Contact: Jim Payne

Other important organisations

The Association of British Factors
Moor House
London Wall
London EC2Y 5HE
Tel: 01-638 4090

Association of Invoice Factors
Jordan House
47 Brunswick Place
London N1 6EE
Tel: 01-623 8462

British Insurance Brokers Association
130 Fenchurch Street
London EC3M 5DJ
Tel: 01-623 9043
Can recommend appropriate local
brokers.

**The Chartered Association of Certified
Accountants**
29 Lincoln's Inn Fields
London WC2A 3EE
Tel: 01-242 6855

**The Chartered Institute of
Management Accountants**
63 Portland Place
London W1N 6AB
Tel: 01-637 2311

Companies Registration Office
keeps records of all limited companies.
For England and Wales these records
are kept at:

Companies House
55 City Road
London EC1Y 1BB
Tel: 01-253 9393

and for Scotland at the:

Registrar of Companies for Scotland
102 George Street
Edinburgh EH2 3JD
Tel: 031-225 5774

For Northern Ireland the same service
is available from the:

Department of Commerce
Chichester House
43/47 Chichester Court
Belfast BT1 4PJ
Tel: 0232 234121

The records kept include financial
statements, accounts, directors' names
and addresses, shareholders, and
changes of name and structure. The
information is available on microfiche
at £2.00 per company, and can be
photocopied at 10p per sheet. This
service is available to visitors only.
There are a number of commercial

organisations who will obtain this information for you. Two such organisations are:

The Company Search Centre
1/3 Leonard Street
London EC2A 4AQ
Tel: 01-251 2566

and:

Extel
37/45 Paul Street
London EC2A 4PB
Tel: 01-253 3400

The charges for this service are about £3.00 to £3.50 for a microfiche of each company, or for a photocopy of the report and accounts, around £8.00.

Company Pensions Information Centre
7 Old Park Lane
London W1Y 3LJ
Tel: 01-408 1933

Corporation of Mortgage, Finance and Life Assurance Brokers Ltd
PO Box 101
Guildford
Surrey GU1 2HZ
Tel: 0483 35786/39126
For commercial mortgages.

Credit Ratings Ltd
51 City Road
London EC1Y 1AY
Tel: 01-251 6675
This company provides an ad hoc subscription service credit report. The cost varies from £15.00 to £12.00 for each report, which can normally be provided within 24 hours. Each credit report provides a company profile, financial performance figures for the past two years, and eight credit ratios (including an estimate of how long the company normally takes to pay its bills). These ratios are then compared to the average for that industry, and are followed by a short commentary bringing important factors to the reader's attention.

Institute of Chartered Accountants in England & Wales
PO Box 433
Chartered Accountants Hall
Moorgate Place
London EC2P 2BJ
Tel: 01-628 7060

The Institute of Chartered Accountants of Scotland
27 Queen Street
Edinburgh EH2 1LA
Tel: 031-225 5673

Small Firms Service
This service is provided by the Department of Employment and operates through a nationwide network of Small Firms Centres. It provides information and counselling services to help owners and managers of small businesses with their plans and problems. Telephone 100 and ask for freefone Enterprise for your local branch.

Publications

Business Format Franchising
Clive Grant
February 1985, The Economist Intelligence Unit
Report No 185
The main emphasis of this special report is on the substance and nature of business format franchising in the UK. Drawing on a major survey recently commissioned by the British Franchise Association and on its own investigations, the EIU presents a detailed examination of the sector in terms of size, turnover, employment, sources of finance and advice and its participants which straddle a wide range of service and retailing enterprises.
A final chapter considers the impact of franchising on the UK economy and forecasts very rapid growth over the next five years with an increasing number of well-established firms, circumscribed by financial restraints, opting for expansion by the business format route. The Report includes 28 tables, including country comparisons, and a series of appendices.

The Complete Handbook of Franchising
Davis D. Selz
Addison-Wesley
This book is not for franchisees, but if you want to turn your existing business into an equally successful franchise organisation, the handbook will help.

Consumer Law for the Small Business
Patricia Clayton
1983 (Kogan Page, 120 Pentonville Road, London N1 9JN, tel: 01-278 0433) price £4.95 paperback.

The Dow Jones-Irwin Guide to Franchises
Peter G. Norback and Crain Norback
May 1983
This is a thorough investigation of franchising, organised by franchise categories. Once again it covers only the American scene, but it does provide some useful pointers.

Financial Management for the Small Business: The Daily Telegraph Guide
Colin Barrow
1984 (Kogan Page, 120 Pentonville Road, London N1 9JN, tel: 01-278 0433) price £5.95 paperback.

The Franchise Newsletter
(Franchise Development Services, Castle House, Castle Meadow, Norwich NR2 1PJ. A monthly publication; free copy on request.)

Franchise Opportunities Directory
available from
Unit 10
Wreford Yard
Ransome Road
Northampton
Tel: 0604 68691
Updated and published each quarter. Gives the names and addresses of around 100 UK franchisors, a couple of lines description of the business and the minimum investment required.

Franchise Opportunity Handbook
(US Government Printing Office, Administrative Division (SAA) Washington, DC 20402, USA).
The handbook provides an interesting insight into the official American views on franchising and also gives an idea of the scope of the franchising phenomenon.

Franchise Reporter
(Franchise Publications, James House, 37 Nottingham Road, London SW17 7EA), has eight issues a year. It is intended to keep you up to date with UK franchise news between the quarterly issues of *Franchise World*.

Franchise Rights, a Self-Defense Manual for the Franchisee
Alex Hammond
(Hammond and Marton, 1185 Avenue of the Americas, New York, NY 10036, USA).
The manual contains perceptive insight into franchisee/franchisor relationships – forewarned is forearmed.

Franchise World
(Franchise Publications, James House, 37 Nottingham Road, London SW17 7EA), has all the latest news on new franchise opportunities, new consultancies and sources of finance. Each issue has a franchise directory, which describes the franchise organisations and gives some idea of the cost of entry.

'Franchising and the Ominous Buy Back Clause' *Burr, Burr and Bartlett,* **Journal of Small Business Management,** Vol. 13 (4), October 1975. The article helps with the crucial question: What happens if I want to sell out?

Franchising and the Total Distribution System
D Izraeli
(Longman, 5 Bentinck Street, London W1, tel: 01-935 0121), 1972. It sets franchising in its context in the economic environment. A good backdrop to see where franchising really fits in.

Franchising in the Economy 1983-1984
(US Department of Commerce, Bureau of Industrial Economies, Washington, DC, USA), January 1985.
Although completely based on the USA, it provides an extremely authoritative view of the role of franchising in an advanced industrial economy. It describes the business environment and the successes and failures in each sector of franchising.

A Guide to Franchising
Martin Mendelsohn
4th edition 1985, (Pergamon Press, Headington Hill Hall, Oxford OX3 0BW, tel: 0865 64881), price £26.

A very sound introduction to the advantages and disadvantages of franchising, it covers the basic principles including the 'franchise contract' which formalises the relationship between the franchisor and the franchisee.

The INFO Franchise Newsletter,
(INFO Press, 736 Centre Street, Lewiston, NY 14092, USA). Does for the world (mainly North America) what *Franchise Reporter* sets out to do for the UK. *INFO* gives advance information on what new franchises are intending to start up in the UK, so it is a way of keeping ahead of the game.

Introducing Marketing
Martin Christopher, Malcolm McDonald and Gordon Wills
(Pan, 18 Cavaye Place, London SW10, tel: 01-373 6070), 2nd edition 1984, price £2.95. Refreshing, practical and set firmly in the UK environment.

The Law and Practice of Franchising
Martin Mendelsohn and Arthur Nicholson
1982 (Franchise Publications). The book has three parts: an overview of franchising; precedents of franchising agreements and clauses with commentary; and the law applicable to franchising. The precedents include a specimen contract for a fast food franchise, and an international area franchise agreement.

The areas dealt with range from trade marks, trade names and goodwill to the UK and EEC competition laws.

Law for the Small Business
Patricia Clayton
5th edition 1987, (Kogan Page, 120 Pentonville Road, London N1 9JN, tel: 01-837 7851), price £7.50, paperback. Explains all the relevant acts and their likely effect on traders.

Planned Savings
Vol. 17, No 3, March 1982. The article 'Franchising – avoiding the pitfalls' presents a useful view of the UK franchising scene.

Small Business Guide
Colin Barrow
2nd edition, 1984, (BBC Publications, 35 Marylebone High Street, London W1). Perhaps the most comprehensive guide to sources of information for small and new business.

The Stoy Hayward Business Tax Guide
Mavis Seymour and Stephen Say
1987 (Kogan Page Ltd, 120 Pentonville Road, London N1 9JN, tel: 01-278 0433), price £12.95.

Working for Yourself
The Daily Telegraph Guide, *Godfrey Golzen*, 9th edition 1987, (Kogan Page Ltd, 120 Pentonville Road, London N1 9JN, tel: 01-278 0433), price £5.95, paperback.

Index of Advertisers

Index